BETWEEN TWO NATIONS

Dual citizenship: Colombia (1991), Ecuador (1995), El Salvador (1980), Panama (1972), Uruguay (1967), Dominican Republic (1996), Mexico (2000?), Argentina, Brazil

St. Vincent, Grenada

2001 – First Latinos elected to city council from Queens, district 21, Hiram Monserrate

Does citizenship eliminate the problem of dual or multiple loyalties? A non-citizen resident of 20 years may be more loyal than a naturalized resident of five. Or both may be equally loyal or not.

BETWEEN TWO NATIONS

THE POLITICAL PREDICAMENT OF LATINOS IN NEW YORK CITY

Michael Jones-Correa

Cornell University Press ITHACA AND LONDON

First published 1998 by Cornell University Press
First printing, Cornell Paperbacks, 1998

Printed in the United States of America

Library of Congress Cataloging-in-Publication Data

Jones-Correa, Michael, 1965–
Between two nations : the political predicament of Latinos in New York City / Michael Jones-Correa.
p. cm.
Includes bibliographical references and index.
ISBN 0-8014-3292-8 (alk. paper).—ISBN 0-8014-8364-6 (pbk. : alk. paper)
1. Hispanic Americans—New York (State)—New York—Politics and government. 2. Immigrants—New York (State)—New York—Political activity. 3. New York (N.Y.)—Ethnic relations. 4. Citizenship—New York (State)—New York. I. Title.
F130.S75J66 1998
305.868'07471—dc21 97-49415

Cornell University Press strives to use environmentally responsible suppliers and materials to the fullest extent possible in the publishing of its books. Such materials include vegetable-based, low-VOC inks and acid-free papers that are recycled, totally chlorine-free, or partly composed of nonwood fibers. Books that bear the logo of the FSC (Forest Stewardship Council) use paper taken from forests that have been inspected and certified as meeting the highest standards for environmental and social responsibility. For further information, visit our website at www.cornellpress.cornell.edu.

Cloth printing 10 9 8 7 6 5 4 3 2 1
Paperback printing 10 9 8 7 6 5 4 3 2

TO MY PARENTS

Contents

Maps and Figures

Tables

Acknowledgments

Though it might seem like a solitary endeavor, writing a book is made possible only with the help of a great many people. I want to acknowledge my friends, colleagues, and family members who listened to, read, and commented on various portions of this work, even when it was rough and incomplete.

First, I thank Nancy Bermeo and Jennifer Hochschild, who in conversations over the years always provided sorely needed perspective, encouragement, advice, and friendship. My deepest thanks as well to Michael Danielson, Jim Doig, Fred Greenstein, Rodney Hero, Bonnie Honig, Peter Johnson, Michelle Lamont, Peggy Levitt, and Sidney Verba, who kindly read versions of many of these chapters and provided many insightful comments and much support. As this book took form, it was aided by my editor at Cornell University Press, Peter Agree, who expertly navigated through the shoals of publication, and by anonymous readers who gave careful and helpful comments.

In the course of completing this project I have had the good fortune to be surrounded by many people who have been both good friends and good critics. I hope I have made good use of their advice. Among them are Dana Ansel, Judith Barish, Jacques Bertrand, Meena Bose, Katrina Burgess, Keith Bybee, Deborah "Cricket" Cohen, Matthew Dickinson, Joshua Dienstag, Rafael Hernandez, Solomon Karmel, Michelle Mulder, and Andrew Richards. Bert Johnson deserves special mention for his help in putting together the maps and the index.

I want especially to express my gratitude to all the people who gave me their time and their trust during my fieldwork in Queens. I cannot thank all of them by name, but I want to thank some without whose support and friendship this project would not have been possible: Alice Cardona, Diana Cruz, Gloria Florez, David Glassberg, Aida Gonzalez-Larín, Araceli Goulding, Merly Landis, Luz Leguizamo, Beatriz Montoya, Nayibe Nuñez-Berger, Hector Rodriguez, Martha Rodriguez, Manuel Rosa, John Sabini, William Salgado, and Guillermo Sanchez.

Modified versions of some chapters were presented at the meetings of the American Political Science Association, the Latin American Studies Association, the Northeastern Political Science Association, and the New York State Political Science Association, as well as at the Workshop on Race, Ethnicity, Representation, and Governance at the Center of American Political Studies at Harvard University, and the ILASSA Student Conference on Latin America at the University of Texas at Austin. I wish to express my appreciation to the participants on these occasions, as well as at the graduate student Women's Studies Colloquium and Political Theory Lunch at Princeton University, and the Gender and Politics Workshop at Harvard University, for their many stimulating comments and observations, which helped to strengthen my work.

Finally, various institutions provided me support, granting the resources and the space to research, think, and write: the National Science Foundation, the Mellon Foundation, and at Princeton University the Latin American Studies Program, the Council on Regional Studies, the Center for Domestic and Comparative Policy Studies, and the Department of Politics. Harvard University provided additional resources with which to finish this work. For all this I am very grateful.

It goes without saying that I could not have done this without my parents. But I will say it anyway: thank you both for all your love and support. And, of course, thanks to Ria Davidis, my best friend and critic, who made it all worthwhile.

M. J.-C.

BETWEEN TWO NATIONS

Introduction: The New Hispanic Immigration

This book reflects three kinds of change under way in the United States today: the increasing importance of Hispanics in American politics, their own increasing diversity, mostly as a result of immigration, and the complex incorporation of these immigrants into American political life.

It is impossible, walking through almost any American city today, to ignore the signs of transformative change. These can be seen in the lettering of signs over the storefronts, which are not just in English but in a panoply of other languages as well; in the faces of store owners, street vendors, waiters, pedestrians, passengers on the bus lines; and in the astonishing mix of national origins in the schools. Over the last thirty years American cities have absorbed the largest wave of immigration to the United States since the turn of the century. In 1994, the Census Bureau announced that 8.7 percent of the U.S. population were first-generation immigrants, the highest proportion since the 1940s, and nearly double the percentage in 1970 (4.8 percent). 22.6 million people—nearly one in eleven U.S. residents—were foreign-born. Four and a half million immigrants arrived in the 1970s, 7.3 million in the 1980s, and another 5 million from 1991 to 1995.[1] These immigrants have settled largely in urban areas across the country.

1 "Census: Immigrants at New High," *Associated Press*, August 25, 1995. Immigrants composed 13.5% of the country's population in 1910. "Percentage of Foreigners in U.S. Rises Sharply," *New York Times*, December 20, 1992. Nonetheless, the 19.7 million first-generation immigrants counted by the 1990 Census was the largest absolute number in the nation's history. Felicity Barringer, "As American as Apple Pie, Dim Sum, or Burritos," *New York Times*, May 31, 1992, section 4, p. E2. For overviews of the new immigration see Jaret 1991: 311; Portes and Rumbaut 1990; Sassen 1985; Waldinger 1989; Massey and Schnabel 1983.

Table 1 Immigration to the United States, 1941–1995

1941–1950	1,035,039
1951–1960	2,515,479
1961–1970	3,321,677
1971–1980	4,493,314
1981–1990	7,338,062
1991	1,827,167
1992	973,977
1993	880,015
1994	804,416
1995	770,461

Sources: Figures for 1941–1992 are from Pachón and DeSipio 1994: 5 table 1; figures for 1993 and 1994 are from "Legal Immigration to U.S. Fell Nine Percent in 1994," Reuters, June 30, 1995; figures for 1995 are from "Immigration to U.S. Continues to Fall," Reuters, March 27, 1996.

Nearly half the new immigrants are from Latin America. In fact, just under half of all Latinos[2] in the United States are first-generation immigrants, and the proportion is likely to increase.[3] This change has important implications for the study of Hispanic politics. A common refrain is that by the year 2010 Latinos will be the largest U.S. minority, surpassing African Americans; from 1990 to 1995 the Latino population grew from 22 million to 26 million (9 percent of the population).[4] Increasingly, to understand Hispanics in the United States, one must understand Latin American immigra-

[2] A note on terminology. "Hispanic" is used by the Census Bureau and most mainstream sources to describe people of Mexican, Puerto Rican, Cuban, Central or South American, or some other Spanish origin (del Pinal and de Naves 1990). In this book I use "Latino"—the term currently in vogue—and "Hispanic" interchangeably. See chapter 2 in Marín and VanOss Marín 1991 for further discussion. "First-generation immigrant" is used here to describe permanent residents in the United States born in another country; the "second generation" are their children.

[3] One survey estimated that 72% of Hispanics in the United States are first-generation immigrants, and 40% have been in the country for less than ten years. This figure comes from a 1992 survey for the Hispanic publication *MONITOR,* produced jointly by Market Development Inc. of San Diego and Yankelovich Partners of Westport, Connecticut. To arrive at this figure, the survey presumably includes Puerto Ricans as foreign-born. See Patricia Braus, "What Does 'Hispanic' Mean?" *American Demographics,* June 1993. Immigration and Naturalization Service (INS) figures, for all their flaws, remain the most valid approximations we have. They indicate that there were about 6.2 million Latin American immigrants from 1950 to 1990. Another two million were legalized by the 1986 amnesty which allowed undocumented aliens living in the U.S. to acquire permanent residency, and about one million Cubans came in as refugees. That makes a total of 9.2 million out of 22.5 million Latinos in the United States—about 41% in 1990. Sixty-seven % of Hispanics in the U.S. are either immigrants or their children. See Jeffrey Passel and Barry Edmonston of the Urban Institute, in Barringer, "Apple Pie."

[4] "Census: Immigrants at New High."

tion. The study of Hispanic politics so far has been in the context of Latinos as a minority, not in the context of Latinos as immigrants.[5] Immigrants and nonimmigrants are both treated unproblematically as members of a single minority group.[6] However, since most of the recent immigration has been voluntary, we might reasonably expect the political incorporation of Latinos to show some similarities to the incorporation of immigrants more generally (Skerry 1993). We need to reexamine our assumptions about Latino politics in this country.

The new diversity of immigration from Latin America, with Latino populations in the United States becoming more differentiated along lines of nationality, class, and generation (Oboler 1995), complicates the notion of a "Hispanic" politics. Thirty years ago one could nearly equate Hispanic politics in New York City with Puerto Rican politics. The same is not true today, for over half the city's Latino population, many of them first-generation immigrants, originate elsewhere in Latin America. This trend is similar in Miami, Houston, Los Angeles, and many other U.S. cities with growing Latino populations. In New York City, Dominicans, Colombians, Ecuadorians, and others make up an increasing percentage of the city's Latin American–origin population, and are beginning to make their way as actors in the city's politics.

An understanding of immigrants and their political incorporation is increasingly essential for a grasp of American politics.[7] About one out of every two new Americans is an immigrant; one of every six new Americans will be a Latin American immigrant.[8] Unlike the common perception of people crossing the border under the cover of night, without documents, these immigrants have all come in through normal legal channels. Many of them become permanent residents; they are all potential citizens. Even though the number of immigrants arriving in the United States since 1965 is ap-

[5] The exception, of course, is Cubans (see for example Portes and Mozo 1988). There is a growing literature on the sociology and economics of new immigrants, but surprisingly little on their political involvement in the United States. The scholarly literature on immigrants and politics is small but growing; see DeSipio and Pachón 1992 (as well as other work by DeSipio); DeSipio and de la Garza 1992; Schmidt 1992; Pachón 1991; Schmidt 1989.

[6] The internal colonialist perspective, at the extreme of this line of thought, interprets the incorporation of Mexican-Americans into the U.S. polity exclusively through the lens of the forcible annexation of the Southwest in 1848; see Acuña 1981; Barrera 1979; Barrera, Ornelas, and Muñoz 1972; Blanuer 1972.

[7] See note 1.

[8] Beck, for instance, claims that "the majority of U.S. population growth since 1970 has come from immigrants and their descendants. They will probably contribute two-thirds of the growth during this decade and nearly all of it after the turn of the century" (1994: 90). According to the census, the population of the United States increased by 22,164,000 people between 1980 and 1990. Legal immigration accounted for about 40% of that increase.

proaching—or has surpassed—the level of the last great wave of immigration to this country from 1880 to 1920, few studies ask how contemporary immigrants are incorporating into the U.S. political system.

This book, based on fieldwork carried out over 1991–1992,[9] focuses on this question of political participation: why do so many immigrants remain outside the formal political arena? In particular, why do so many Latin American immigrants hesitate before becoming American citizens? Having hesitated to naturalize, what do immigrants then do instead?

The Political Incorporation of Immigrants

In this addressing these questions I have illustrated the costs of and barriers to the political incorporation of immigrants in the United States by describing the political life of Latin American immigrants in Queens, New York, which I believe can provide certain answers regarding the general issue of the inclusion of immigrants into our formal political system. If the case of Latin Americans in Queens is any indication, the policy of incorporation that we have today is failing a large number of recent immigrants. I contend that this situation has come about because the burden of political incorporation falls entirely on the new arrivals. Citizenship and entry to participation in the political system has come to be seen as a test to be passed, and not as something in the best interests of both the new citizen and the polity. Recent immigrants, faced with making a decision to naturalize as citizens of this country, a decision that would irrevocably close off any formal links with their country of birth, hesitate. This hesitation can extend over decades, leaving immigrants adrift in a political limbo.

During this period of irresolution, immigrants do not cease to exist. And it isn't as though in the absence of formal participation Latin American immigrants have no political life at all, or cease to be political actors. Immigrants continue living in cities around the United States, going to work, paying taxes, having children who are born American citizens, and sending them to school. They are members of organizations and associations, and work toward various communal ends. In short, they act like other residents of the United States. But they are not citizens, and the price of making the transition to citizenship, and full membership in the polity, is high.

[9] The fieldwork consisted of open-ended semistructured interviews and participant observation conducted in Queens, New York City, over an eighteen-month period. This qualitative work is complemented by an analysis of census and survey data. For further elaboration of the book's methodology see the Appendix, as well as Chapter 3.

The political environment in Queens is not particularly welcoming for immigrants. The constraints to participation they encounter are not so much economic (downward socioeconomic mobility, vulnerability in the marketplace, continuing obligations in the country of origin expressed through remittances, and so forth), as they are political. In the first place, immigrants receive a chilly reception from political parties. While the muscle of the political machine may have atrophied, the Democratic Party in Queens still keeps its skeleton alive. The party acts as a gatekeeper to the political system by monopolizing candidacies and appointments. With limited resources at its disposal, the party is not eager to mobilize new constituencies such as recently arrived immigrants. While not actively discouraging immigrant participation, the party does nothing to encourage it either.

Second, native-born residents and immigrants have competing conceptions of what political community means, which are based on territorial notions of politics. Residents, often second- and third-generation immigrants themselves, see themselves inhabiting a political community which is the physical space that surrounds them. First-generation immigrants, for their part, maintain ties to a national community of origin which are kept alive in memory by the desire to return. The longer immigrants stay in the United States, the greater the tension between these two conceptions. The problem is that loyalties to different territorial political communities are often seen as irreconcilable. To belong to two distinct political communities is like being in two places at the same time—it isn't supposed to be possible.

The political institutions and communities of the home country and the receiving country present immigrants with a Hobson's choice. American politicians want immigrants' votes before they will accept them as full-fledged political actors. To vote, immigrants must become citizens. To become an American citizen, one is required, at least by law, to renounce allegiances to a former nationality. Likewise, by becoming American citizens, Latin American immigrants can lose their previous citizenship and forfeit the possibility of return as full members of their countries of origin. Immigrants are increasingly caught between competing desires: their wish to demonstrate their loyalty to their home countries and their interests in the country in which they reside.

To escape these irreconcilable choices, immigrants resist institutional pressures to make irrevocable decisions about membership in political communities. They avoid taking on new citizenship in the United States, while also strategically distancing themselves from the demands of the state they have abandoned (by not taking part in elections in which expatriate residents can participate, for instance). These actions are not simply a rejection or acceptance of either the country of origin or the United States. Nor are they simply a strategy of avoidance. On the contrary, Latin American immigrants in Queens combine instrumental strategies and a sense of the continuity with their own histories to construct a fluid politics of identity. The managing of past and present constraints—loyalty to memory and present desire—are all expressed through a constantly renegotiated set of identities.

The attempt to reconcile the irreconcilable is seen most directly in the attempts of various national groups to petition their home countries for the recognition of dual citizenship. But other reconciliations of sorts take place through the practices of a politics of identity—with immigrants simultaneously maintaining distance and ties to both polities through the assumption of multiple identities that draw on continuities from their countries of origin, but are tailored to respond to their situation in this country. By pursuing a politics of in-between, Latin American immigrants can emphasize cultural loyalty while minimizing the institutional political constraints they feel acting on them from the two polities. In Queens, this is expressed through the breaks and continuities in the forms of organization and repertoires of action that permeate immigrant social life.

Immigrants do not passively accept the barriers that keep them from affirming their membership in both societies and from active participation in the country they live in. Immigrants in Queens pursue two different strategies to reduce the costs they face to enter into formal political membership and participation in the United States, differences that are are fundamentally gendered. Latin American immigrant men tend to monopolize the leadership positions in social and cultural organizations. Activist first-generation immigrant women, on the other hand, are more likely to seek the roles of intermediaries between immigrants and the American political system. Their distinct positions in the immigrant community lead to starkly different approaches to resolving the dilemma of marginalization. In general, while mainstream immigrant organizations, dominated by men, are oriented toward their home country, activist women attempt to circumvent the obstacles to local participation placed there by the once supposedly helpful political party structure.

Latino political behavior can only be explained with an understanding of the costs immigrants face as they make the decision whether to become full members and participants in the American polity. The context to which immigrants arrive and their ties to their home country both conspire to make the choice of citizenship and political participation a difficult one. While their political strategies certainly help carve out a space for independent action, an arena where they can escape the pressures from the irreconcilable demands of nation-states, this is not enough to guarantee their membership in the broader polity in which they live. In the end, there is no better protection or guarantee of rights in a participatory democracy than full membership through citizenship.

Organization of the Chapters

This book is divided into four parts. The first sets the context for the question of citizenship and immigration in New York City, beginning with an illustration in Chapter 1 of the impact of immigration on a changing city and on the neighborhoods to which immigrants move. The dilemma is that while immigrants and older residents may share public spaces in the city, immigrants' position on the margins of these spaces reflects their broader marginalization in political life.

Why is this a problem? Chapter 2 explores the curious absence of discussion of political incorporation from our contemporary debates on immigration and concludes that this silence potentially undermines democratic participation. The value we place on democratic participation requires that we pay more attention to the political incorporation of newcomers and others on the margins of our political system, and to their inclusion in the full membership of citizenship.

Most of those seeking an explantion for low rates of formal participation place the blame on the differential effects of socioeconomic status. But Chapter 3 finds that this status does relatively little to explain the inordinate length of time that immigrants take to become citizens—and their consequent political marginality. Instead we must look to the *costs* that immigrants face to explain why making the decision to naturalize and participate in American politics is so difficult.

Part II describes these costs. Chapter 4 focuses on the exclusionary logic of political parties, and in particular how machine politics in Queens snubs marginal political actors, including newly arrived immigrants. Chapter 5 looks at the internal structure of these new immigrant communities, and the pressures against individuals realigning their political loyalties. Latin American immigrants in Queens face resistance from both within and without as they face the decision whether to naturalize.

Part III addresses immigrants' attempt to reconcile these alternative visions of political community through a "politics of in-between." Chapter 6 looks at how Latino identity, constructed from the tensions between instrumentalism and history, can become the basis of a conscious strategy balancing one set of demands against the other. Chapter 7 describes the construction of an "in-between" politics among Latin American immigrants in Queens.

Finally, in Part IV, I look at how immigrants break out of the constraints placed on them by competing polities. As both women and men struggle within a new context, they choose markedly different (though not incompatible) strategies for dealing with the dilemma of irreconcilable political communities.

Neither economic constraints, which are ameliorated over time, nor political barriers, which are mostly passive, are sufficient explanations for why immigrants are not active participants in American political life. Nonparticipation can persist for decades after arrival in this country, long after many immigrants have stabilized their economic situations and have established themselves professionally. Many Latin American immigrants acquire residency as soon as they are able, but not citizenship. To understand why this happens we must turn to the costs immigrants face as they try to make the decision to naturalize.

Although it describes people in a particular time and place, this book also illuminates some larger issues of immigrant political socialization and acculturation. It responds to questions of community mobilization and alternative politics, in particular, by linking the location of politics to notions of identity and by looking at a "politics of in-between." The book also has something to add to our notions of Latino politics in the United States; although my argument may have more to say about immigrant political socialization than about the experience of Latinos in the United States, it is important to recognize that the Hispanic experience in this country is increasingly an immigrant one and that the two have become intertwined.

The development of the idea of a politics of in-between adds to our understanding of who participates and why, and suggests possibilities for how political participation can be encouraged among marginalized social actors. Finally, this project addresses the anxiety that American identity is being eroded by immigrants who fall outside the bounds of citizenship and the nation's core values. For those who wish to hold onto a static vision of America, this book's views of first-generation immigrants will not be very reassuring; the United States is an evolving project, and that will hardly end now.[10]

[10] Among those who are concerned about the impact of immigration on American political culture are Johnson 1994; Walzer 1990; and Schuck and Smith 1985. See also Samuel Huntington, *American Politics: The Promise of Disharmony* (Harvard University Press, 1981); Eugene McCarthy, *A Colony of the World: The United States Today* (Hippocrene Books, 1992). See also Felicity Barringer, "Land of Immigrants Gets Uneasy about Immigration," *New York Times,* October 14, 1990, Week in Review, p. 4.

Given that the social changes brought about by this most recent immigration are here to stay, the challenge is to see that new and marginal members of our society are encouraged to participate to the fullest extent possible. I suggest ways in which this is not presently being done, and how it might be done better.

I

SETTING THE CONTEXT

1

Intimate Strangers: Immigration to Queens

As I rode the number 7 train to Queens late one winter afternoon, I watched the other people in the car and jotted down some impressions in my notebook.

> It's cold and the light is already gray. The car is full of Latina women in wool overcoats, carrying bulging, lumpy handbags, things picked up on the way home from work, the afternoon shift just ended. It's after school. There are teenagers on the train too, boys and girls—black, Asian, Latino most of them. Talking in English to one another, slipping into Spanish, back and forth. Mostly English. The guys dressed in baggy pants, black shoes.
>
> There's a man practicing English, moving his finger along the lines of his workbook. People passing the time reading the paper—the *New York Post*, the *Daily News*, the occasional *El Diario*, the Chinese or Korean papers. People reading small Bibles they can tuck into their pockets. Very few with books. Women reading magazines—health, beauty, true crime stories.
>
> At night the train is full. Indians, Mexicans, Chinese, Colombians, Koreans. Guys in leather or nylon jackets, getting off work in restaurants, stores, factories at one or two in the morning. Leaving the train and walking home, usually alone, looking down, looking at no one.
>
> There are some Asian men in some kind of betting game with coins. Hold out their hands—bet on the number of coins—on their combinations, on predictions of how many will be held out? The Latino men looking on, interested, amused. I fall asleep, and wake up on a quiet train.[1]

[1] Author's fieldnotes, March 30, 1992.

When you ride the elevated number 7 train from Manhattan through Elmhurst, Woodside, Jackson Heights, Corona, ending finally in Flushing, you can easily see that New York is a city in transition. Some changes are visible—the sari shops on 86th Street, the Colombian nightclubs on Roosevelt Avenue, the Korean stores lining Broadway in Elmhurst. Others are less obvious but just as striking. They have occurred in the privacy of neighborhoods and apartment houses: Russians living next to Puerto Ricans living next to Koreans, who themselves are neighbors with Dominicans, Guyanese, or Argentines—the permutations in Queens are practically endless. There are clusters of nationalities, buildings or blocks of buildings where one group predominates, but the overall impression is of a mélange of new languages, cultures, experiences. There is resistance to change on the part of residents who remember the neighborhood streets as they were ten or twenty years ago, and who want to preserve what they see as a way of life—*their* way of life. In spite of this, the city's transition is relentless—the cumulation of thousands of individual decisions to come to the United States.

This chapter begins by outlining the economic and demographic shifts that have taken place over the last four decades in New York and other cities. These structural transformations have in turn brought about other changes which may be less obvious, but just as crucial. The people who come to the city find themselves sharing a common physical space, but little else. They may not have a language they can all speak together, or customs or ideology to bind them. But they do share a space, the neighborhood, the streets, parks, and public transportation that make up the public space and infrastructure of New York City. In these public areas, new and old residents pass each other by every day, but only infrequently interact. A ride on the number 7 train into Queens is a metaphor of sorts for this kind of experience. Immigrants and older residents, factory workers and office-bound commuters, school children and retirees all ride the subway. The space is communal, but the experience, while usually not unfriendly, is generally solitary. The challenge is finding or constructing a communal space that goes beyond mere physical proximity to include all the city's residents in shared interactions and common projects. The different ways in which residents, old and new, define and experience community make this goal more difficult.

Immigration to New York

In 1960, the city was about three-quarters white—now it's less than half. Much of this racial and ethnic change has taken place as the result of im-

Table 2. Changes in race and ethnicity of New York City population, 1960–1990

	Percentage of total population				
Ethnicity/race	1960	1970	1980	1986	1990
White	76.5%	63.2%	52.0%	44.1%	43.2%
Black	13.1	19.2	24.0	25.9	25.2
Hispanic	9.2	15.2	20.1	24.6	24.4
Other	1.3	2.3	3.8	5.4	7.2

Source: Brecher and Horton 1993: 6, table 1.1.

migration. Just as white residents began moving out in the 1960s, immigrants were taking their place (see Table 2). Except perhaps for Los Angeles, New York has felt the strongest impact of the newest wave of immigration. About 900,000 immigrants—one out of every seven arriving in the United States—settled in New York City in the 1980s.[2] Rates of legal immigration into New York City rose from an average of 57,000 a year in the 1960s to 78,000 a year in the 1970s, and then approximately to 86,000 annually in the 1980s.[3] By 1990, about 29 percent of the city's population was foreign born, the highest level since 1930.[4]

More than half this immigration was from Latin America and the Carib-

[2] The *New York Times* has slightly different figures for immigration to the city. According to Deborah Sontag, "A City of Immigrants is Pictured in Report," *New York Times*, July 1, 1992, p. B1, the census indicated that 953,000 New Yorkers had entered the U.S. in the 1980s. By contrast, Edward Fiske, "New York Growth Is Linked to Immigration," *New York Times*, February 22, 1991, p. B1, also cited the Census Bureau to claim that 854,000 immigrants arrived in the city between 1980 and 1989. Finally, Sam Roberts, "New York Exports Its Talent as a Migration Tide Turns," *New York Times*, March 6, 1994, p. A1, citing the 1990 Public Use Microdata Sample (PUMS) gives a figure of 680,000 immigrants for the decade. The Department of City Planning, for its part, counted more than 609,379 new legal immigrants between 1983 and 1989. Salvo and Ortiz 1992.

[3] These figures almost certainly undercount the city's immigrant population. The Census Bureau itself estimated that it had undercounted the total number of people in the city by probably 300,000, and according to city officials many of those overlooked lived in neighborhoods "where residents do not speak English, or fear the Government because they are illegal aliens, or live illegally doubled up in public housing"—neighborhoods, in other words, with large concentrations of immigrants. Richard Levine, "Big Gain Predicted in New York City if Census Is Adjusted," *New York Times*, April 20, 1991, p. 25.

[4] Immigration continued at a rapid clip through the mid-1990s: Census Bureau estimates indicate that about 460,000 immigrants arrived between 1990 and 1994, even as the city lost more than one-tenth of its population to other parts of the country. See Celia Dugger, "Immigrant Voters Reshape Politics: Idealistic New Citizens Attract Both Attention and Debate," *New York Times*, March 10, 1996, p. 1. See also Robert Friedman, "Huddled Masses by the Millions; Immigration Surge Accents New York Life," *New York Newsday*, June 24, 1990, p. 5.

Table 3. Comparison of selected Latin American immigration populations, 1982–1989

Country of origin	Immigration to N.Y.C.[a]	Immigration to the U.S.	% total immigration settling in N.Y.C.	Rank among new immigrants to N.Y.C.	Total immigrant population in N.Y.C. 1989[b]
Dominican Republic	116,000	190,000	60.8%	1	350,000
Colombia	23,000	85,000	26.7%	6	110,000
Ecuador	18,000	36,000	49.9%	9	90,000
Honduras	8,000	33,000	26.3%	14	26,000
El Salvador	8,000	82,000	10.0%	15	47,000
Peru	7,000	42,000	17.6%	19	32,000

Sources: Figures are from the INS annual immigrant file tapes, 1982–1989; unofficial figures that include illegal immigration are significantly higher. Data from Salvo and Ortiz 1992: 29.

[a] New York City received 15% of all legal immigrants in 1980, down from 20% in 1940.

[b] Data derived from 1990 that include census microdata sample in Institute in Puerto Rican Studies, 1992.

bean (see Table 3). New York attracts a disproportionate share of the immigration from many of this region's countries.

Forty percent of all Caribbean immigrants settle in the city, and 35 percent of all South American immigrants. Sixty-one percent of all Dominican immigrants—the single largest immigrant group to New York since 1965—settle in the city. Latinos now make up a quarter (or more, if one counts the numbers of undocumented immigrants) of the city's population.

Immigration to Queens

About a third of all recent legal immigrants have gone to the borough of Queens, joining those already established in the area's neighborhoods. This immigration, from over a hundred different countries, changed the composition of some Queens neighborhoods dramatically over the decade. In 1990, 36 percent of the population of Queens was born outside the United States, up from 29 percent in 1980. The number of Asians in Queens increased by 154 percent to 238,000; the number of Latinos increased 45 percent to 380,000.[5] Some indication of the diversity of the new population can be gauged by the fact that by 1990 the borough of Queens had substantial populations of Chinese, Guyanese, Dominicans, Colombians, Jamaicans,

[5] Edward Fiske, "New York Growth Is Linked to Immigration," *New York Times*, February 22, 1991, p. B1; M. P. McQueen, "Immigrants Flooding into U.S. Have Helped Transform Queens into a Brave New World," *New York Newsday*, August 1, 1993, p. 1.

Figure 1. Latin American immigration to Queens, by years of entry

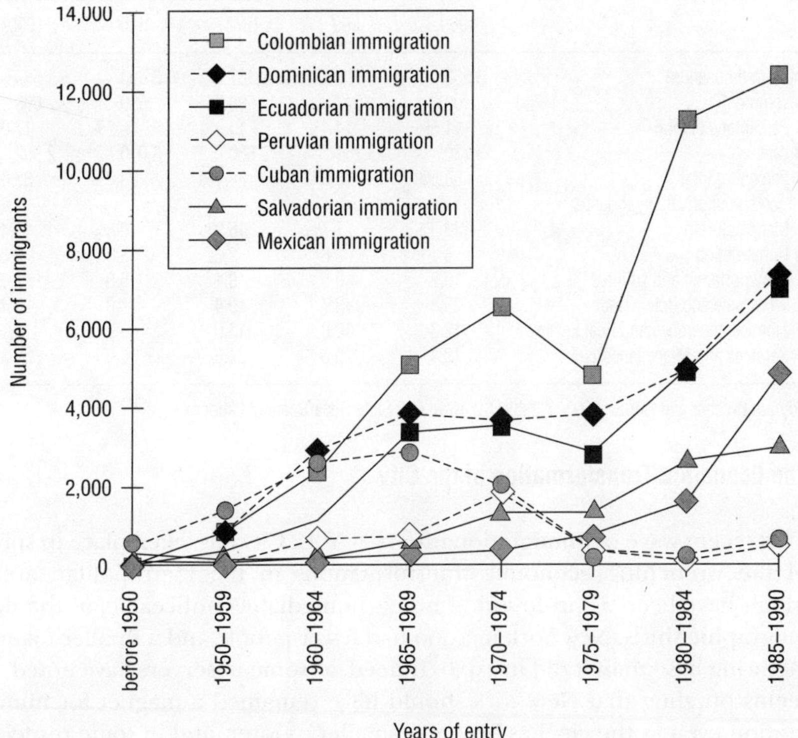

Source: 1990 Census Public Use Microdata Sample

Koreans, Indians, Ecuadorians, Filipinos, Romanians, Pakistanis, Iranians, Salvadorans, and Greeks, among immigrants of many other nationalities (Jackson 1995: 966–69). Asians accounted for 36 percent of new immigrants in the borough in the 1980s, while South Americans totaled about 24 percent. Figure 1 indicates the flow of the seven largest Latin American immigrant groups into Queens from 1950 to 1990, extrapolating from the 5 percent Public Use Microdata Sample in the 1990 census. The influx into northwest Queens was particularly large; this area received 48 percent of the borough's new immigrants. The neighborhoods of Astoria, Sunnyside, Woodside, Jackson Heights, Elmhurst, Corona, and Flushing absorbed 88,400 recent immigrants in a six- year period in the 1980s alone.[6]

[6] From 1983 to 1989, 184,000 legal immigrants moved to Queens. See ibid.

Table 4. Employment in New York City, 1960–1990

	1960	1969	1977	1987	1990
Total (in thousands)	3,538	3,797	3,187	3,590	3,569
Government	408	547	508	580	608
Percentage of total	11.5%	14.4%	15.9%	16.2%	17.0%
Private	3,130	3,251	2,680	3,010	2,962
Percent of total	88.5%	85.6%	84.1%	83.8%	83.0%
Percentage of private by industry					
Manufacturing	30.3%	21.7%	16.9%	10.6%	11.4%
Construction	4.1	2.8	2.0	3.3	3.8
Transportation and Utilities	10.2	8.5	8.1	6.0	7.6
Wholesale and Retail Trade	23.8	19.7	19.4	17.8	20.4
Finance, Insurance and Real Estate	12.3	12.3	13.0	15.3	17.5
Services and Miscellaneous	19.4	20.6	24.6	30.9	39.3

Source: Brecher and Horton 1993: 7, table 1.2; New York State Department of Labor.

The Economic Transformation of the City

This recent wave of immigration into New York City has taken place in spite of the wrenching economic transformations in the metropolitan area, which have been as profound, if not as immediately noticeable, as the demographic shifts. New York in 1990 had fewer people and a smaller manufacturing base than it did in 1956. Indeed, as some observers have noted, it seems puzzling that New York should have remained a magnet for immigration even as the city has become "smaller, poorer, and in some respects a less economically important part of the region and nation" than it was thirty years ago (Drennan 1991: 26; see also Waldinger 1989: 220). Overall employment levels in the city, which had dropped precipitously in the 1970s, only reached their 1969 level a decade later, when the city was enjoying a brief spate of rapid growth in the late 1980s (see Table 4). But this growth was significantly different from that which had driven previous cycles of economic expansion in the city. Manufacturing employment in 1990 was one-third of what it had been in 1960. On the other hand, the percentage employed in service industries had almost doubled, while employment in the so-called FIRE sector (finance, insurance, and real estate) had grown substantially during the period.[7]

Immigrants arriving in New York are no longer being swept into blue-

[7] For a review of the economic transitions in the city, and the city's role in an increasingly internationalized economy, see Waldinger and Bailey 1992; Drennan 1991; Waldinger 1989; Waldinger 1986–1987; and Sassen-Koob 1985. For a particularly bleak and scathing review of the city's development policies from 1960 to 1990 see Fitch 1993.

collar jobs in large factories, as they had been in the early decades of the twentieth century. Stable union jobs in the manufacturing sector have been rapidly disappearing, as these industries moved either elsewhere in the United States or overseas. Instead, immigrants are becoming the source of low-skilled labor in the new nonunionized jobs in the service and light manufacturing sectors of the economy.[8] The shift in the city's job base to services, together with white flight to the suburbs (there were almost 500,000 fewer whites in the city in 1990 than in 1980[9]) has created a demand for workers willing to work at low-skilled, low-paying jobs (Waldinger 1989: 221).

Immigrants to the city often operate on the margins of the economy, filling economic niches as self-employed entrepreneurs, owning small businesses dependent on the larger fortunes of the city. Their precarious position was made evident in the downturn in the city's economy from 1987 to 1992, when the city lost 337,000 jobs—11.2 percent of its total job base—wiping out all the employment increase between 1976 and 1988.[10] Over 100,000 of these jobs were in manufacturing.[11] This downturn pushed even more immigrants into self-employment, often not quite within legal bounds.[12] An estimated 17 percent of the city's economy is unregulated and off the books.[13]

Changing Neighborhoods, Constant Maps

The 1980s and 1990s saw immigrants increasingly moving into areas of the city which had been, until recently, all white. More than half of all neigh-

[8] The garment industry, long a magnet for immigrant labor, lost 45,000 jobs between 1980 and 1991. Many of these jobs moved elsewhere; many of those that stayed survived as nonunionized low-paying employment. Eben Shapiro, "This Is Not a Rags to Riches Story," *New York Times*, January 5, 1991.

[9] Fiske, "New York Growth." Another three-quarters of a million people left the city in the early 1990s, mostly to be replaced by almost half a million new immigrants. See Richard Perez-Peña, "New York's Foreign-born Population Increases," *New York Times*, March 9, 1996, pp. 1, 25; Sam Roberts, "Migration Tide."

[10] Thomas Lueck, "Job Recovery in New York Called Slowest: Recession Analysts See Region First In, Last Out," *New York Times*, May 3, 1992.

[11] Sarah Bartlett, "New York Logs 500,000 Jobs Lost since 1989," *New York Times*, April 16, 1992, p. B1.

[12] Donatella Lorch, "Ethnic Niches Creating Jobs That Fuel Immigrant Growth," *New York Times*, January 12, 1992, pp. 1, 20; Deborah Sontag, "Unlicensed Peddlers, Unfettered Dreams," *New York Times*, June 4, 1993.

[13] Deborah Sontag, "Émigrés in New York: Work off the Books," *New York Times*, June 13, 1993, pp. 1, 40.

borhoods in the city are now racially and ethnically diverse.[14] In spite of the marginalization of immigrants in the economy, one could interpret the demographic and residential diversity of the city as an indication of the integration of immigrants into the fabric of local communities, and of their revitalization of decaying neighborhoods (Winnick 1990).[15] This optimistic view, while not entirely false, does give a false impression. For the moment, immigrants and the older residents they encounter live in the same neighborhoods, but they experience these neighborhoods in very different ways.

In this situation maps, which are meant to guide visitors to a new area, are next to useless as indicators of "communities." Labels on maps are meant to correspond to the way in which people refer to the urban geography around them. A good street map of Queens, say, will indicate boundaries and names, not just of streets, but of areas. Within the borough, names are assigned to each neighborhood; in northwestern Queens, from west to east, from the East River to Flushing Meadows Park, these are Long Island City, Sunnyside, Woodside, Elmhurst, Jackson Heights, and Corona.[16] These names are meant to invoke an image of neighborhoods as separate and coherent communities. As Richard Sennett writes, it seems as though "in its garden variety definition, a community is a neighborhood, a place on a map; this definition makes good common sense now precisely because of the atomizing of the city which took place in the nineteenth century, so that people living in different places in the city lived different kinds of lives" ([1974] 1992: 221).

Mapmakers seem to *assume* that neighborhoods are communities; sociologists have been doing the same for a half-century or more. But what does "community" really mean?

"Community" is an odd word, carrying various and sometimes contradictory meanings. It has a long history of use in the social sciences; in these disciplines, it has had multiple definitions, at times stirring furious debate. But on the whole it has come to signify a particular kind of place—a space distanced from the rest of the world, separated by some sort of boundary,

[14] "Ethnically diverse" means containing significant numbers of at least three racial/ethnic groups: Asian, Latino, black, or white (Alba et al. 1995). Alba et al. note that all-white neighborhoods, in particular, are much less common, and that most whites now live in ethnically and racially diverse neighborhoods.

[15] Massey and Denton, in *American Apartheid* (1993), are considerably less sanguine, arguing for the likely continuation of urban segregation by race and class. On Latinos see especially chapter 5.

[16] Interestingly, these areas aren't marked by boundaries on street maps. Street maps are for strangers who only need to recognize their general location; residents are supposed to be familiar already with their neighborhood geography.

where what remains enclosed somehow has a unitary nature.[17] Locating "community," giving it a physical immediacy apart from whatever solidaristic ties exist, seems an attractive solution to the problems of discussing a concept so inherently ambiguous.

The hegemony of this territorial idea obscures alternative ways of thinking and talking about community, and the political consequences these differences can have. This is particularly true in the case of immigrants. Latin American immigrants to Queens are not fully part of the immediate neighborhood communities. The descendants of earlier European immigrants (or "white ethnics," as I will call them) relegate newer immigrants to the margins, literally, of the "community" as they conceive it. Latin American immigrants, for their part, do not see themselves as being bound to a territorial community that is physically present, but to one that exists mostly in memory. This community of memory both enables and constrains their social organization and political participation.

The White Ethnic Community

Northwestern Queens is, for the most part, a middle-class residential area, just across the East River from Manhattan—but much farther away in reality. In Queens, people refer to Manhattan as "the City," which means that in their minds at least, Queens isn't part of it. The sociologist Robert Park once expressed shock at "a city of two millions of people [in which] there are no hotels! Which means, of course, that there are no visitors."[18] This very nearly describes Queens. The only people in the borough are those who live there—almost two million in 1990.[19]

[17] See, for example, G. A. Hillery's review of definitions of community (1955). Hillery counted 94 definitions of community in the sociological literature alone, but 69 of these stress locality as one of the characteristics of community, as well as common ties and social interaction. More recent work continues to identify community as a territorial phenomenon. Charles Tilly's main concern in his influential article "Do Communities Act?" is the question of "collective action on a territorial basis" (1973: 212). See also Austin and Baba 1990: 59; Lyon 1987: 7; Guest and Lee 1983; and Keller 1968.

[18] Park (1925: 11) borrowed this observation from Walter Besant, who was describing East London.

[19] There is a surprising lack of research and writing on Queens. A notable exception is Roger Sanjek's direction of ongoing research on the borough since 1983 for a project on "New Immigrants and Old Americans" (Sanjek 1988). See also Vincent Seyfried, *Corona: From Farmland to City Suburb, 1650–1935* (New York: Edigan Press, 1987), Richard Lieberman, *City Limits: A Social History of Queens* (Dubuque: Kendall-Hunt, 1983), and Jon Peterson, ed., *A Research Guide to the History of the Borough of Queens* (Flushing: Department of History, Queens College CUNY, 1987).

In 1900 this area was still mostly farmland. Development began in 1900 when the Pennsylvania Railroad bought out the Long Island Railroad and increased service to Manhattan, electrifying the route (1905–1908) and opening up tunnels under the East River (1910)—bringing most of Queens within commuting distance of Manhattan. Queensboro Bridge was opened in 1909, providing access by trolley and, for those that had them, by car. The story of the development of Queens is the story of the expansion of mass transit in New York City.

Development really took off in 1917, with the completion of the number 7 subway and elevated line into Manhattan. The Queensboro Corporation had been buying up hundreds of acres of land in what is now Jackson Heights, and built up the entire neighborhood around a series of low-lying ornately designed garden apartments which set the pattern for apartment building in the area. Much of the housing in these neighborhoods was constructed between 1920 and 1960, and bought up by second- or third-generation immigrants moving out from "the City" to the quieter areas of the outlying boroughs. By 1960, the area was almost completely built up (Jackson 1995).

The neighborhoods in northwestern Queens were originally composed of European immigrants and their descendants: Italians, Irish, and Jews—second- and third-generation "white ethnics." The 1965 Immigration Act, which allocated immigration more equally among countries, and shifted its emphasis toward family reunification, changed all this. Even before 1965, there was, however, already a steady trickle of new immigration into the area. Cuban and South American professionals settled in the area as early as the 1930s.[20] These residents became the sponsors for a much larger wave of immigrants arriving after 1965. Little by little over the last thirty years, the white ethnic population has been displaced by newer immigrants, many of them from Colombia, Ecuador, the Dominican Republic, Peru, Cuba, Mexico, and the other countries of the hemisphere, but also immigrants from China, Korea, and India. Today European immigrants and their descendants are a minority in these neighborhoods.

For example if we look at one of these neighborhoods, Jackson Heights, on a map (see Map 1), the area delineated closely corresponds to the area covered by the post office's zip code designation.[21] New York City's Planning

[20] Elsa Chaney, "Colombian Migration to the United States (Part 2)," in *The Dynamics of Migration: International Migration*, Occasional Monographs Series, no. 5, vol. 2, pp. 87–141 (Washington, D.C.: Interdisciplinary Communications Program, Smithsonian Institution, 1976); cited in Sanjek 1988.

[21] Probably the best, and certainly one of the easier, ways of distinguishing neighborhood areas.

Office breaks down its immigration figures (working from census data) by zip code, and these indicate that Jackson Heights received 11,375 legal immigrants from 1983 to 1989.[22] The surrounding neighborhoods received a good deal of new immigration as well: Elmhurst received 17,176, Woodside 11,666, and Corona 14,255. But looking at immigration data this way reifies the idea of separate neighborhood communities, and suggests that immigrants are fitting into an existing framework of neighborhoods.[23] This is only partly true.

White ethnics in Jackson Heights, particularly those who are more actively involved in local associations, have often lived much of their lives there. For them the neighborhood has always seemed something changeless and *known*. Demarcations between neighborhood and neighborhood are commonly acknowledged: the railway lines, the Brooklyn-Queens Expressway, Roosevelt Avenue, Northern Boulevard, Junction Boulevard.[24] For instance the City Council member for the district explains how he sees the community:

> Now, traditional community boundary lines is like a railroad, OK, like the connecting railroad by the BQE. Or an expressway. Very little commerce, pedestrian traffic, [a different] mindset. There are very few people who live on 73d Street and Broadway who do business in Woodside—they do it in Jackson Heights. Now it may be closer in some ways to 61st Street and Woodside, but you just don't find that happening.
>
> Northern Boulevard has always been a boundary in Jackson Heights. Between [here and] the northern part of Jackson Heights, which some people call Trains Meadow . . . [or] East Elmhurst . . . [B]ut it's a different housing stock—it's one-family and two-family homes, and on the other side of Northern is largely apartments. Plus it's a large busy highway, so that a lot of people don't cross . . . it's a totally different mindset.

[22] Jackson Heights in 1990 had 129,000 residents: 43% Hispanic, 28% white, 15.5% black, 11.5% Asian. Like much of northwestern Queens, it is among the most diverse areas of New York City.

[23] Other bureaucratic designations reinforce the idea of communities traced by neighborhood boundaries: the districts covered by the community boards, the board of education, and police precincts.

[24] Residents speaking at the public hearings held by the state reapportionment task force, for instance, defined communities territorially, using streets to mark boundaries: "The community is defined by these streets: 43rd Avenue to the south, 149th Street to the west, 23rd Avenue to the north, Broadway to the east; [these streets] help us to define our identity . . . an identity of interests." Or: "Jackson Heights has been divided in half. The traditional borders of Jackson Heights have always been Northern Boulevard, Roosevelt Avenue and Junction Boulevard." Author's fieldnotes, public hearing, New York State Legislative Task Force on Demographic Research and Reapportionment, Queens Borough Hall, February 13, 1992.

Map 1. North-central Queens

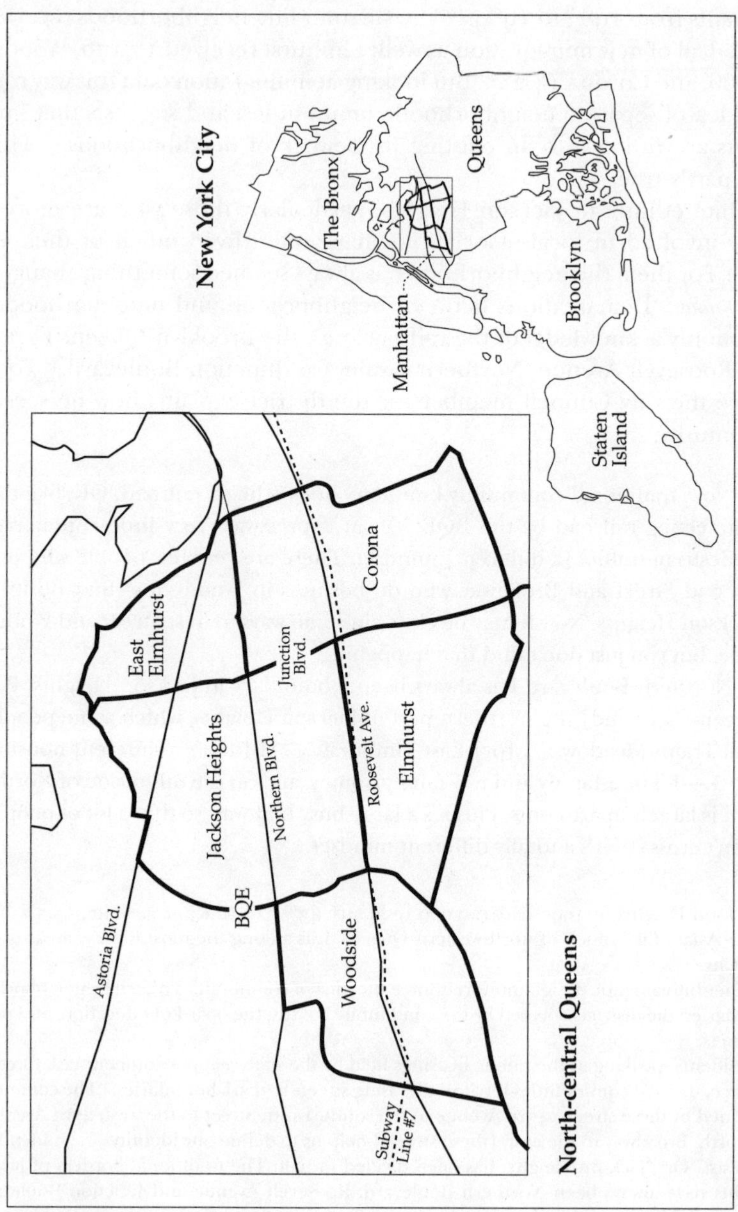

Source: CUNY Data Center

> Roosevelt is another traditional boundary, separates Elmhurst from Jackson Heights. . . . People who live on one side of Roosevelt Avenue don't cross to the other side of Roosevelt Avenue, because they live in Jackson Heights and they do their business in Jackson Heights. And the people who live in Elmhurst do their business on Broadway. That's just the way things are . . . my mother has never been to a store on the other side of Roosevelt in her life.[25]

In white ethnics' imaginations neighborhood frontiers are forever fixed. Older residents still navigate around the same landmarks as they always have. To a large extent, for them community *is* the neighborhood with its boundaries. The idea of community doesn't shift, even though the neighborhood has been changing, and continues to change. The community still encompasses the neighborhood, where everyone is supposed to know everyone else,[26] where everyone supposedly spends their lives—even as they know this is no longer true (if it ever was), even as they feel "their" neighborhoods changing.

This may be why, while some of the neighborhood's boundaries seem "natural" (in the same manner as a Chicago School sociologist might have seen it: the Brooklyn Queens Expressway a six-lane canyon cutting through Queens, and Northern Boulevard with three or four lanes going in each direction), others seem less so. Why should Roosevelt Avenue or Junction Boulevard be considered natural boundaries? Roosevelt has two lanes of traffic, with the number 7 train built overhead—a major transportation route into Manhattan. The street is lined with shops, restaurants, and travel agencies.[27] It is a vibrant and congested street, and an important public space for pedestrians. Roosevelt has become the main thoroughfare for newer immigrants in the area, but most older white ethnic residents avoid it. For them it has "a completely different lifestyle. It's South American, Hispanic. . . . Completely different. It's almost like you are in a different country." Whites resent this: Latin American immigrants

> come from a different culture. And we people who have been here all these years are not used to their culture. They [white ethnic residents] object. You

[25] Interview, Council member, 25th District, January 9, 1992. Note how closely this description of the neighborhood resembles Wirth's description of the Chicago ghetto, enclosed by "natural boundaries" (Wirth 1925).

[26] The president of the Jackson Heights Neighborhood Association, who has lived in the area for 26 years, described his discomfort with transients: "We have a community driveway down the back—but I want to know who my neighbors are. I want to know the face. I want to know whether they belong on my driveway or not." In his mind, most immigrants are just transient: "The intention of the newer immigrants is not to stay." Interview, April 29, 1991.

[27] There are 168 businesses on the stretch along Elmhurst and Jackson Heights alone, and another 60 where Roosevelt runs through Corona. See Yuan 1986.

see them with the radios. The kids with radios in their cars, with the fringes, all that fancy stuff. Well, we don't do that. . . . They [white ethnics] resent it. . . . The fact that there are all those Hispanic restaurants. So few American restaurants. They won't even go to a Spanish restaurant, even though a Spanish—Hispanic—restaurant gives them better food for less money. They're afraid to try it, they don't want to try it.[28]

Intermingled with the worry about the changes taking place is the fear that comes with the association of immigrants with drug-dealing, prostitution, and crime.[29] Roosevelt Avenue is seen as the center of illegal activity in the area, perpetrated by new immigrants.[30] On a tour of the street at night, the district attorney exclaimed, "I was shocked . . . Roosevelt Avenue in the middle of the night is like a Turkish Bazaar." Mary Sarro, for many years the Community Board 3 district manager, called it "a zoo, a horror show."[31]

[28] Interview, member, Community Board 3, April 13, 1991. Similar fears surface in older residents' views toward Asians as well. On the reaction to Asians in Flushing, for instance: "The rapid rate of Asian immigration has created a situation in which many of the new residents do not speak English well. Some of the people who used to call Flushing home no longer feel any sense of identity walking the streets. With the increasing presence of Asians, a certain amount of inter-ethnic conflict has already surfaced in community life in Flushing. Long time residents feel that they are being locked out of their own neighborhoods. They complain bitterly about the non-English signs on the local shops and business establishments. They feel anxious about going into the restaurants, afraid they will not be able to read the menus, speak to the waiters, or eat the food. Some of our respondents told us that they have difficulty getting served in the Chinese and Korean restaurants. If they do manage to get the attention of the waiter, they often have to suffer the indignity of being shepherded into the 'foreigners' section of the restaurant, which is often close to the kitchen or the toilets. Some report that they are treated ungraciously—given forks to eat instead of chopsticks, being shown only simplified menus, and charged higher prices than Asian customers" (Smith 1995: 78).

[29] For instance, it is rumored that the Peruvian Shining Path has established its North American headquarters in Jackson Heights, and that in the 1980s Jackson Heights was one of the most important centers for Colombian cocaine traffic in this country. "All Mixed Up," *New Yorker*, June 22, 1992. A retired police officer living in Jackson Heights said to me: "This is the city of fear. When I go to the city now, to go the restaurant or to the theater, I carry my 9 mm. I take it because I'm scared. If I feel this way, and I carry protection, what do other people do? Here I just carry this small thing" (flipping open his jacket to show me the pistol clipped to his belt). Author's fieldnotes, May 1, 1992.

[30] Police call Roosevelt Avenue the largest center of prostitution in the city outside of Manhattan. "Sordid Business Booms in Queens," *New York Times*, January 30, 1992; "Survival of the Feistiest: Neighborhood Fights Summer Crime Surge," *New York Newsday*, July 28, 1992. Jackson Heights is also supposedly one of the main centers in the city for drug-dealing and money-laundering. For an example of sensationalistic and overblown reporting, see Ian Fisher, "A Window on Immigrant Crime: In Jackson Heights, Drugs, Dirty Money, and Prostitution," *New York Times*, June 17, 1993, pp. A1, B8.

[31] "Roosevelt Avenue Vice Eyed," *Jackson Heights News*, November 18, 1991.

Junction Boulevard and Roosevelt Avenue, central for immigrants in the vicinity, are borders for older white ethnic residents; illegal activity only serves to confirm the avenue's marginalization.[32]

In so much of their public rhetoric, white ethnics defend Jackson Heights as a *place,* and it is the place, the physical structure of the neighborhood, they regard as the community. By this logic, if you don't reside in the neighborhood, then you aren't a member of "the community." Every year, for instance, there are three Latin American immigrant parades, among others, which march down 37th Avenue through the interior of Jackson Heights, from west to east. The manager of the Jackson Heights Community Development Corporation recalled opposition to the Latin American parades: "One of the big bitches the community has, and I bitch about it too, is that every year . . . it seems that every other Hispanic Parade goes marching down 37th Avenue. And the organizers of the parades are citywide groups, with none of their leadership or members within the community, so everyone feels like 'why are they disrupting our community?' Nobody would bitch if it was a parade done by a local group."[33] Rhetorically, at least, white ethnics' objections are to outsiders, not to Latin American immigrants per se; neighborhood residents presumably are accorded more tolerance and a different set of rights. When a cultural awareness group was set up to allow people to explain differences between immigrants and white ethnics, one meeting was set up for Colombian immigrants. The CDC manager recounted the story: "Two lawyers from Jackson Heights said, oh, we'll be there and we represent [Colombians in Jackson Heights], but they didn't. They didn't live in the community. So they really weren't representative of the community."[34] Not living in the neighborhood means not belonging.

However, living in the neighborhood is not sufficient to be part of the community, because white ethnics' idea of community is not purely territorial in nature—it includes the espousal and protection of a way of life. In large part this plays out as the difference between the familiar and the foreign, which is manifested in two ways. The first is language. Speaking English becomes a measure of one's commitment to being part of the community. The manager of Community Board 4 draws distinctions, for example, between the older European immigrants and the newer Latino and Asian residents: "They never consider this their home. The children are citizens. But they never speak to them in English. I grew up in an Italian

[32] For discussions of the equation of marginalization and illegality, see Norton 1988: 68–69, 160–64, and Hobsbawm [1969] 1981.

[33] Interview, May 6, 1991. The CDC is a city-funded nonprofit organization.

[34] Ibid.

neighborhood. . . . And I never spoke to my girlfriend to this day—we've been friends since kindergarten—I've never said an Italian word to her. We weren't brought up that way. Yet you see these kids, they are talking . . . to each other in Spanish and they were born here. They . . . never speak English."[35] Second, being part of the community means keeping to certain standards of decorum. The manager of Community Board 3 claims that newcomers are accepted as long as they uphold these standards. Most immigrants, she says, do not.

> They come from countries where they can do many things, you see, many of the complaints that we receive is that they don't maintain community standards. Like someone will come in—this is very basic, but we deal with very basic emotions here. Say someone buys a house, and there's a beautiful dogwood tree in the front yard. And they cut it down. Which offends the neighbors tremendously. Or they don't put their refuse out properly. Or they don't really maintain their home properly. Although you get the other side where many of them do and upgrade their property. I think basically, truly, it is a class distinction. If you maintain your property, maintain the standards, you are very quickly accepted, they really don't care who you are. It's when you don't, and you do whatever you care on the street, which [we] find very offensive, and you block driveways, and you play loud music. You know, party all night and you are boisterous, then that becomes very offensive . . . that may be normal behavior, but to the established resident that is not normal behavior.[36]

To be accepted as a member of the community by second- and third-generation white ethnics, immigrants not only have to live in the neighborhood, they also have to "be good neighbors," accepting neighborhood standards and traditional ways of doing things. These standards can be enforced

[35] Interview, April 22, 1991.

[36] Interview, April 9, 1991. In her study of immigrants in a Philadelphia neighborhood, Goode (1990) also noted the importance older residents placed on immigrants' "keeping to the rules": "Transgressions abound: not knowing which day is trash day; 'throwing slop on the porch'; loud blaring multi-speaker car radios; using up all the parking spaces on the block with multiple vans of a family business; outdoor parties at odd times; inappropriately hanging around the school yard during recess and bringing children prohibited snacks in dangerous glass containers; remodeling buildings as churches and businesses without proper permits. These are all talked about as rule infractions which should be corrected through stern and patronizing lectures by community authorities and law enforcers. There is," she concludes optimistically, "nonetheless a strong expectation that newcomers will learn" (135). See Michael Efthimiades, "Peddler Crackdown," *Jackson Heights News*, July 30, 1992, p. 1; and Michael Efthimiades, "Doggie Doo Patrol Created to Catch Violators," *Jackson Heights News*, July 23, 1992, p. 1.

by residents, at times brutally. In one instance, a Dominican youth caught spray-painting graffiti in the Italian enclave in Corona known as "Spaghetti Park" was chased down the street and beaten to death by several men with baseball bats.[37]

Immigrants in the Neighborhood

Suppose we show the data on the number of immigrants in New York differently from the way it is shown by the City Planning Office—instead of emphasizing zip code areas, we look at ethnicity by census tract. If we shade in those census tracts with a plurality or majority population of Latin American origin (see Map 2), we see another picture emerge. The physical space occupied by Latinos is centered on Roosevelt Avenue and Junction Boulevard, those very streets designated as "boundary lines" by white ethnics. Much of the recent immigrant settlement is on either side of those streets. This shouldn't be surprising; immigrant settlement falls on either side of the main public transportation route into Manhattan.[38] Is Roosevelt a border, or is it the main street for the community? Perhaps neither spatial representation fully captures the way people living in the area think about and act in their surroundings.

In some ways Roosevelt Avenue, and to a lesser extent Junction Boulevard, serve as the physical core of the Latin American immigrant community. Every day dozens of immigrant vendors illegally set out their goods along the sidewalks of Roosevelt and Junction.[39] When Colombia won a playoff game for the 1990 World Cup in soccer, immigrants came out onto Roosevelt to celebrate en masse, blocking traffic.[40] After journalist Manuel de Dios Unanue was assassinated in a local restaurant, a funerary protest march of several hundred persons marched down Roosevelt.[41] But these incidents do not show that Latin American immigrants think of themselves as inhabiting their own physical community in Queens, with its own boundaries.

[37] Author's fieldnotes, meeting with district attorney Richard Brown, December 17, 1991.

[38] The City Planning Office notes that proximity to public transportation is a major determinant of immigrant settlement patterns, particularly in Queens and Brooklyn (Salvo and Ortiz, 1992: 161).

[39] Much to the dismay of store owners and older residents. See Efthimiades, "Peddler Crackdown."

[40] The celebration led to a confrontation between immigrants and police, resulting in a minor riot. This incident is one more reason Roosevelt has a bad reputation with white ethnics. Interview, director, Jackson Heights Community Development Corporation, May 6, 1991.

[41] Author's fieldnotes, March 27, 1992.

Map 2. Ethnic concentrations in North-central Queens, 1990

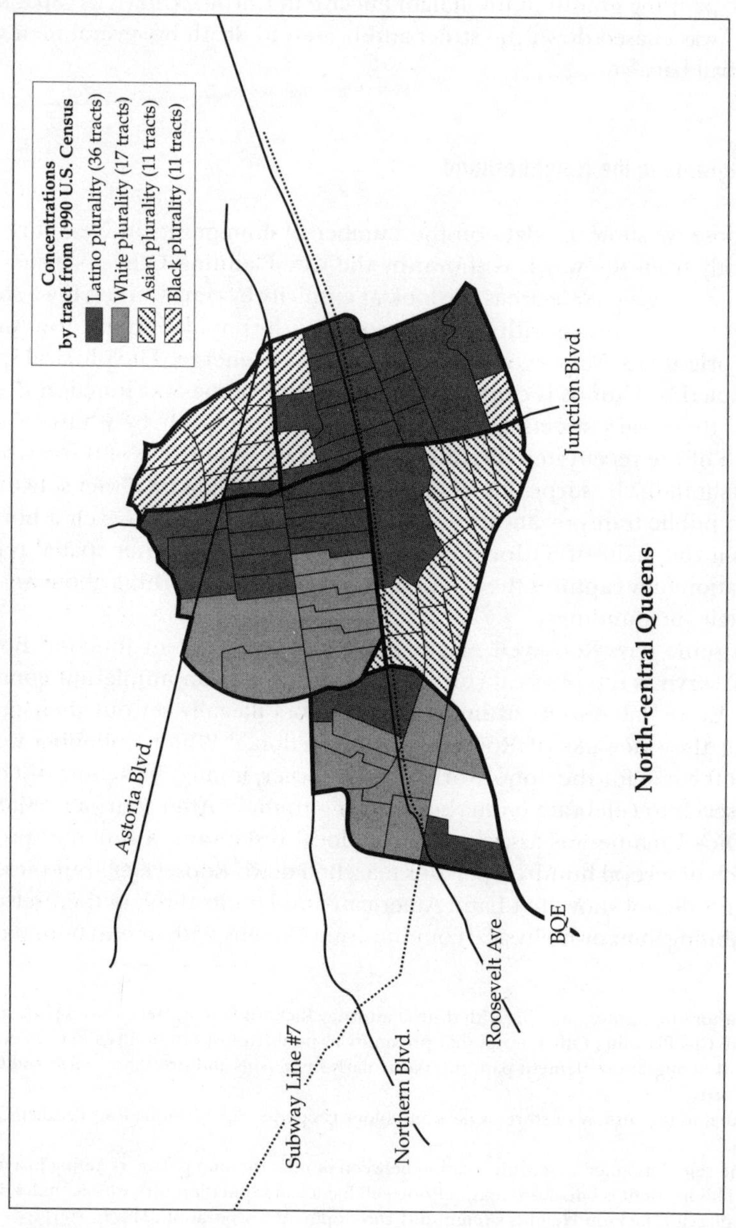

Source: CUNY Data Center

Immigrants may see themselves as living in a place and yet not being *of* that place. Ira Katznelson, in his study of northern Manhattan in the 1970s, describes how "for most Washington Heights–Inwood residents, the block and neighborhood provided the most tangible experiences and ties of daily life. Indeed, for most people, the block and its surrounding turf was so important that it shaped their entire identity" (1981: 104). He notes, however, an exception to this description: Greeks in Washington Heights were not involved in the physical space of the neighborhood. For this group, the Greek Orthodox church provided the focus for social relations. "Through its schools, perpetuation of the Greek language, and the provision of a whole set of activities such as singing, dancing, and talk and slide presentations on Greece, the church provided a relatively complete social world. One consequence was that there was little place for any kind of social life outside the set of activities that it sponsored . . . Greek involvement in non-Greek networks, including political ones, was minimal" (ibid.). Katznelson sees the Greek case—a complete withdrawal from the social space of the neighborhood—as atypical. But it is not atypical for recent immigrants to conceptualize and experience space differently from the way long-term residents might.

Immigrants are newcomers to a place, and their perceptions of it will differ substantially from those of long-time residents. The differences will be not only of space but of time. Describing northern Manhattan, Katznelson writes that the neighborhood "was divided in new ways between groups that did not share essentially similar pasts" (ibid. 107)—in other words, their history of the place colored their experience of it. "Neighborhoods enclose people who, like automobile drivers on a highway, move 'at different speeds, and have no mode of communication and little mutual understanding about how to stay out of each other's way in unforeseen circumstances.'"[42] Though somewhat overstated, the point is well taken. People can share the same space and perceive it in very different ways. Each group of people may have its own landmarks—the churches they attend, stores and restaurants they patronize, or the particular bars they frequent. Distinct groups of people in a neighborhood may have overlapping experiences in a shared space and yet their lives may hardly touch at all.

What role does territoriality play for Latino immigrants? Geography is still a part of Latin American immigrants' conception of community, but it is largely the geography of memory, which lends a certain vagueness to their experience of community; not being immediate, it lacks concreteness. An-

[42] Katznelson 1981: 107, quoting Murray Edelman, "Space and Social Order," discussion paper presented at the Institute for Research and Poverty, University of Wisconsin, August 1978.

derson recounts how the creation of a reading public allowed the creation of national "imaginary communities," with each provincial reader aware that others shared the same thoughts and experiences ([1983] 1992: 188). In the same vein, for Latin American immigrants in this country community is based in the shared memory of the geography of the home country. The more time they spend in the United States, however, the more this territory becomes entirely imagined, existing neither in this country, nor any longer in the country left behind.

Communities Overlapping but Not Touching

Immigrants and older white ethnic residents live side-by-side in the neighborhoods of northwestern Queens. But the communities they live in, while they overlap, may not quite touch. At least in the dislocations and transitions experienced by this first generation of immigrants, neighborhoods are more likely to contain multiple communities than to constitute a community itself. The signs of this in neighborhoods like Jackson Heights are clearly evident.

Older residents are intent on keeping public spaces intact and familiar. For instance, when the city was considering budget cuts in its public transportation system, one of the first items up for consideration were the buses running from the outer boroughs into the city. Many middle-class, mostly white, commuters use these buses, which run parallel to the subway, to get to and from work every day. The buses are seen as being safer and faster than the subway, and are used much less by the working-class immigrant and minority commuters, who use the elevated trains to get to Manhattan. When the city held public hearings on the planned cut-back, the City Council member for Jackson Heights said it was "the biggest political issue here in the last five years."[43]

Another example might be the attempt by the Jackson Heights Beautification Group to designate the apartment buildings making up the older core of Jackson Heights—a thirty-six block area—as a historic district.[44] The buildings of the area, they argued, while not necessarily architecturally distinct in and of themselves, as a whole created a unique architectural space which they felt merited preservation. Whatever the aesthetic merits of the argument, the effect of the proposal would have been to continue the

[43] Author's fieldnotes, April 16, 1992.

[44] Steven Lee Myers, "Historic Preservation Comes of Age in Queens," *New York Times*, February 3, 1993, p. B1.

character of the upper-middle-class (and mostly white ethnic) ownership of the apartments. Only this type of owner could afford to keep the buildings up in their pristine historic condition. In this sense, the creation of a historic district would have reinforced the effect that the conversion of most of these buildings to co-op status had in the 1980s—to keep that section of Jackson Heights as a middle-class, mostly white enclave in a rapidly changing Queens.[45]

The immigrant and white ethnic communities, like the commuter bus route and the subway, run parallel but separately. The older residents in the neighborhood are not inveterately opposed to including the newcomers, at least in principle. But to be included in this community one must accept the rules laid down by the older residents. Goode, in her ethnography of white ethnic neighborhoods in northeastern Philadelphia that were also coping with immigrant transitions, writes that in the eyes of established residents

> newcomers to America are construed as guests and established residents as hosts. The host-guest relationship asserts priority rights for the established residents over community institutions and standards of behavior. Guests can "learn the rules" and become incorporated. Newcomers should be welcomed. They are assumed to be escaping from terrible economic and political situations and have the "right" to come. Hosts are obligated to accept newcomers and teach them about the community and its ways. However, they must allow newcomers to keep some limited aspects of their own ways. These safe, sanitized emblems of their peasant culture, folk music and traditional foods should be performed at events to create appreciation and mutual respect. . . .
>
> As a return for their welcome, newcomers should show gratitude and be loyal to America. They are obligated to learn the language and the rules of the community as quickly as possible. They should not try to change the rules (1990: 134).

Of course until immigrants "learn the rules" they are kept at arm's length, literally relegated to the margins of the community, areas in Queens designated as "criminal" or "dirty" (see Sibley 1995: chap. 4 and 5).

Until immigrants learn the rules, they're kept at the margins. They are expected to learn the rules on their own, and when they do, they can be al-

[45] Christopher Gray, "Waiting in Queens for Historic Status," *New York Times*, June 28, 1992, section 10, p. 7. The attempt to designate a historic district also continues Jackson Heights' unfortunate history in trying to keep out "undesirables": when the apartments were first constructed, there were covenants to keep out Jews, blacks, and others (Jackson 1995).

lowed in the community—asked to join neighborhood associations, sit on community boards, and the like. It can be a very long time, however, before immigrants navigate their way among these rules. Having a different sense of community and seeing the neighborhood in a different way, immigrants are as likely to keep to their own rules, or perhaps eventually even change the rules, as to adopt the established rules as their own. Until then immigrants and older residents continue to run on their separate, but parallel, courses.

The isolation of new and old residents from one another, the absence of any kind of interaction that goes beyond the sharing of the physical space of the neighborhoods in which they live, is problematic. What is happening in these neighborhoods in Queens, among passengers on the number 7 train and in other public spaces in the city exemplifies the social and political isolation of immigrants and others on the margins throughout American society. With citizenship, too, immigrants are expected to learn the rules on their own, and are only allowed in when they manage to do so. Until then, they float untethered to formal politics. It's this dilemma, and why it matters, that we turn to next.

2

Participation in the American Polity: Why Citizenship Matters

The common political identity under which Americans have traditionally acted is that of citizenship. This shared membership facilitates discussion and mobilization for communal projects. Immigration can be problematic because it allows people into the polity who do not share this identity. They are not automatically included as members, and in fact may not wish immediately to become members. However, every polity includes residents who are not full members, whether by choice or law. Children, criminals, and foreigners rarely have the same rights as full members. So merely having neighbors who do not share membership in the polity is not in itself problematic. However, a new situation arises when, as is happening today, incorporation and membership are not even part of the discussion.

This chapter considers the implications of the absence of any mention of citizenship from the current debate on immigration, and makes the case for why we should be concerned if immigrants are not full members under the umbrella of citizenship. Aside from the very real dangers of their exploitation by the unscrupulous, the marginality of immigrants and others in the polity has three very damaging consequences: it undermines the processes of representation and accountablity which are central to representative democracy, it reinforces our undervaluation of participation in the political process, and it encourages our willingness to see immigrants as outsiders instead of as potential citizens.

Immigration Anxiety

Americans have always felt ambivalent about immigration, and events in the 1990s have only raised public anxiety about it. Islamic fundamentalists, some residing in the United States illegally, were convicted of the World Trade Center bombing in 1993, and another group was tried for participating in a conspiracy to blow up New York City's tunnels and bridges. A shipwreck off the Long Island coast with nearly three hundred illegal Chinese immigrants aboard turned attention to the smuggling of foreigners into the United States.[1] The number of illegal migrants apprehended at the borders has risen once again to well over one million a year.[2] Commentators have increasingly spoken of immigration spiraling out of control, of American borders in chaos.

Surveys asking about immigration have drawn increasingly negative responses. In 1993 a *New York Times*/CBS poll elicited the highest negative response ever to the question of whether immigration levels should be kept at current levels or decreased: 61 percent favored a decrease—as opposed to 49 percent in 1986, 42 percent in 1977, and 33 percent in 1965.[3] This is only one in a series of polls that have tracked Americans' disenchantment with the newest wave of immigration.[4] Respondents are not necessarily unhappy with immigration in principle, or even with individual immigrants,[5]

[1] Jaclyn Fierman et al., "Is Immigration Hurting the U.S.?" *Fortune*, August 9, 1993, p. 76.

[2] David Johnston, "Rise in Crossings Spurs New Actions to Seal U.S. Border," *New York Times*, February 9, 1992, p. A1.

[3] Seth Davis, "Poll Finds Tide of Immigration Brings Hostility," *New York Times*, June 27, 1993, p. 1; see also Tony Freemantle, "Anti-immigrant Sentiment Rises; Impact a Matter of Debate," *The Houston Chronicle*, July 4, 1993, p. 1.

[4] Many recent polls have shown similar findings. See for instance the 1993 Gallup poll cited in Richard L. Berke, "Politicians Discovering an Issue: Immigration," *New York Times*, March 8, 1994. The "Empire State Survey" in 1993 indicated that a majority of New Yorkers believed relations between immigrants and natives were tense (second only to black-white relations) and that there were too many immigrants in the city. Rob Polner, "Us and Them: Poll Shows Harsh Divisions over Race and Immigration," *New York Newsday*, October 25, 1993, p. 7. For overviews of attitudes of the U.S. public on immigration issues, see Espenshade and Hempstead 1996; Simon and Alexander 1993; Hoskin 1990.

[5] In a 1993 *New York Times*/CBS poll 67% said newcomers to their neighborhood would be welcomed, about the same percentage which gave that answer in 1968; James Adams, "New York Bombers Blunder into the Arms of FBI Agents," *New York Times*, June 27, 1993, p. 1. On the other hand, in a 1996 poll of probable voters 36% of respondents said that recent immigrants have burdened their community while 31% thought recent immigrants made a contribution. The remaining 33% thought recent immigration was not an issue. See "Americans Divided on Immigrants," United Press International, March 20, 1996. In addition, some observers have noted a rise in anti-immigrant actions. See Deborah Sontag, "Across the U.S., Immigrants Find the Land of Resentment," *New York Times*, December 11, 1992, pp. A1, B4.

but with what immigrants have come to represent. A *Newsweek* poll in 1993 indicated, for instance, that 60 percent of Americans see current levels of immigration as a bad thing, while 59 percent simultaneously believe that immigration in the past was good. Fifty-nine percent say that "many" immigrants wind up on welfare, and only 20 percent think America is a melting pot.[6] Some observers write of "a kind of xenophobic fever spreading"—certainly hyperbolic language, but also indicative of the rising level of anxiety.[7]

Both Republican and Democratic politicians "want to see, and be seen at, a get-tough effort to control immigration." In California, Republican governor Pete Wilson's call for a crackdown on illegal immigration became the basis of his 1996 campaign for the presidency.[8] The state legislature passed a number of laws trying to curb illegal immigration, and in 1994 voters approved Proposition 187, which authorized cuts in medical, welfare, and education benefits to immigrants.[9] At the national level, Congress introduced legislation in 1994 to cut the number of both legal and illegal immigrants into the United States, and a group of twelve Republicans and two Democrats has proposed a constitutional amendment that would deny citizenship to the American-born children of illegal immigrants.[10] Even President Clinton joined what seems to have become the new consensus, announcing in 1993, together with a proposal to spend additional hundreds of millions of dollars to bolster the Border Patrol and to crack down on visa fraud and phony asylum cases, that "we must not—we will not—surrender our borders to those who wish to exploit our history of compassion and justice."[11]

[6] Tom Morgenthau et al., "America: Still a Melting Pot?" *Newsweek*, August 9, 1993, pp. 16ff.

[7] Penny Loeb et al., "To Make a Nation," *U.S. News and World Report*, October 4, 1993, pp. 47–53.

[8] Berke, "Immigration."

[9] Four of these bills, backed by the Federation for American Immigration Reform, an anti-immigrant lobbying organization, were passed in 1993 denying drivers' licenses to illegal immigrants, prohibiting local sanctuary ordinances, enabling easier deportation of prisoners, and blocking government job placement to undocumented residents. See Patrick J. McDonnell et al., "FAIR at Forefront of Push to Reduce Immigration," *Los Angeles Times*, November 24, 1993, p. A1. The implementation of Proposition 187 was stalled by its opponents in the courts. See "Judge Keeps Ban Intact against California Immigration Law," Reuters, December 14, 1994; "Prop 187 Challenge Proceeds," Associated Press, March 14, 1995.

[10] Berke, "Immigration," and Deborah Sontag, "Calls to Restrict Immigration Come from Many Quarters," *New York Times*, December 13, 1992, p. E5. The news commentator Cokie Roberts noted that "what is happening is that there's . . . an amendment on every single bill that's coming up saying that none of the money in that legislation can go to illegal aliens" ("This Week with David Brinkley," *ABC News*, July 25, 1993).

[11] Morgenthau et al., "Melting Pot." See also "INS Chief Hails Spending Bills," Associated Press, August 10, 1995. The budget for the Immigration and Naturalization Service was $2.6 billion in fiscal year 1996, more than 20% over the previous year's levels, and the highest in the agency's history.

Clinton echoed an earlier statement made by Republican president Ronald Reagan, almost word for word. Immigration in the 1990s has truly become a bipartisan issue.

The overwhelming worry is about the economic rather than political consequences of immigration. The concern is whether immigrants take away jobs from native-born Americans and consume rather than contribute to public resources. Economists argue incessantly over the costs and benefits of immigration.[12] Environmentalists worry about the degradation of natural resources,[13] some Hispanic Americans wonder whether illegal immigrants lower wages,[14] and African-American interest groups are split over whether immigrants take jobs away from the black working class.[15] The debate is not

[12] Julian Simon, an economist at the University of Maryland and contributor to the *Wall Street Journal*, Gregory de Freitas at Hofstra University, and Jeffrey Passel of the Urban Institute have all argued that recent immigrants are, in the long run, beneficial to the economy. See Simon 1989; Tomás Rivera Center, Claremont, "A $30 Billion Mistake: Ground-breaking Study Shows California's Anti-immigrant Research Fed by Flawed Research," news release, February 22, 1994; and Rebecca Clark and Jeffrey Passel, "Studies are Deceptive," *New York Times*, op-ed, September 3, 1993. Donald Huddle, professor emeritus of economics at Rice University, and Harvard economist George Borjas have argued to the contrary. See Huddle, "A Growing Burden," *New York Times*, op-ed, September 3, 1993, p. A23; and Borjas 1990. Borjas, for instance, claims that "new immigrants are joining the welfare system at a much higher rate than the older immigrants. It's a net loss for the country. They're taking more out than they're putting in. They seem to be more unskilled and they have less education." Quoted in Robert Reinhold, "In California, New Talk of Limits on Immigrants," *New York Times*, December 3, 1991, p. A20. See also Larry Rohter, "Revisiting Immigration and the Open Door Policy," *New York Times*, September 19, 1993, Week in Review, p. 4; Center for Immigration Studies, "The Costs of Immigration: Assessing a Conflicted Issue," backgrounder, September 1994; and Tomás Rivera Center, "Why They Count: Immigrant Contributions to the Golden State," June 1996.

[13] "In California the Sierra Club, concerned that immigrants are causing a population explosion harmful to the environment, joined forces with three groups that favor immigration restrictions to create the Coalition to Stabilize Population." Sontag, "Calls to Restrict Immigration." See also comments by Larry Orman, executive director of the Greenbelt Alliance, a nonprofit group that promotes the preservation of undeveloped land around San Francisco, in Reinhold, "Limits on Immigrants." See also Bouvier and Grant 1994.

[14] An overwhelming majority of Hispanics polled in the 1989 Latino National Political Survey said there is too much immigration. Roberto Suro, "Hispanic Pragmatism Seen in Survey," *New York Times*, December 15, 1992, p. A1. A 1995 telephone survey of English-speaking legal immigrants in the United States found that 61% would favor some kind of national identification card to distinguish citizens and legal residents from illegal immigrants. However, only 30% said immigration should be reduced; 44% said it should remain at current levels, and 15% said it should be increased. See "Poll: Immigrants Favor ID Card," Associated Press, July 5, 1995.

[15] The Black Leadership Forum, headed by Coretta Scott King and Congressman Walter Fauntroy, has lobbied to maintain sanctions against employers hiring illegal immigrant labor on the grounds that immigrants and the native working class compete for the same jobs. Wade Henderson, director of the Washington office of the NAACP, argues otherwise: "You can't blame immigrants for the problems of the black poor." Their plight, he says, stems mainly from failures in domestic social policy rather than immigration policy. "Is Immigration Hurting the U.S.?"

at all concerned with immigrants' incorporation, as Americans, into American political life.

This is very different from earlier discussions of immigration. Throughout the late nineteenth century and well into the twentieth there were fierce debates on the merits of immigration. But these had a strong political as well as economic component. The focus on political integration occurred however, not because people were less concerned about immigrants taking away jobs. On the contrary, two major recessions during this time contributed to the worry that immigration would lead to the loss of jobs among the native-born. Mayo-Smith, for instance, writing in 1898, worried a great deal that immigrants would undercut the wages of native-born laborers, echoing the same concerns that labor unions express today (1898: 8, also chap. 7). But commentators were equally concerned about how immigrants would fit into political life. Certainly there were disagreements about whether immigrants might make good citizens, and whether they would ever truly become "American," but no one doubted the importance of the questions.

There were a number of different strains to these debates, three of which I will highlight here. In the first, critics agonized over the "dilution" of "native stock" by the new immigration. "No nation can suffer such a turnover in its population origin," wrote one pair of observers, "and retain its essential character" (Grant and Davidson 1930: 160). Immigrants degraded the cultural heritage of the United States and weakened the common culture, the loss of which, some believed, could mean the end of the nation. "A group of people does not become a nation until it is animated by common standards of life and thought . . . common tradition and common loyalty . . . like-mindedness, and above all, common backgrounds and traditions to which appeal may confidently be made. Until a nation has these it is only a geographical expression. When it loses them, it becomes again a geographical expression" (Lewis 1928: 144–45). Less extreme, but perhaps more worrisome, was the possibility of the loss of specific cultural traits believed to be necessary for democratic self-governance.

> We are told that capacity for self-government is not an inborn trait, that it can be acquired, and that the peoples of other nations have not had a chance to show their powers. . . . One sometimes wonders if the sober restraint, the initiative, the independent self-reliance, the ability at team-play, which are essential to self-government are in any way native to the populations of southern and eastern Europe and whether, if they come to dominance, our politics

Fortune, August 9, 1993. See also the exchange between George Will and Dan Stein, "This Week with David Brinkley," *ABC News*, June 20, 1993.

may not entirely change its tone and become the fevered or fitful record of alternate despotism and revolution (Lewis 1928: 333).

These are the kinds of musings which led many critics to advocate terminating immigration from anywhere other than northern Europe. If culture was ingrained in immigrants' "race," then there was no hope of their becoming good citizens.

A second view of immigrants was equally skeptical about their capacity to adapt to democratic practices, but emphasized their lack of experience and training in the *habits* of democracy rather than their racial attributes. Mayo-Smith, for example, wrote:

The continued addition to our electorate of hundreds of persons who have had no training in self-government, who have other and quite different traditions of state action—will this not tend to weaken our capacity and self-reliance? Will it not also affect the adjustment of our institutions to our people—an adjustment which is so necessary if the institutions are to work successfully? If the new bearers of our political life have neither the aspirations which our ancestors cherished nor the experience which we have inherited—will not the homogeneousness of our social organization be seriously imperiled? A free ballot which was safe in the hands of an intelligent and self-respecting democracy, is no longer safe in those of an ignorant and degraded proletariat (1898: 6).

The first generation was always suspect in this regard. They would never truly acquire the mind-set needed to become good Americans. One could only hope that their children would.

Universal suffrage admits the immigrant to American politics within one to five years after landing. But the suffrage is not looked upon today as the sufficient Americanizing force that a preceding generation imagined. The suffrage appeals very differently to the immigrant voter and to the voter who has come up through the American schools and American life. The American has learned not only that this is a free government, but that its freedom is based on Constitutional principles of an abstract nature . . . when he contemplates public questions these abstract principles have more or less influence as a guide to his ballot. But the immigrant has none of these. He comes here solely to earn a better living. The suffrage is nothing to him but a means of livelihood. Not that he readily sells his vote for money—rather does he simply "vote for his job." He votes as instructed by his employer or his political "boss" because it will help his employer's business or because his boss

> will get him a job, or will, in some way, favor him and others of his nationality. There is a noticeable difference between the immigrant and the children of the immigrant in this regard. The young men, when they begin to vote, can be appealed to on the ground of public spirit; their fathers can be reached only on the ground of private interest (Commons 1907: 220–21).[16]

The habits of democracy, it seemed, would only come about through experience, and experience would only come with time. With this in mind, this group of critics called for some kind of moratorium on immigration (at the very least), to give the nation time to absorb the new immigrants.

Finally, a third group of critics believed that new immigrants *could* acquire the skills necessary for good citizenship, but the acquisition of these skills needed to be nurtured. Noting concerns about immigrant absorption, for instance, the Inter-Racial Council of New York City argued that the fault was not the immigrants'. Rather, the problem was that

> immigrants upon arrival in the United States receive no information concerning the country and its institutions. Their transit to destination is without official supervision. Few systematic provisions are made for connecting them directly with opportunities or contacts in their new home. This is a direct consequence of the failure on the part of our governments, federal, State and municipal, to recognize the necessity of taking affirmative action that will make it possible to incorporate into our national life, as integral parts of it, the uprightness, the industry, the thrift, the devotion, and the steadfastness of the immigrant (Inter-Racial Council 1920: 6).

If immigrants were guided through the process of learning about democratic skills and values (a process that should by no means be left to the political machine), then they could enter as full participants into political life. This view led, of course, to calls for "Americanization" programs to initiate immigrants into democratic political life.[17]

16 "No one can be called a true American who retains a particle of direct personal tradition not native to this country. Immigrants, however worthy, bring other than American traditions from their old countries. Something of these, their children are apt to preserve, sometimes their grandchildren. Only when these traditions have faded into dim knowledge of whence a family came—without any definite personal memories—can full American nationality declare itself." Barrett Wendell, *Barrett Wendell and His Letters* (Boston: Atlantic Monthly Press, 1924) p. 254, quoted in Lewis 1928: 159. Lewis also quotes Congressman William S. Bennett, testifying before a Senate committee: "And I want to say right here . . . that no man born in a foreign country, coming here after forty years of age, ever gets to be as good an American citizen as one born here" (1928: 162).

17 William Barr, then president of the Inter-Racial Council in New York City, proposed that "if we admit immigrants, we must accept only those who are potentially good citizens, and having

There are clear tensions among these three points of view. Proponents of "Americanization" and expounders of racial theories came from very different starting points. But all three sets of commentators took citizenship and the practice of politics seriously. They all regarded democratic politics as something precious and, therefore, as something to be protected and *limited*.[18] As one commentator noted: "Some people say nobody should be admitted to this country who doesn't agree from the moment he arrives here that he will become a citizen on the first day possible. I don't believe in that idea. I regard citizenship as the most precious privilege that can be bestowed on a human being. It must be deserved. It must be earned."[19]

This view was the basis of the compromise that eventually prevailed. Citizenship and the right to be involved in politics were something to be earned, and it was agreed they shouldn't be earned easily. In 1906 Congress gave the Bureau of Immigration (now the Immigration and Naturalization Service) control over naturalization, and naturalization was conducted only by federal naturalization courts. Qualifications for aliens seeking citizenship were standardized and enforced: immigrants had to provide information on lawful admission and residence; have the ability to speak, read, and write the English language; have knowledge of the history and government of the United States; and prove good character (Commons 1907: 189).[20]

These three kinds of arguments from the debates about the last wave of immigration are echoed today, and now, as then, the most clamorous voices call for restrictions on immigration. Critics charge that the United States has lost control of its borders, that immigrants bring undesirable traits to this country, that they refuse to Americanize, that they represent a threat to the cultural integrity of the United States (Brimelow 1995; Lutton and

---

accepted them, we must provide the means that will make them good citizens" (Inter-Racial Council 1920: 20–21).

[18] The logic being, I suppose, that if what is rare becomes precious, then what is precious must be *made* rare. Whether this logic is correct is another matter altogether.

[19] F. Charles Schwedtman, vice-president of the National City Bank of New York, quoted in the *Proceedings of the National Conference on Immigration* (Inter-Racial Council 1920: 48–49).

[20] Nor did the Federal government act alone. Just as southern states were putting in place literacy tests, vagrancy taxes, poll taxes, and property clauses to disenfranchise blacks, by the late nineteenth century in the North and West there was a counterreaction to the relative ease of access immigrants had to citizenship. Connecticut (1855) and Massachusetts (1857) led the way early on, refusing to enfranchise those who could not read the Constitution. By the turn of the century, six other northern and western states—Wyoming, Maine, California, Washington, Delaware, and New Hampshire—had set up barriers against those who could not read or write English (Commons 1907: 220–21). States that had allowed aliens to vote after filing first papers (signaling intent of citizenship) had repealed that privilege by early in the twentieth century (Higham 1955).

Tanton 1994; Nelson 1994; Brimelow 1992; Auster 1991; Stacy and Lutton 1986). Patrick Buchanan's speech at the 1992 Republican convention in Houston, in which he called for block-by-block fighting to "take back our culture" was representative of this culturally conservative position, seeing immigrants as the bearers of foreign traits threatening the concept of America as an ethnically European nation with certain Christian core values (Fukuyama 1993: 26). This theme has also been taken up in certain quarters of the press. *The Washington Times* in Washington, D.C., for example, notes that "earlier immigrants tended to be European and so were already at home in the European-based civilization of America. Assimilation wasn't difficult. For immigrants today, overwhelmingly from Latin America or Asia, this isn't true. The newcomers today arrive with entirely different cultures in their baggage—differences in religion, political values, family structures, work habits and languages."[21]

Though the author here wants to distance contemporary immigration (bad) from its historical precedents (good), he is echoing the very same complaints that earlier critics had made of previous waves of (largely European) immigrants. The difference from the turn-of-the-century cry about immigrants' incompatibility with America is that, despite the occasional reference to immigrants' lack of certain "political" or "democratic" values, immigrants' role in American politics is almost absent in this critique. Instead the argument is almost entirely cultural.[22] Whereas a hundred years ago the question of political incorporation seemed inescapable, now it is hardly even an issue.

Perhaps there is less of a sense today that immigrants are potential Americans. They remain outsiders, foreigners, so there is no wish to hasten their incorporation. There are two reasons for this perception. First, many people hold the mistaken belief that most immigrants are illegal—which is far from the case. In a 1993 *New York Times*/CBS poll, for instance, 68 percent of respondents said they believed that "most immigrants who have moved to the United States in the last few years are here illegally" (the actual ratio of illegal to legal immigrants is closer to one in seven).[23] This belief places *all*

[21] Samuel Francis, "Fencing out the National Culture," *The Washington Times*, May 25, 1993, p. F1.

[22] And it is racial, borrowing again from the turn-of-the century debates which tended to blur our current distinctions between race and culture. See Peter Brimelow's reflections (1992) on riding the New York subway, which reveal deep-seated fears of dark-skinned people speaking foreign languages operating in some subterranean world into which whites would not want to venture.

[23] Adams, "New York Bombers."

immigrants, legal and illegal, outside the domain of public life and public responsibility in this country.[24]

A second group of commentators does not reject the possibility that immigrants, or their children, could eventually become Americans. Like their counterparts in the last great debate on immigration, they believe that assimilation is possible, pointing to the assimilation of immigrants in the past as an example. What has changed, they charge, are cultural conditions in the United States. Whereas before there was the sense that everyone was a potential American, and that American values were universalizable, these hopes have been weakened, so the argument goes, by an institutional culture that promotes multiculturalism and affirmative action, which has a corrosive effect on the tenuous civic and cultural fabric of the republic (Schlesinger 1992; Glazer 1983). The proponents of this view are convinced that immigrants exhibit a perverse intransigence to adaptation, which reflects doubts among elites about whether there is any coherence to the notion of being American (Beck 1994). This argument is mostly about culture and cultural politics, but again it is not about democratic participation.

The third group in the early debate argued that immigrants could be educated in the skills to become citizens, which led to wide-scale educational and civic experiments in the "Americanization" of immigrants. There is no real equivalent to such efforts today. One might point to orientation programs for Asian refugees, or those for Russian Jews, but these are limited and local. Likewise, programs promoting citizenship are virtually nonexistent. Politicians hardly worry about the political integration of immigrants because, as I argue in Chapter 4, it is not usually in their interests to do so. The silence of entrenched U.S. Latino interest groups is not all that surprising—the entry of a large number of Latin American immigrants into American political life portends the emergence of a large and unpredictable political force that may threaten the hegemony of these groups as Hispanic spokespersons and political agenda-setters.[25] The one major exception has been the National Association of Latino Elected and Appointed

[24] My argument is not meant to imply that we do not have some obiligations to incorporate illegal immigrants as well. For example, see Walzer 1983. For the most part, however, this book describes the political choices facing legal immigrants.

[25] "One obstacle to . . . pan-Latinism has been the myopic, opportunistic raving of some Latino elected officials and other leaders, who fuel nationalistic rivalries to obscure their own inadequacies. For example, a bill calling for non-citizen voting, which would augment Latino political strength, was thwarted by some Puerto Rican elected officials, who mistakenly viewed the bill as a Dominican initiative. The bill was subsequently introduced by an African-American state senator." Howard Jordan, "Latino Mayoral Vote: The Margin of Victory," *New York Newsday*, October 24, 1993, p. 29. For a largely cynical view of the national Latino leadership, and their position on the new Latin American immigration, see Skerry 1993, particularly chapters 9–11.

Officials (NALEO), which has set up a number of naturalization campaigns over the years, particularly in California and Texas. NALEO had a U.S. citizenship hotline from 1985 to 1988 to provide information on the immigrant amnesty program then in effect and has continued to run ads and campaigns to encourage naturalization.[26] It has also sponsored, directly or indirectly, much of the extant research on Latino immigrant citizenship (see Pachón 1989; Pachón 1987; NALEO 1984).[27] But these efforts, however earnest, remain the exception, touching only a small fraction of those eligible. There has been minimal exertion at the national or state level to bring immigrants and other marginal political actors into formal politics.[28]

Why this stark contrast in the tone of the two immigration debates? Why was immigrant political participation central to the debate at the turn of the century, and so peripheral a hundred years later? Why the lack of concern? The answer to these questions may lie in the changing importance attached to political participation itself. While critics then saw participation as a key civic virtue, for many American commentators today it simply doesn't matter whether people participate or not. "Democratic" government will continue to function even if the participation of citizens is infrequent and superficial. The "division of labor"—so the argument goes—"allows most citizens to pay relatively little attention to public affairs. Politics and government are peripheral rather than a central concern in the lives of most citizens" (Milbraith and Goel 1977: 145; see also Dahl 1961: 224–25 and Lipset 1960: 227–29).

> As we think about the role of the average citizen, then, we should not expect him to give a lot of attention to, and be active in resolving issues of public policy. Nor should we expect him to stand up and be counted on every issue that comes along. The most we can expect is that he will participate in the choice

[26] Linda Rosier, photograph, *New York Times* 1993. The caption reads: "Maria Betancourt and her husband, José, leaving the club on 108th Street in Corona Queens yesterday with nephew and niece, after she filled out an application for citizenship." The registration drive, sponsored by NALEO and a local club, is held once a month. The banner in the photo reads: "Citizenship Workshop: Citizenship . . . The Better Way." The interest of other Latino organizations and some elected officials has been piqued by the rise in Latino immigrant naturalization rates after 1994, and the possibility of translating these new citizens into voting power. But this interest has yet to be translated into a concerted program or effort.

[27] The contemporary literature on naturalization and immigrants remains underdeveloped: see Alvarez 1987; North 1987; Pachón 1987; Portes and Curtis 1987. For a review of the earlier social science literature on immigrant naturalization see DeSipio 1987.

[28] There was a brief moment in 1995 and 1996 when the INS made a commitment to ease the backlog of immigrants who had requested citizenship by committing more resources to streamlining the naturalization process. This program was scaled back in the face of criticism that immigrants with criminal records were becoming citizens undetected.

of decision makers and that he will ask to be heard if an issue comes along that greatly concerns him or on which he can make some special contribution. Many citizens do not even vote or speak up on issues, yet their passive role has the consequence of accepting things as they are. Indeed, it is impossible to escape at least a passive role in the choice of decision makers. The choice process can proceed and government can continue to function even if many citizens choose to be so inactive as to fail to vote (Milbraith and Goel 1977: 146–47).

It is thus presumed that even if people do not participate, their interests will be taken into account because others who hold similar views will act on their behalf. Is this perspective correct, and does it matter? Should we be troubled that immigrants do not become citizens and are not involved in formal politics? What are the implications of their political marginality? I believe there are three reasons why we should be concerned with immigrants' incorporation into American political life.

First, there is the problem of representation and accountability. The argument for ignoring problems of representation is that, in the end, it doesn't matter because those who are unrepresented hold views similar to, and in similar proportions to those who actually are represented.[29] But this argument is unlikely to hold if a distinct group of people is unrepresented, rather than just random individuals, and if this group has special needs and unique views in a number of important areas (Verba et al. 1993). While immigrants may hold representative views about, say, who should be elected president, they will probably have distinct views on a number of issues that affect them directly, but affect most Americans only tangentially—questions of immigration restrictions, language policy, English as a second language. To ignore the question of representation is to overlook the absence of accountability of the politicians and bureaucracies who purport to represent recent immigrants. The inadequate representation of immigrants' views results in many of their needs—in education, housing, and health—being poorly met, and in an increase in their vulnerability to exploitation, which is inherently greater than that of many other members of the polity.

Second, and more important, we should attempt to include those on the margins of the polity because democratic decision-making is not simply a matter of reflecting people's previously held views. If it were, the above ar-

[29] See for example Gant and Lyons 1993; Bennet and Resnick 1990; and Wolfinger and Rosenstone 1980: chap. 6. The League of Women Voters released polling data in 1996 along the same lines. See Richard Berke, "Non-voters Are No More Alienated than Voters, a Survey Shows," *New York Times*, May 30, 1996, p. A21.

gument might be right: if participants and nonparticipants held the same views, then it might make little difference whether people participated. However, people do not enter the polity with their interests already formed, and their minds already made up.[30] Participation is about more than simply assuring adequate representation; it is one of the key ingredients of democratic deliberation. In the process of deliberation views are not only aired, but opinions changed, new options considered, old questions discarded. Participation matters because deliberation is about the *process* of democracy rather than about its outcome. We should be paying more attention to the formal incorporation of immigrants into politics because *politics matters*—particularly if we believe in, and care about, the virtue of democratic participation.[31]

Third, and certainly most crucial, we should be concerned about the political marginalization of immigrants because they are all, every one of them, potential American citizens. The absence of any mention of citizenship in the immigration debate implies seeing immigrants only as the "other," not as potential members in a common polity. Focusing only on the economic costs or cultural dangers of immigration, the public discussion thus far has drawn a line between "us" and "them," not recognizing immigrants as being "one of us." We cannot afford to have a significant portion of our own population remain disenfranchised for a generation—most of their adult lives—participating in neither the formal political systems of the country they arrive from, nor those of the country that takes them in. Nor does this marginalization end with the first generation. The disenfranchisement of the parents is reflected in the apathy of their children. This is an unsustainable state of affairs. As Michael Walzer has noted, any regime whose legitimacy rests on the assumptions of democratic consent and citizen participation is presented with a political dilemma when its populace contains large numbers of noncitizens outside the bounds of formal partici-

[30] We can't assume, if nonvoters were to enter into the political sphere, that their views would remain the same, or even that the menu of issues on the table would stay the same. Nor can we assume that the issues currently on the table accurately represent all the issues that might arise if the process were more open. As Verba et al. note: "Comparisons between voters and nonvoters in terms of their policy attitudes cannot fully address the issue of the representativeness of activist publics in that they focus only on differences in preferences as revealed in questions about public issues pre-selected by authors of surveys. These policy issues are not necessarily the matters of most concern to respondents" (1993: 304).

[31] For spirited advocacy of democratic participation see Barber 1984 and Pateman 1970. Many of the classic defenses of participation do so with the presumption that the main argument for participatory democracy is a moral one—people become better persons if they participate, so the argument goes. My argument is somewhat different: the polity is a better polity as a result of participation and deliberation.

pation (Walzer 1983). As long as such a situation persists, doubts about justice and legitimacy in the polity will remain.

Encouraging the full incorporation of those on the margins is one solution, but the United States has not opted for this alternative. Instead it has left the decision to naturalize entirely in the hands of each new arrival. Given this situation, Latin American immigrants take a very long time before naturalizing as American citizens. Why? The next chapter begins to answer this question.

3

Explaining Participation:

Why It Takes So Long to Become a Citizen

The majority of adult Hispanics do not participate in formal U.S. politics—even in the fundamental act of voting—primarily because of low citizenship rates. Why do naturalization rates remain so low? The traditional explanation for participation and turnout has been a socioeconomic model, which argues that rates of participation are closely correlated with people's social and economic resources; we can predict people's level of participation, that is, by their socioeconomic status. The higher an individual's educational level, for instance, the higher the expected level of participation (Conway 1991; Milbraith and Goel 1977). But according to this argument one would expect middle-class Latin American immigrants to have high rates of political participation, particularly in one of the most basic political acts, and the first step toward political integration—taking the oath of citizenship.

Judging from 1990 census data for Queens, the standard socioeconomic explanation does not seem to account for the low levels at which immigrants become members in the polity. These data indicate that standard socioeconomic variables do little to explain the nonparticipation of immigrants in formal politics, while length of stay is highly significant. But the finding that naturalization is correlated with length of stay is not, in itself, an explanation. *Why* do people take so long to naturalize and enter as participants in formal politics? To explain why length of stay is significant, we turn to a model emphasizing the *costs* that immigrants face in making the decision to participate politically, rather than simply measuring the resources at their disposal.

Table 5. Voting turnout, 1990 congressional elections, by race and ethnicity

	Total voting-age population	% registered	% voting
Hispanic	13,756,000	32.3	21
Black	20,371,000	49.0	33
White	155,587,000	60.0	44

Source: Jennings 1991: 16–17.

Latino Political Participation

Latino political participation in the United States as a whole is low. According to the Census Bureau, at the time of the 1990 mid-term congressional elections there were 13,756,000 Hispanics of voting age in the United States (see Table 5). Of these, 4,442,000 were registered to vote—about 32.3 percent. Of those registered to vote, 2,894,000 actually voted—21 percent of the total Latino population eighteen and over (Jennings 1991: 16–17). Perhaps these figures might not seem as significant given the context of general American voter apathy (Abramson 1983: 5–8). In these same elections, for example, 60 percent of voting-age whites were registered and 44 percent actually voted. Forty-nine percent of the black voting age population was registered and 33 percent voted. But the percentages for Hispanics are markedly lower than those for either whites or blacks.[1]

In the 1992 presidential elections the picture is similar. The Census Bureau estimated that the total Hispanic population eighteen and above in the United States was 14,688,000. Of these, 5,137,000 were registered, or 35 percent, and 2,921,000 actually voted—29.5 percent of those Hispanics of voting age (see table 6). The turnout for a presidential election is several percentage points higher than an off-year election, but even so only one in three Hispanics of voting age actually cast their ballots.[2] The turnout for whites and blacks was twenty to thirty percentage points higher than that for Latinos.

For New York State, the Census Bureau estimated there were 1,172,000 Hispanics of voting age in 1992; 38.3 percent of this population was registered, and 32.6 percent voted (Jennings 1993: 27). In 1990 voter turnout

[1] Previous research has reached similar conclusions. See Longoria, Wrinkle and Polinard 1990; Wrinkle and Miller 1984; Atunes and Gaitz 1975; Welch, Comer and Steinman 1975 and 1973.
[2] Also, the usual increase in voting in a presidential year is lower for Latinos than for whites or blacks (see Tables 5 and 6).

Table 6. Voting turnout, 1992 presidential elections, by race and ethnicity

	Total voting-age population	% registered	% voting
Hispanic	14,688,000	35.0	29
Black	21,039,000	63.9	54
White	157,837,000	70.1	64

Source: Jennings 1993: 4–5.

had been significantly lower: of an estimated 1,480,000 Hispanics of voting age in the state, 34 percent were registered and 23 percent voted (Jennings 1991: 37). Likewise, in the city voter registration among Hispanics was lower than for the population as a whole (Rodriguez et al. 1995: 44–45). Estimates for New York City indicate that of a voting age population of 1,158,476 Hispanics in 1991, only 39 percent were registered and about half of these voted in 1992.[3] Registration rates in electoral districts that had heavily Latino immigrant populations were even lower. In predominantly Dominican electoral districts the registration rate was 32 percent; in South American electoral districts it was 21 percent. Of registered voters only 56 percent turned out in 1992 in Dominican electoral districts and 62 percent in South American districts (Rodriguez et al. 1995: 44–46). In some of these heavily immigrant districts, under 10 percent of the voting age population went to the polls.

Nor does the picture change if we look at other indicators of political participation. Calvo and Rosenstone conclude that "Hispanics are less likely to participate in politics than other Americans" (1989: 2; see also Cohen and Capsis 1978); in their measures of political participation, Hispanic participation was significantly lower than non-Hispanic. Although the ratio for "attending a public meeting" was essentially equal at .95, Hispanics were only three-quarters as likely as non-Hispanics to "turn out to vote" (.78), "try to influence others to vote" (.78), and "belong to a political club" (.75).

[3] See Baca 1991; Rodriguez et al. 1995: 45. Note that in Baca these estimates of Hispanic voters in New York City are based on counts of Spanish-surname voters on the city's electoral roles, not on voters' self-identification as Hispanics. This may result in some distortion of the results. Rodriguez et al. come up with significantly higher voter registration rates: they estimate that 51% of voting-age Latinos were registered in 1992. This higher figure may result from their methodology: they estimated registration and voting rates by overlaying electoral commission data over census tract data. So if an election district had a majority Dominican population according to the census, this was matched to the electoral commission data, and tallied as "Dominican turnout." Needless to say, these results are very rough. For a discussion of this methodology and their results, see Rodriguez et al. 1995: 43–50.

"For none of the other forms of electoral participation (e.g. attending political rallies, working for parties or candidates, contributing money) or nonelectoral participation (e.g. writing to a congressman, signing a petition, doing committee service for a local club, or belonging to a political club or group) did the Hispanic to non-Hispanic ratio reach .70. Thus, 'as the cost of participation rises, Hispanic participation trails further and further behind that of other Americans'" (Hero 1992: 62, quoting Calvo and Rosenstone 1989).

Much, if not most of this nonparticipation can be ascribed to noncitizens (Pachón and DeSipio 1994: 6; Uhlaner, Cain, and Kiewiet 1989). Breaking the numbers down, it is apparent that more than a third of those Hispanics of voting age who are not registered, and of course not voting, are first-generation immigrants who have not become citizens (Jennings 1991: 37; Jennings 1993: 27). How do we explain the nonparticipation of Latin American immigrants?

Socioeconomic Status and Political Participation

One of the most reliable conclusions of the literature in American politics has been that political participation correlates with socioeconomic standing. While the central claim is that there is a relationship between social status and voting turnout (Avey 1989: 5; Wolfinger and Rosenstone 1980: 13), researchers usually suggest that socioeconomic characteristics also influence other kinds of political participation. Milbraith and Goel, for example, look not only at whether people voted, but also at party and campaign activity: participation in a political party between elections, activity in a political campaign, donating money, registering people to vote, joining a party, convincing people to vote, running as a candidate, and joining groups to improve community life (1977: 13). Verba and Nie find that high socioeconomic status generally correlates with greater participation in various types of voluntary activity, either directly in electoral politics or in community and social organizations (1972: 126).[4] "Middle-class persons are ex-

[4] Among the sixteen different kinds of activity they looked at were: voting in national elections, voting in local elections, acting in at least one organization involved with community problems, working with others in trying to solve some community problem, attempting to persuade others to vote for certain candidates, actively working for a political party, contacting a government official about some issue or problem, giving money to a party or candidate during an election campaign, and being a member of a club or organization (Verba and Nie 1972: 31).

posed to more stimuli about politics than working-class persons," explain Milbraith and Goel (1977: 38) in their review of the literature. A whole slew of political scientists have concluded that those with higher measures of socioeconomic status—indicated by income, occupation, and education—are more likely to participate in politics, broadly defined.

Wolfinger and Rosenstone, for instance, note that the correlation between socioeconomic status and political participation "holds true whether one uses level of education, income, or occupation as the measure of social status" (1980: 13). Some researchers lump the three together as a single variable (Verba, Nie, and Kim 1978; Verba and Nie 1972). However, education is often assumed to be the more significant of the three (Wolfinger and Rosenstone 1980: 17; Barber 1969: 11–14; Campbell et al. 1960: 476–78). The finding that "people with higher levels of education tend to participate at a higher level than those with less education" is widely documented.[5]

The arguments for the relationship between education and political participation are often stated in sweeping terms (Milbraith and Goel 1977: 47; Verba and Nie 1972: chap. 8; Campbell et al. 1960: chap. 17). Wolfinger and Rosenstone, for example, conclude:

> Education, we have argued, does three things. First, it increases cognitive skills, which facilitates learning about politics. Schooling increases one's capacity for understanding and working with complex, abstract and intangible subjects such as politics. This heightens one's ability to pay attention to politics, to understand politics, and to gather the information necessary for making political choices. Thus education is a resource that reduces the costs of voting by giving people the skills necessary for processing political information and for making better political decisions. Second, better educated people are more likely to get more gratification from political participation. They are more likely to have a sense of citizen duty, to feel moral pressure to participate, and to receive expressive benefits from voting. Finally, schooling imparts experience with a variety of bureaucratic relationships: learning requirements, filling out forms, waiting in lines, and meeting deadlines. This experience helps one overcome the procedural hurdles required first to register and then to vote (1980: 35).

[5] Milbraith and Goel (1977: 98) cite numerous studies that support this finding: Rosenau 1974; Verba and Nie 1972; Olsen 1973; Nie, Powell, and Prewitt 1969; Alford and Scobie 1968; Dahl 1961; Lipset 1960; Campbell et al. 1960; Lane 1959; Campbell, Gurin, and Miller 1954; Riesman and Glazer 1950.

Rosenstone and Hansen argue that education fosters skills needed for political participation, and inculcates a sense of duty and efficacy. "Education helps citizens to negotiate the maze of demands that participation places on them. To cast a ballot, citizens must figure out how to vote; they must make sense of the candidates and the issues; [and] they must locate polling places" (1993: 13). All of these tasks, presumably, are aided by the skills gained with education. In short, they and others believe that education increases resources and skills, and lowers the information costs associated with political participation (Conway 1991: 21–27; Wolfinger and Rosenstone 1980: 14; Lane 1959).

The broad scope and general nature of these arguments lead one to believe that they would apply as well to immigrants as to any other set of political actors. Indeed, the effect of higher socioeconomic status on the political participation of immigrants is supported by a number of authors (Hoskin 1989: 350; Portes and Bach 1985; Richmond 1981; Kritz, and Keely and Tomasi 1981; Chiswick 1976; and Handlin 1959). Hoskin, for instance, argues that those with higher socioeconomic status can use the resources at their disposal to adapt to their surroundings on their own terms (1989: 352). Examples might include the incorporation of Cuban émigrés into American politics (Perez 1992) and the formation of ethnic enclaves (Bonacich 1972). Nonetheless, active political participation by immigrants is not extensive. Immigrants often try to keep a low profile—they are even characterized as passive and apathetic (Hoskin 1989: 360).

Arguably, if immigrants have cultural backgrounds that differ significantly from the culture of the receiving country, they will have a difficult time adapting to political life in their new society (Hoskin 1989: 351; see also Power 1979; Freeman 1979; Rist 1978; Castles and Kosack 1973; Handlin 1959: 44). But Latin American immigrants share at least as many aspects of U.S. political culture—experience with representative political systems, a liberal tradition, and so forth, as they have differences—for example, their experience of authoritarianism (Portes and Bach 1985). One would think the cultural gap would be much greater for Asian immigrants than for Latin Americans, yet Asians naturalize at much higher rates than Latin Americans.[6] A simplistic cultural explanation is clearly inadequate.

[6] Barkan 1983; for a general overview of recent Asian immigration, see Wong 1986. Though Asians have much higher naturalization rates than Latin Americans, once they become citizens they still have very low participation rates in electoral politics. Once Latin American immigrants become citizens, on the other hand, they register and vote at rates comparable to those of native-born whites. Obviously the meaning of citizenship differs between the two groups; this requires further exploration.

Latin American Immigrants in Queens: The 1990 Census

Quantitative information about Hispanic political attitudes and behavior is slight. Latinos were not included, for example, as a distinct group in many of the earlier studies on political participation, and in general, they are underrepresented in survey data and exit polls (de la Garza 1987). Hispanics were not distinguished as a separate category by the Census Bureau until 1970, and these data were further elaborated by national grouping and immigrant status only in 1980 and 1990. To test the findings that socioeconomic status is a major predictor of political participation, especially the act of choosing citizenship, we must turn to the data from the 1990 census. The 1990 Census Public Use Microdata Sample (PUMS) gives us a sense of socioeconomic status—occupation, household income, and education—in relation to citizenship among first-generation Latin American immigrants in Queens.[7]

The census data show that there is, in fact, a slight positive correlation between higher socioeconomic status (measured by education, income, and occupation) and rates of citizenship. The relationship is weak, however, in the cases of education and income, and muddied in the case of occupation. Citizenship rates for first-generation Latin American immigrants remain low despite relatively high levels of household income and education. Only 44,200 out of the 166,160 Latin American immigrants the 1990 census counted in Queens—26.5 percent—were citizens (see Table 7). The high rate of Cuban naturalization reflects, most probably, the unique circumstances of their arrival as refugees in the 1960s. The diminishing chances of return made American citizenship appear all the more attractive to them. On the other hand, the low rate of naturalization for Mexicans is due, in part, to their recent arrival. Most have arrived in the last ten years, many in the last five.

Occupation, according to the 5 percent sample of households from the 1990 (PUMS), has only a slight positive relationship with citizenship.[8] Noncitizens outnumber citizens in every profession, and immigrants are concentrated in occupations where the margins of noncitizenship are greater. In addition, occupation is particularly problematic as a measurement because immigrants either experience substantial shifts in employ-

[7] The PUMS is a 5% random sample drawn from the 1990 Census of Population and Housing (U.S. Census Bureau, 1993b).

[8] A meaningful correlation between the two variables, using Pearson correlation coefficients, is not possible to establish since occupational categories are discrete, not continuous, and cannot be clearly ranked according to status.

Table 7. Citizenship votes, first-generation immigrants in Queens, 1990 (seven largest national groups)

Country of origin	% citizens	Number of citizens
Cuba	62.4	10,420
Dominican Republic	30.0	27,580
El Salvador	22.3	8,080
Colombia	21.9	43,460
Ecuador	19.6	23,320
Peru	19.1	11,440
Mexico	11.2	7,860

Source: 1990 Census Public Use Microdata Sample

ment or because recent immigrants answer the occupation question on the census form with answers indicating what they consider as their profession, not their current employment.

In the first place, what immigrants put down as their answer may not reflect much more than a snapshot of that moment in time. Immigrants have some initial downward occupational mobility from their home country, followed by high job turnover particularly in their first years after arrival to the United States, and the census gives only an imperfect idea of this. We can compare the immigrant cohort arriving in 1985–90 to that which arrived in 1980–84 and see that there was a shift in the kinds of occupations they claimed: in 1990, for instance, the most common occupations of the later cohort were household help, food preparation, and construction. Food preparation and construction were among the top three occupations held by the earlier cohort, but skilled labor was the third. For the 1975–80 cohort, the top three occupations were owner-operated business, textile factory work, and building maintenance. The data seem to suggest a shift away from unskilled to semiskilled labor in the ten to fifteen years after arrival to the United States. But of course, the data could indicate just as well a shift in the pool of immigrants arriving to this country. The problem is that there is little continuous data for any immigrant group over a period of years (Portes and Bach 1985 being a rare exception).

Second, immigrants' answers on the census forms may reflect their training and status in their home country, not the position they hold in this one. For example, under the question asking for occupation, the 1990 PUMS has a response category for "judge." The data indicates that there were four Colombian respondents in Queens who identified themselves as judges. If we were to extrapolate from this 5 percent sample, we might reach the conclusion that there were, in 1990, eighty judges of Colombian descent living in

Queens. However, in 1990 there was only *one* judge of Hispanic descent in the whole of Queens county—a Puerto Rican—and few others in the city as a whole. So where did all these Colombian judges come from? It must be that some respondents put down their previous professions (or what they believed to be the nearest equivalent from the complex list of census options), or simply misunderstood the question. Another instance of probable confusion is that about 30 percent of Latin American immigrants identifying themselves in 1990 as working with the police or fire protection services had only come to Queens between 1980 and 1990, and 15 percent had arrived after 1985. It is difficult to imagine, in the context of New York City's civil service requirements, that newly arrived immigrants would gain easy access to unionized city agencies (some of which also require U.S. citizenship as a prerequisite to employment). Again, a number of immigrants must have responded to the question of occupation by putting down their previous profession, not their current employment. These examples indicate an uncertainty that taints the entire set of responses.

Immigrant household income, as measured by the 1990 PUMS sample, has only a slight positive relationship to citizenship. This is reflected in the measure of the correlation between the two variables, which is only .09 ($p <$ .0001).[9] By income level, the percentage of those who are citizens ranges only from about 22 percent for those at the low end of the income scale to about 35 percent at the high end. Even at the high end, almost two-thirds of Latin American immigrants are not citizens. So income by itself tells us little about why immigrants acquire (or resist acquiring) U.S. citizenship.

It is important to note that household income for Latin American immigrants in Queens is actually quite high. The average for this group is close to $36,000 a year; median income is probably closer to $30,000 (see Figure 2). In 1989 median income for New York City as a whole was $29,823.[10] Table 8 provides data on the median household income for Latinos nationally. Latino immigrants in Queens have substantially higher household incomes than every group except possibly Cuban Americans. The higher household income of Latin American immigrants in Queens reflects higher wages and costs of living in the New York metropolitan area, and higher incidence of dual-income families. But it also indicates that many first-generation Latin American immigrants in Queens are, by U.S. standards, middle-class.

[9] Pearson Correlation Coefficient, N = 8182.

[10] Josh Barbanel, "Census Data Show Boom before Bust," *New York Times*, April 16, 1992, p. B4. The median income for Latinos in Queens is also not far below that of whites in the city as a whole: whites' median income in 1989 was $36,454 (Rodriguez et al. 1995: 33, table 10).

Figure 2. Household income of Latin American immigrants in Queens, 1990

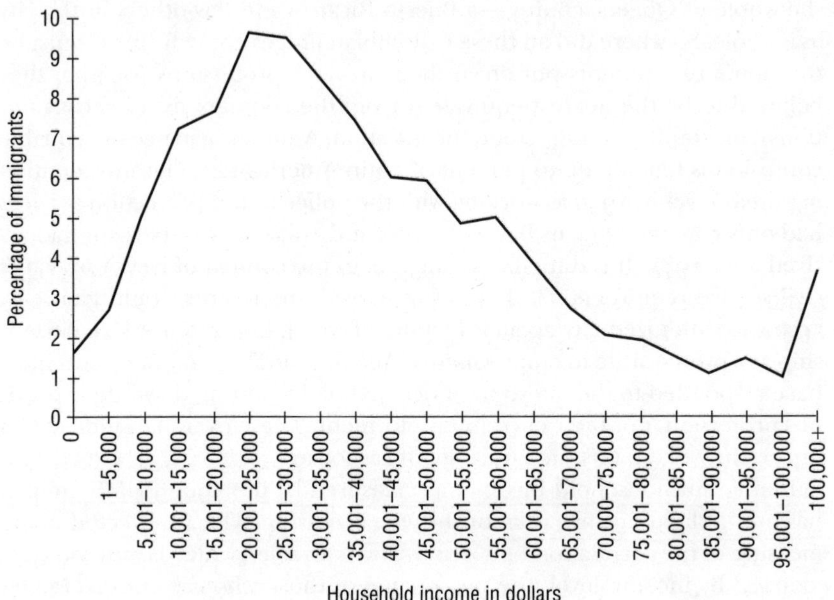

Source: 1990 Census Public Use Microdata Sample.

Table 8. Median household income of U.S. Hispanics, 1991

	Median household income (in dollars)	% below poverty level
All Hispanics	23,431	25.0
Mexicans	23,240	25.0
Puerto Ricans	18,008	37.5
Cubans	31,439	13.8
Central and South Americans	23,445	22.2
Non-Hispanics	36,334	9.5

Source: Garcia and Montgomery 1992. See also Cattan 1993.

Of the three socioeconomic variables I examine, the strongest correlation of citizenship for first-generation Latin American immigrants is with level of education. The correlation between the two is .17 ($p < .0001$),[11]

[11] Pearson Correlation Coefficient, N = 8182; there is a 55% match between predicted probabilities and observed responses, with another 12% tied. Somer's D is 0.23.

which indicates that the higher an immigrant's level of education, the more likely they are to be a U.S. citizen. This finding supports those on Mexican immigrants by Fernandez, Frias, and Gonzales (1984), Garcia (1981), and Ramirez (1979). At the low end of the scale, we see that only about 15 percent of immigrants with low levels of education are U.S. citizens, while those with Ph.D.s have citizenship rates over 75 percent. Even so, this relationship does not explain citizenship and noncitizenship among immigrants as well as we might have expected. First, the positive correlation between education and citizenship is not terribly strong. This may be, in part, because the level of education among the population of immigrants is not evenly distributed. There are relatively few immigrants who have masters and doctoral degrees, so the impact of their high citizenship rates is relatively slight. More important, it's likely that some of the difference in the naturalization rates between those with higher educational levels (particularly M.A.s and Ph.D.s) and those with less education has little to do with their level of education. Professionals who arrived before 1970, for instance, often became citizens because doing so made it possible for them to practice their professions and find jobs with government agencies, not necessarily because they wished to become active participants in American politics.[12]

The bulk of Latin American immigrants to Queens fall under three educational peaks—those with elementary school education, those with a high school degree or some college, and those with a college degree. Those who have less than a ninth-grade education make up about 21 percent of the Latino population twenty-five and older. Forty-eight percent, by far the largest proportion of adults, have gone through four years of high school. Those with college degrees make up 10 percent of the population. The educational level of Latinos in Queens matches or betters that of Hispanics nationally (see Table 9). There is still a considerable gap between them and non-Hispanics, but most Latin American immigrants come to Queens with a significant amount of educational training and human capital.

The census data present Latin Americans in Queens as an established, successful immigrant population. Their educations and incomes place many of them well within the American lower middle class, and just at or above the median for New York City. Given their situation, the literature linking socioeconomic status with involvement in political life would predict that these immigrants would be participating more fully in formal political life. However, this is not the case. Though all three socioeconomic variables

[12] Through the early 1960s many states had laws that required citizenship for a wide range of jobs dealing with the public: dentist, undertaker, doctor, attorney, police officer, etc. These laws were challenged in court, and eventually dismantled.

Table 9. Educational attainment of U.S. Hispanics, aged 25 or older, 1991

	% with four years of high school	% with four years of college
All Hispanics	51.3	9.7
Mexicans	43.6	6.2
Puerto Ricans	71.8	11.5
Cubans	61.0	18.5
Central and South Americans	60.4	15.1
Non-Hispanics	80.5	22.3

Source: Garcia and Montgomery 1992.

available in the census are positively related to citizenship, the correlations are rather weak. It seems that these variables only partly account for the outcome of citizenship or noncitizenship.

Length of Stay and Citizenship

The explanatory power of the socioeconomic variables is overshadowed by the effect of immigrants' year of entry into the United States (see Figure 3). For example, 82 percent of Latin American immigrants who arrived before 1950 are citizens, compared with less than 10 percent of those who arrived between 1985 and 1990. The correlation between citizenship and year of entry is high at .46 ($p < .0001$). The earlier an immigrant has arrived to the United States—and the longer he or she has stayed in this country—the more likely he or she is to become a U.S. citizen.[13] A logistical regression model indicates that immigrants' year of entry into the United States is the best single predictor for the outcome of citizenship among first-generation immigrants, accounting for 75 percent of the cases observed.[14] In fact, adding other variables to the regression equation seems to make little or no difference to the general fit of the model.[15]

[13] Pearson Correlation Coefficient, N = 8182. There is a 75% match between predicted probabilities and observed responses, with another 9% tied. Somer's D is 0.59.

[14] The LOGISTIC procedure fits a parallel lines regression model that is based on the cumulative distribution probabilities of the response categories, rather than individual probabilities. Thus the model may be used to determine the probability of binary outcomes, or ordinal outcomes with a small range of values. In this model, citizenship is the dependent variable; year of entry and other variables are independent, explanatory variables.

[15] For instance, a logistical regression with the variables for year of entry, level of education, age, household income, sex, and marital status still accounts for only 80.5% of the cases. A regression equation with only the variables for year of entry and level of education accounts for 79.9% of the cases, with a Somer's D of 0.61. This minor difference between the two equations may be due in part to the multicolinearity among some of the variables. Education, income,

Figure 3. Citizenship rates of Latin American immigrants to Queens, by years of entry

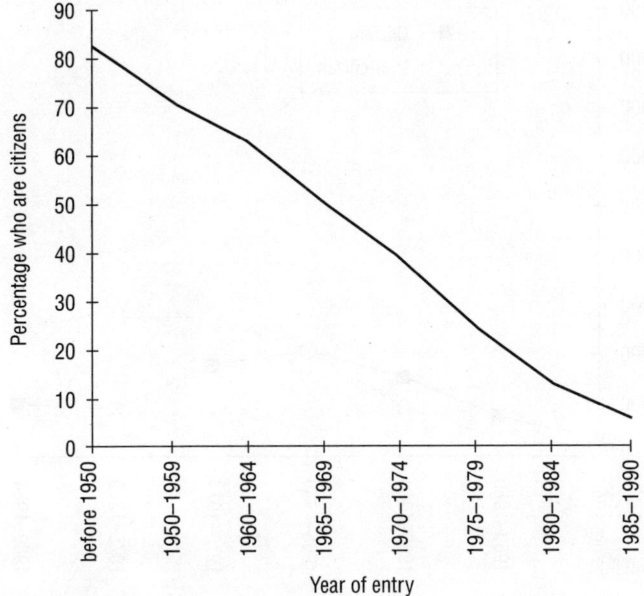

Source: 1990 Census Public Use Microdata Sample.

This result is not entirely unanticipated in the literature on political participation. Milbraith and Goel note that "the longer a person resides in a given community, the greater the likelihood of his participation in politics" (1977: 113). Lane notes that "people who first come into the community are likely to have fewer associational ties, less information on community affairs, few political contacts, and fewer emotional and material stakes in the group tensions that express themselves in politics" (1959: 267). Milbraith and Goel note that this finding is supported by the work of other social scientists: Alford and Scobie 1968; Agger, Goldrich, and Swanson 1964; and Lipset 1960. Garcia (1981), working on Mexican immigration to the United States, notes that length of residence is one of the major factors contributing to naturalization. But it is not just one of many predictors, along with education, occupational stability, and economic mobility, as Garcia suggests.

---

and occupation are all interrelated, of course (Pearson's R between 0.19 and 0.17), as are age and year of entry (0.22). So the variables "year of immigration" and "education" may be, in part, serving as markers for other variables. However, while the correlations are significant, it is still true that these two variables, and year of entry in particular, carry by far the most weight in predicting the outcome of citizenship or noncitizenship.

Figure 4. Citizenship of Latin American immigrants in Queens, by year of entry

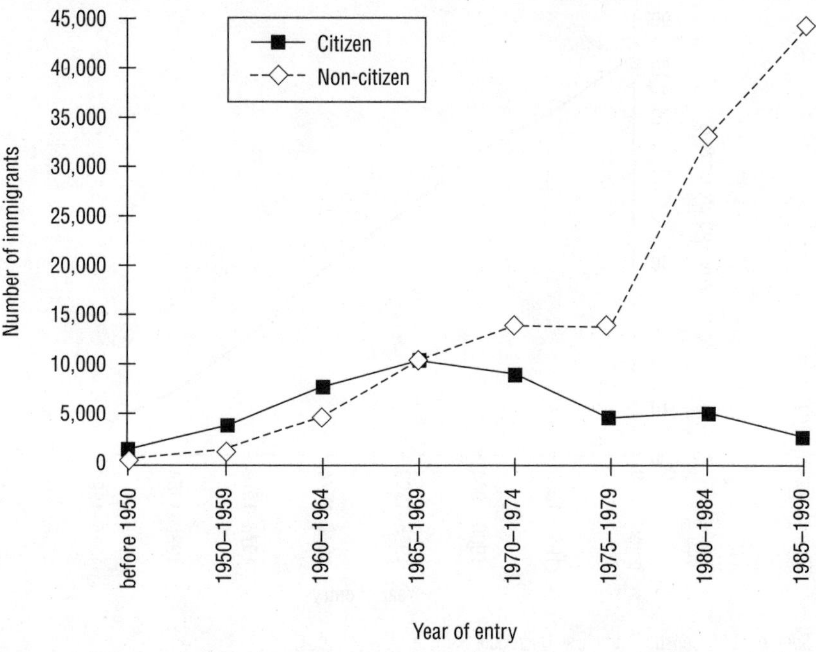

Source: 1990 Census Public Use Microdata Sample.

Among the indicators measured by the census, length of stay is overwhelmingly the most important predictor of citizenship in the United States.

Given that length of stay gives a good indication of the likelihood of becoming a citizen, what is surprising is that the interval between the time of arrival and the decision to become a citizen is so long. After twenty to twenty-five years, only a bare majority (50 percent) of the 1965–69 cohort of immigrants had become citizens (see Figure 4). Assuming things stay the same,[16] then we can expect that it will take at least twenty years before 50 percent of the most recent cohort become citizens. If the average age for immigrants in Queens at the time of their arrival in the United States is be-

[16] This is a problematic assumption. For instance, national origin and some socioeconomic characteristics have changed from 1965 to 1990. New York City has changed as well. Economic prospects for immigrants in the early 1990s were not what they were in the mid-1980s, which may have resulted in declining immigration into the city (a trend also reflected somewhat at the national level). Political changes under way affect the context immigrants arrive to as well. What effect all this will have is of course unclear.

tween twenty and thirty-five,[17] and it takes twenty years for a majority of immigrants (just over 50 percent) to become citizens, most are becoming citizens only well into middle age.

The passage of time is not really an *explanation* of why Latin American immigrants become citizens—it is simply a predictor. We also know that socioeconomic variables make relatively poor predictors for citizenship. Traditional accounts of political participation, looking at socioeconomic status through survey data, fail with this large and growing segment of the population, who have been arriving in increasing numbers since 1965. We have to turn elsewhere to answer the question of why Latin American immigrants, even those with relatively high socioeconomic status, remain outside direct political involvement—particularly the most basic form of political participation, acquisition of citizenship.

The Costs of Participation

One way to account for the delay in citizenship acquisition, and hence in political participation, is to think of the decision to naturalize less in terms of the availability of resources and the possibility of acquiring benefits by expending these resources, and more in terms of the *costs* and *constraints* that people encounter as they choose to implement the resources they have on hand. In *Voice and Equality*, Verba, Schlozoman, and Brady (1995: 283–87), suggest inverting the standard question "why do people become involved in politics?" to ask instead "why *don't* people become involved in politics?"[18] The answers, they suggest, have more to do with the constraints and demands on people's resources than simply with the resources themselves.

Every individual faces real costs to political participation. As Verba, Schlozman, and Brady point out, "money given to a candidate is not available for other purposes; time devoted to an informal community effort is

[17] The NALEO Educational Fund's National Latino Immigrant Survey estimated that the median age at which respondents come to live permanently in the United States is 22 (Pachón 1989: 8). The median age of all Hispanics is 34.7; for Mexicans it is 34.7, for Puerto Ricans 36, for Cubans 46.5, for Central and South Americans 34.5. The median age of non-Hispanics is 41.1 (Cattan 1993).

[18] The authors give three answers: "because they can't; because they don't want to; and because nobody asked" (15). "They can't" suggests the choices people have to make with always limited resources: people never have enough time, money, and skills to do everything they want to do, so they allocate their resources among the choices available to them. "They don't want to" focuses on the absence of political engagement—people who don't participate may display little interest or concern with public issues. "Nobody asked" implies isolation from the networks of recruitment through which citizens are mobilized to politics (16).

time away from work, family, recreation or sleep" (1995: 284). Yet even given the resources at their disposal, Latino immigrants have much lower rates of involvement than native-born citizens. Some of the difficulties immigrants face in participating politically may be accounted for by their socioeconomic standing, but this alone is not enough to explain the difference between the native-born and immigrants. Rather, as the aspiring middle-class immigrants of Queens demonstrate, the resources they have do not seem to be easily translatable into formal political participation. This would suggest that they face additional costs not borne by the average voter (or perhaps face them in different ways).[19] If the low rates of participation among Latino immigrants in Queens are not solely derived from a lack of resources, but also from costs they face, what accounts for these costs?

Commentators who have noted the hurdles facing immigrants as they decide whether to become American citizens and enter into the political process have tended to focus on the administrative hostility and bureaucratic hurdles inherent in the naturalization process (DeSipio 1994: 11–12; DeSipio and Pachón 1992; North 1987; Alvarez 1987; NALEO 1984). One advocate noted, for instance: "We have eliminated voter literacy exams in the South, but we still retain the tradition of arbitrariness in testing for the citizenship exams. . . . Examiners can make the process a living hell. They can obviously overstep their discretionary authority, as in one instance where someone was asked if they ever had sex before marriage. Or they can perversely ask the kind of civics questions that most Americans could not answer."[20] While these concerns are not insignificant, it's doubtful that in themselves they account for the low levels of naturalization among Latin American immigrants. Fear of the INS and the impact of bureaucratic hurdles may be overstated; data from the National Latino Immigrant Survey, for instance, indicate that a majority of Hispanics going through the naturalization process found the INS helpful (Pachón and DeSipio 1994: 105). Less than 2 percent of those who had delayed applying for citizenship said they had done so because of fear of the INS (ibid.: 110). Most of those who had applied and completed the naturalization process reported feeling very or somewhat satisfied with the process (ibid.: 119).[21] Eighty percent indicated that the examiner was helpful (NALEO 1989: 20). The bother and

[19] The role of costs, and immigrants' rational calculation of these costs in making their decision about naturalization, are developed, respectively, by Hammar (1990b: 142–47) and Bauböck (1994: 102–15).

[20] Deborah Sontag, "Immigrants Forgoing Citizenship While Pursuing American Dream," *New York Times*, July 25, 1993, p. 33.

[21] Percentages ranged from 60% for South Americans to 86% for Cubans, with Mexicans, Dominicans, and Central Americans falling in between.

cost of applying for citizenship might be an additional factor in deterring people from making the decision to naturalize, but it is unlikely that they are the main reason for people's reluctance to naturalize.

If it takes a generation for even half of the largely middle-class Latin American immigrant population in New York to become citizens, the overwhelming majority will spend twenty to thirty years on the margins of political life. The reason for their hesitation is not found simply in socioeconomic explanations, nor, I argue, in bureaucratic impediments. Instead immigrants have to confront a set of costs which other members of the polity are not likely to have to face.

In the chapters that follow I argue that immigrants face two primary costs  before they are able to participate fully in the polity: one from without, and the other, as it were, from within. First of all, immigrants, residing as they do on the margins of the polity, face costs in terms of access to and recruitment to the formal political arena. Political parties are not eager to expend their resources on what they see as "high-risk" potential voters. Hegemonic parties in particular have an interest in keeping to a minimum their winning coalitions. Why should they try to incorporate and mobilize new actors—unknown quantities in the political process, who might conceivably tip the balance the parties have so precariously established—when by assembling the same group of voters who voted them into office in the past, party leaders can continue to win elections? To enter into politics, then, immigrants must overcome the inertia of the political system to be taken seriously as political players. Immigrants have to mobilize themselves first before parties will pay enough attention to consider expending resources to respond to their needs and demands. Second, immigrants face costs from within their own communities. Making the decision to participate as full members of the American polity implies paying a price as members of the polities of their countries of origin. Taking on the privileges and responsibilities of American citizenship means not only losing benefits and foregoing duties in their home countries, but paying the psychological cost of separation as well. This is made even more difficult by the uncertainty, in their own minds, of their stay in the United States, an uncertainty reinforced by their own community's resistance to the idea of staying in the United States. The combination of these costs from without and within makes the choice for immigrants to naturalize and participate in American political life all the more difficult.

II

THE COSTS OF CHOOSING

4

Resistance from Outside: Machine Politics and the

The United States has received immigrants throughout its history, and the long experience has created its own mythology. Part of the popular imagery has it that earlier in this century the ships bringing immigrants were met at the dock by the political boss, a basket of food or clothing draped over his arm, waiting to receive the newcomers and recruit them as part of the city's political machine.[1] A New York politician recalled in an afterglow of nostalgia that when immigrants arrived, the party ward heeler "took them as fast as they came [and] flung them into his melting pot . . . he naturalized them, registered them and voted them for Tammany Hall" (quoted in Henderson, 1976: 10). The urban political machine is now mostly remembered as a quintessential Americanizing institution; immigration policy allowed immigrants entry, but the machine made them voting citizens.

This memory of the political machine, which emphasizes its role as an integrating mechanism into democratic politics, is acquiring renewed relevance today as the United States again becomes the destination for millions of immigrants from around the world. Over eight million immigrants arrived in this country in the last decade, more than at any other time since the last great wave of immigration from 1900 to 1910. The United States

1 The boss's role did not end at the docks. Oscar Handlin writes that "under a variety of designations there was in every ward a place where a man could go and see the boss, or see someone who would in turn see the boss." He quotes an imaginary ward leader: "'I think that there's got to be in every ward a guy that any bloke can go to when he's in trouble and get help—not justice and the law, but help, no matter what he's done'" (1951: 191). This rudimentary welfare safety net was repaid at election time by the votes of grateful recipients.

receives twice as many immigrants as all other nations combined (Hoskin, 1990: 35). Most of these become permanent residents; many may eventually become citizens. Are they being integrated into the electoral process? How relevant is the popular historical view? What role do political parties and urban political machines currently play in the integration of immigrants into American political life?

Social scientists differ on how political machines actually work. A generation of social scientists which included Robert Dahl, Robert Merton, and Raymond Wolfinger generally portrayed political machines in a positive light.[2] Their writing was deeply influenced by instrumentalist explanations for party politics like those of Joseph Schumpeter and Anthony Downs, which posited that cost/benefit rationales drove all political behavior. Their economic modeling of party behavior laid the groundwork for an explanation of the machine's integration of immigrants. A more recent interpretation of the urban political machine, represented by Steven Erie's work, partly challenges this view. Erie makes the case that political machines only occasionally mobilized immigrant voters, in large part because machines were rarely competitive. In most cases, the machine tried to retain a monopoly on access to the political process by systematically limiting participation or demobilizing participants.

The present situation of Latin American immigrants in Queens neatly illustrates Erie's case. Democratic machine politics in Queens, though weakened, still functions. But rather than playing the integrating role in which it has been cast in the popular imagination, it aims to keep political mobilization within tightly constricted bounds, and to direct and control that mobilization for its own ends. Rather than lowering the entry costs for marginal political players, the Queens Democratic party, like the hegemonic party organizations Erie describes, raises them instead. If actors are at the margins of electoral politics, as immigrants are, then they are ignored; if political players rise to challenge the machine, they are thwarted. Only if new political actors succeed in mobilizing themselves on their own does the party organization attempt to bring them into its circle.

The strategy of the party organization in Queens is very simple: it places all the costs of mobilization and incorporation on those on the margins of politics. Successful entry into the formal political arena requires passage over a series of hurdles.

[2] See Cornwell 1964: 27–39. For a cautious synthesis of this position, see Greenstein 1964. Robert K. Merton's *Social Theory and Social Structure* (1957) had a significant effect on many of these writers.

Instrumentalist Views of the Political Machine

The popular view of the political machine leached into the social science literature in the 1950s and '60s, abetted and reinforced by revisionist scholars who rebutted earlier opinion that the machine was the root cause for corruption and decay in American politics, and who created a vision of the urban political machine as a democratizing influence. Drawing from the example of New Haven's integration of immigrants in[illegible]ectoral process, Robert Dahl asserted, for example, that "[illegible]ntry . . . the political stratum has seen to it [illegible]uld, have been properly trained [illegible]ls . . . The result was as astonishin[illegible]and cultural assimilation as history can provid[illegible]. The key point to this reinterpretation was that the loc[illegible] mobilizing effort was the machine. It brought outsiders into the political system, and that process was initiated by political insiders, elites in the political parties.

The assertion that the party machinery worked to integrate immigrants drew directly from instrumentalist theories of party politics, which drew in turn on economic models of political behavior. Joseph Schumpeter, in *Capitalism, Socialism, and Democracy*, was one of the earlier and more influential proponents of this view. The theory, wrapped in militaristic metaphors, is relatively simple: given a competitive environment with open elections and two parties, "the first and foremost aim of each party is to prevail over the other in order to get into power or stay in it" (Schumpeter, 1942: 279). Rivals and alternative programs will be co-opted, lest they challenge the central players: "There are," Schumpeter writes, "cases in which the political engine fails to absorb certain issues. . . . Such issues may then be taken up by outsiders who prefer making an independent bid for power to serving in the ranks of one of the parties" (ibid.: 281). Democratic politics are inherently competitive, the theory goes, because the main interest of each player is to acquire power. Politicians, being competitive, will mobilize potential players to keep the extra edge over their opponents; otherwise outlying issues and actors will be picked up by the opposition.

The driving assumption is that players in the political game will seek to maximize support (Downs, 1957: 10).[3] This assumption adopted in the literature of immigrant mobilization, is stated most clearly by Dahl: "In a competitive political system within a changing society, a party that neglects any

[3] This assumption is echoed by contemporary authors. See Arian et al. 1991: 151; Enelow and Hinich 1984.

important source of support decreases its chances of survival . . . as new social strata emerge, existing or aspiring party leaders will see and seize opportunities to enhance their own influence by binding these new elements to the party . . . new social elements are likely to be recruited into one of both of the parties not only as subleaders but ultimately as leaders" (1961: 114).

Competitive parties will choose to mobilize not only active players in the system, but potential or marginal players such as immigrants:

> Since political leaders hoped to expand their own influence with the votes of ethnic groups, they helped the immigrant overcome his initial political powerlessness by engaging him in politics. Whatever else the ethnics lacked they had numbers. Hence the politicians took the initiative; they made it easy for immigrants to become citizens, encouraged ethnics to register, put them on the party rolls, and aided them in meeting the innumerable specific problems resulting from their poverty, strangeness and lowly position. (ibid.: 34)

Immigrants didn't even need to be citizens to be incorporated, because the politician guided them through the court system as fast as—or faster than—the law allowed, making them citizens and leading them to the polling booths. This made sense in the economy of machine politics, which traded in specific, tangible benefits (Erie, 1988: 192). Raymond Wolfinger writes that "votes mattered to American politicians, who solicited [immigrants] with advice, favors, petty gifts, and jobs. . . . Each nationality group in a city had leaders who bargained with politicians, trading their followers' votes for money, favors and jobs" (1965: 898).[4]

Social scientists such as Dahl, describing the history of immigrant political integration into American life, wrote at the juncture of common belief and economic models of politics. The economic model provided a rationalization of the popular image of political machines by providing the hypothetical figure of the boss, waiting with a basket at the pier where the immigrants' ships landed, with a rational calculus for his actions. Written in a language convincing to social scientists, Dahl's and others' essentially populist vision became the accepted account of the political machine.

Writing a generation later, Steven Erie argues that political machines never really attempted to incorporate immigrants wholesale. "Throughout most of their history," he writes, "urban machines did not incorporate im-

[4] See also Oscar Handlin (1951: chap. 8) and William Foote Whyte (1943: chap. 6) for other accounts of machine incorporation of ethnic voters.

migrants other than the Irish" (1988: 6). The argument of Dahl and others is wrong on two counts. First, it assumes that the electoral arena will remain competitive. In a competitive environment, instrumentalist logic would require that the party out of power attempt to mobilize marginal voters to build a coalition to recapture political office. Political machines, however, are not in the business of being merely competitive. Machines are not interested in maintaining a dual or multiparty system where there is free competition. The aim of the machine is to drive competitors out of business and become monopolies. Machines only mobilize potential voters until they establish control of the political system, after which their purpose is to keep core constituencies satisfied; then they can demobilize or ignore marginal or outside players (ibid.: 69). This was the case through the nineteenth century and well into the twentieth in many U.S. cities. "Having already constructed a minimal winning coalition among 'old' immigrant—that is Western European—voters, the established machines had little need to naturalize, register, and vote later ethnic arrivals" from southern and eastern Europe (ibid.: 6).[5]

Erie also believes that Dahl and others are wrong to assume that the machine had unlimited inducements to mobilize voters. Machines were constantly trying to create resources to meet ethnic demands—demands which, Erie notes, "nearly always exceeded the machine's available supply" (9). Even if they wanted to do more, the urban machines could only reward or encourage mobilization in drips and drabs. The solution the Irish-run machines at the turn of the century found was to allocate most of the choice rewards to a core group of reliable supporters, and to apportion what was left among marginal voters. The newer immigrants were among the latter group. They were given the less valuable benefits the machine had to offer: symbolic recognition, support in getting social services provided by the state government, and lobbying for state labor and social welfare legislation (69).

Notwithstanding his criticisms of prior interpretations, Erie's analysis of the urban political machine is not revolutionary. He provides an important corrective to Dahl and others' analyses of the machine in particular by attaching an addendum to the earlier instrumentalist model. Dahl (and to a

[5] For example, in the Lower East Side, where "as early as 1910 [the] district was 85% Jewish and Italian, and only 5% Irish . . . the Irish maintained firm control over the party apparatus. As late as 1932, three-quarters of Tammany's district leaders on the Lower East Side were Irish while less than one-fifth were Jewish. The first Italian leader was not selected until 1931. With a lock on the party organization, the Irish monopolized nomination to elective office. Between 1908 and 1933 every Tammany candidate for the Board of Aldermen, the State Assembly, and the Senate from the Lower East Side was Irish" (Erie 1988: 101).

lesser extent Wolfinger[6]) makes generalizations about the urban machine based on a single example—in Dahl's case New Haven—and assumes that because conditions there were competitive, such conditions also existed elsewhere. Erie demonstrates that cities like New Haven are much more the exception than the rule. Political incorporation of marginal players will only take place to the extent that, first, there is competition, and, second, the supply of resources can be stretched to cover the demand. In cases where these conditions do not apply, machines will tend to act like monopolies, demobilizing and ignoring marginal players. "Embryonic machines," he writes, "are mobilizers. They face competitive pressures to increase the number of partisan voters. Entrenched machines, in contrast, are selective mobilizers. Having defeated the other party's machine and rival factions, consolidated machines need only bring out their traditional supporters. There is little electoral incentive to mobilize newer ethnic arrivals" (10). What Erie adds to the discussion of party politics is a corollary about how parties act under noncompetitive conditions.

Contemporary Machine Politics in Queens

The machine politics existing today in New York City are not those of eighty or even forty years ago; they face different conditions and incentives. Tammany Hall, the notorious Manhattan-based New York City machine, was already crumbling by the early 1930s, under the pressure of reformist mayors and governors. By 1961 the atrophy of the Tammany clubhouses led to the capture of the Democratic Party by reformers and the end of a citywide machine (Arian, 1991: 9–11). New York City, however, has in reality always had not one but five political systems—one in each borough of the city (Adler and Blank 1975: 136).[7] Although reformers may have killed off the overarching centralized machine in Manhattan, machine politics have continued operating in the outer boroughs to the present day (Mollenkopf 1990: 80). Electoral politics in Queens, for instance, are dominated by a Demo-

[6] Wolfinger has a more sophisticated and nuanced view of machine politics than Dahl, but works within similar instrumentalist paradigms. See Wolfinger 1972a and 1972b: 383–85.

[7] "Tammany Hall" was in fact an amalgam of five separate county (borough) organizations since New York State law sets out party organization at the county, not city level (Erie 1988: 175). County leaders agreed among themselves to endorse particular candidates. "Their endorsement of a candidate and their subsequent ability to 'deliver' the support of the local assembly district clubs in their boroughs by collecting nominating position signatures and getting the vote out on primary day would, in turn, be the basis for their claim on the mayor for patronage and other favors" (Arian 1991: 9).

cratic organization operating out of the political clubs and Borough Hall. Even though this organization was wracked by the 1986 suicide of Donald Manes, the county Democratic leader and borough president,[8] and may have decayed still more with the revision of the city charter in 1989,[9] machine politics are alive and well in Queens (Mollenkopf 1990: 78). The president of the community board in Jackson Heights summed up the situation: "It hasn't changed [since Manes's suicide]; especially to get an appointment to the court, to be a judge . . . You can go into a primary without party backing, but it's hard . . . in a general election . . . hard to win. The clubs back the machine candidates, collect their petitions, go door to door. . . . Most of these guys started out as reform candidates," he said, waving his arm at the roomful of local politicians and their aides. When asked if they still were outside the machine, he shook his head.[10] The reformers have ended up running the machine, and the reform clubs, like the JFK club in Jackson Heights, have taken the place of the old machine's clubs.[11]

Machine politics in much of Queens continues to be organized around these Democratic clubs, with one in every state assembly district, and about two hundred members in a typical club (Adler and Blank 1975: 65). Club members provide the party with a cadre of experienced volunteers for petition-gathering to nominate candidates, canvassing, and guaranteeing voter turnout during the primary. In return, what patronage the machine

[8] Donald Manes's death was particularly damaging because it came in the midst of investigations into influence peddling, bribery, and corruption. The broader FBI investigation eventually led to a number of indictments, convictions, and resignations involving two borough presidents (Manes and Stanley Friedman of the Bronx) and several state legislators, commissioners, and city hall aides (Arian 1991: 39–40). For a closer look at the seamy side of the Koch regime, particularly in its declining years, see Newfield and Barrett 1988.

[9] Called the most dramatic change in the structure of city government since its incorporation in 1898, the city charter revisions were approved by the city's voters in 1989 (in the same election which made David Dinkins the first black mayor of New York City) by a five to four margin. The charter revisions were the culmination of a lawsuit filed in 1981 which charged that the old Board of Estimate acted as a de facto legislative body and that its boroughwide basis of representation violated the constitutional norm of one person, one vote. After a series of suits and countersuits going all the way to the Supreme Court, in 1989 the final ruling was decided against the city. An appointed charter commission came up with a plan that expanded the numbers of City Council seats from 35 to 51, with the express intent of drawing district lines that would increase the number of minority representatives. The revisions also, for the first time, gave the City Council legislative and budgetary authority. At the same time, the revisions increased the power of the mayor and the operating agencies which the mayor controlled. In short, the City Council and the mayor divided the powers once held by the Board of Estimate (McNickle 1993: 313–14).

[10] Conversation, May 27, 1992.

[11] Talk at the JFK Democratic Club, Jackson Heights, by state senator Leonard Stavinsky, May 27, 1992.

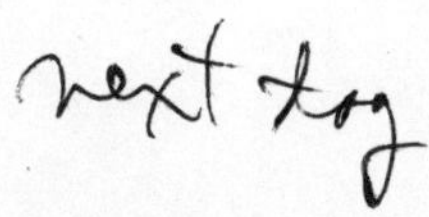

has left is usually dispersed to Democratic club members: "The use of a club's good offices in finding jobs for members—both in government directly (as in numerous non-civil service court posts) and with contractors who feed at the public trough—is still a continued welfare activity in the clubs . . . so is . . . behind the scenes negotiating in matters involving minor offenses by club members, such as parking violations and failing to answer jury notices" (ibid.: 141).

This practice continues in Queens today. As one long-time Democratic Party activist put it: "Yeah, you're a member of the club, so when you found a club, your district leader tells you who you are going to work for. That's how you get the job of being an inspector, and then that's it."[12]

Fixing parking tickets and the like may no longer be as prevalent in the wake of the Manes scandal, but providing club members with paid positions as poll watchers or recommending them for judicial clerkships and city and borough posts continues (Mollenkopf 1990: 80; Mollenkopf 1987: 494).

Democratic machine politics in Queens has two principal characteristics. First, it has inherited the remnants of a long-established machine operating in a noncompetitive environment. The Democratic presence in the area is overwhelming; the Republican Party is relegated to being a permanent minority (in 1991, Republicans accounted for only 18 percent of the borough's registered voters, as compared to 65 percent of voters who were registered Democrats [Baca, 1991]). Second, with Democratic political clubs functioning, the infrastructure of the political machine still exists in Queens. However, with the changes in the city's charter, which transferred power from the Board of Estimate to an expanded, elected City Council, the borough machinery has lost significant resources it once had at its disposal.[13] So though the Queens machine exists, it operates in weakened form. Erie's argument that an established political machine in a noncompetitive situation will hold onto its core constituency and attempt to demobilize marginal or potential players would seem especially true during periods in which resources are constricted (1988: 188–90). If Erie is correct, the combination of these two characteristics in Queens machine politics—the absence of competition and the atrophy of the patronage system—would mean that the political machine in Queens would have little interest in bringing new players into the system. This seems indeed to be the case.

[12] Interview, June 10, 1991.

[13] The chief loss is control over the borough's budget. Before 1990, the budget was decided at the borough level, and the borough presidents sat on the city's Board of Estimate, having a great deal of input into the overall shape of the city budget. Since the city's charter revisions the borough's budget is drafted by the borough president's office, but reviewed and approved by the City Council.

In the last thirty years the Queens immigrant population has increased enormously. The 1990 census put the borough's Latino population alone at 381,000, about 20 percent of Queens' total population—most of these being first-generation immigrants. This represents an increase of more than a hundred thousand people from the count in the 1980 census. As previously established groups leave for areas lying outside the city, the Latino presence is growing rapidly in the area.[14] The north-central area of the borough, once composed almost entirely of middle-class Jewish, Irish, and Italian neighborhoods, is now among the most diverse in the city, with majority Asian and Latino populations. Despite the changing demographics of these neighborhoods over the last twenty-five years, however, political organization has remained overwhelmingly white. No Latino holds elected office in the borough, nor has the county Democratic machinery endorsed any Latino (or Asian-American) candidate—which would, in much of Queens, be tantamount to election to office. Several Latino candidates have run for office against machine incumbents at the level of district leader, City Council, State Assembly, and Congress, but none has succeeded. There is only one Latino judge. Having languished for years in the county housing court, the lowest rung in the judicial hierarchy, he has recently been elected to the civil court.

At the turn of the century the urban machines used sometimes brutal methods to, as Erie puts it, "deflate demand" for political resources: "As oligopolists of the working-class market, the bosses drove rival producers and product lines out of town. Both repression and corruption were used to defeat the machine's labor and Socialist Party rivals. The machine's henchmen intimidated labor party speakers and voters. The machine-controlled police force broke up Socialist meetings, revoked the business licenses of insurgent immigrant entrepreneurs, and enforced Sunday closing laws to stifle Jewish dissidents" (1988: 218; see also Wirth 1925: 193). These tactics of force and intimidation are hardly in use anymore. The machine has no need for these to demobilize its potential challengers. Instead it demobilizes passively, not by doing anything in particular, but by doing nothing. People are not turned away; they are just not invited. Those who invite themselves are let in, but not necessarily welcomed or made to feel at home. Activists are co-opted, but the population as a whole is left alone except during election time. The passivity of modern machine politics is evident in Queens in the following three areas: citizenship, voter registration, and political club membership.

[14] CUNY Data Services, cited in Baca 1991.

Once under the purview of political parties, the acquisition of citizenship is now left entirely to immigrants themselves. The entrepreneurial activism of the machine boss who guided the immigrant through the citizenship process (however limited it may have been) withered away with the passage of the Naturalization Act of 1906 which made it more difficult for political machines to manipulate the court system, implemented literacy tests in English as a requirement for citizenship, and required proof of five years of continuous residence in the local area prior to naturalization (U.S. Government, 1907: 596). Changes in state electoral laws ended alien suffrage by 1910, so that even before changes in the immigration laws restricted their numbers in 1917 and again in 1929, newly arrived immigrants had lost much of their appeal to the machine as potential players.[15] Today no mechanism currently operates in the political parties to integrate noncitizens. Whereas toward the end of the ninteenth century being a noncitizen did not necessarily mean being outside the political system, in contemporary Queens it does, and immigrants can be ignored.

For those who *are* citizens, voter registration is rarely encouraged by local machine politicians. Party-sponsored registration at any time other than the quadrennial presidential election year drives is practically nonexistent; one Democratic club member maintained that "the club does voter registration drives, at least once a year we do it. But as far as anyone in organized politics doing outreach getting everyone registered to vote, be serious. They don't."[16] What little attempts there are to register Latin American immigrants are carried out by immigrant organizations themselves. These tend to be haphazard and small-scale due to the lack of resources, but have been picking up in frequency and scope in the last several years. At least three Colombian organizations as well as the Queens Hispanic Coalition completed registration drives during the 1992 campaign, for instance.[17] Spanish-surnamed registrants in Queens now make up 8 percent of enrolled voters

[15] Thirteen midwestern and western states allowed voting by immigrants who had filed only their "first papers" (declaring their intention to become citizens). Aliens were disenfranchised following the surge of the Republican Party in the 1890s (Erie 1988: 93), and this trend finally culminated with the anti-immigrant backlash following World War I.

[16] Interview, director, Jackson Heights Community Development Corporation, May 6, 1991. CDCs are city-authorized and financed, but run by local political appointees.

[17] Registration drives have been organized by Latin-American immigrant groups before many local and national elections. For instance a respondent interviewed on February 24, 1992, talked about having organized a voter registration campaign in 1980. A conversation with a respondent on August 23, 1991, mentioned a group of Hispanics who had gotten together after the 1988 Democratic convention and started a registration campaign in Queens. Each election stimulates small, concerted attempts to register voters.

in the borough (up from 7 percent in 1988).[18] Even so, Latino registration in Queens is far below their proportion of the population (20 percent in 1990).

It seems curious that the same machine politicians who make almost no effort to register Latinos then use voting as a measure of political influence. The language equating voting and influence is pervasive: "Politics comes to two things: money and votes."[19] Latinos are not perceived to have the votes. "For years," said a Democratic district leader in Jackson Heights, "I have heard talk about [Latinos] delivering votes. . . . In all my years as district leader I haven't seen anyone deliver more than a pizza."[20] Claire Shulman, the Queens borough president, reportedly asked one Latino activist why Queens politicians should pay attention to Latinos when they don't vote. She said she would deal with Latinos when they voted, and they don't vote now.[21] A Latina described a conversation she had with state assemblyman Ivan Lafayette, who represents the Jackson Heights area: "Lafayette said, 'you need to get your community organized.' He said, 'many years ago Latinos came to me, but they did nothing. I didn't get one vote. I've been elected all these years without the Latino vote.'"[22]

Not only are Latinos perceived as nonvoters, but local politicians have no stake in seeing that they *do* vote. The Democratic Party has an organization built up in Queens with a core group of political club regulars to do the crucial petitioning and mobilizing before and during primaries and elections. Politicians of all stripes, in all situations, tend to focus their attention on those constituents who are already active (Verba et al. 1993: 303), and this is particularly true in Queens. Politicians can, and do, still win elections without the Latino vote.[23] Party outreach becomes, as one Queens insider put it, a kind of "preaching to the choir."[24] The Democratic Party could reg-

[18] Spanish-surname voter registration in Queens increased 12% from 1988 to 1991, but was still below the overall city increase of 17% (Baca 1991).

[19] Meeting of Queens Hispanics with Christopher Hyland, Clinton campaign, June 2, 1992.

[20] Meeting, Queens Hispanic Coalition, July 13, 1991.

[21] Conversation, September 10, 1992. In another reported conversation Congressman Tom Manton, the county Democratic leader, said something to the effect of "You guys don't vote, so why should I listen to you? You don't count because you don't vote." Interview, Ecuadorian activist, June 19, 1991.

[22] Meeting, Queens Hispanic Coalition, July 13, 1991.

[23] They can do this—for the time being—because the largest bloc of voters in Queens remains non-Latinos over the age of 55; this group make up 40% of registered voters in the borough (Baca 1991).

[24] "The political and civic clubs are not giving civic lessons. They get down there, they discuss club business, they have a speaker, and . . . it's like, you know, preaching to the choir." Interview, Helen Sears, Democratic district leader, Jackson Heights, June 14, 1991. James Dillon, an

ister and mobilize Latino voters, but mobilization would only mean additional competition for scarce political resources.[25] Queens politicians can afford to marginalize Latinos in part because the Latinos in Queens who do participate in the electoral process tend to be Democrats in any case, regardless of the way they are spurned by the local party organization (see Table 10). As noted previously, Queens is an overwhelmingly Democratic county. The Republican Party's organizational base hardly exists, and there is no effective competition in many areas of the borough. The Republican Party has not been successful at attracting large numbers of Latinos, in spite of their willingness to support some Hispanic candidates.[26] A slightly higher proportion of Latinos than non-Latinos lean toward the Republican party, but whether out of ideological sympathy, or simply for the pragmatic reason that it is better to work with the party in power than with the permanent minority, most stay with the Democratic Party, in spite of their discontent and periodic threats to leave it.[27]

Membership in the party's political clubs seems to be relatively open—it can be as simple as being a registered Democrat and paying $10 in dues every year. Applicants for membership to the clubs are rarely, if ever, turned away (although there is no attempt at recruitment either). Yet there are curious gaps and omissions in club membership. In a borough where a fifth of the population is Latino—higher in areas of north-central Queens—the composition of the clubs is almost entirely white. Maureen Allen, president of the JFK Democratic Club, said new immigrants were not interested in participating: "At least they haven't reached out to us. They may be forming

---

independent candidate for City Council in the adjoining district noted that political clubs rarely reach out to the white community either. Interview, June 14, 1991.

[25] Nor is this the case only in Queens. *Campaigns and Elections*, the political campaign manager's trade magazine, advises that "Get Out the Vote [campaigns] should not concentrate on all the people who live in the district. It should concentrate only on those who will vote and are likely to vote for you." This kind of strategy marginalizes unincorporated potential voters. Cathy Allen, "GOTV: Campaign and Elections' Grassroots Blueprint for Success on Election Day," *Campaigns and Elections,* October/November, 1990.

[26] The Republican district leader in Jackson Heights had an opening for a woman district leader, but there were no takers. "The problem," he said, "is the low level of interest. People aren't interested. There's no one out there . . . I give it to [Latinos] on a platter, without an election or anything, and they still weren't able to get anyone. Not one person." Conversation, June 20, 1991. The Republican Party has also backed at least one Latino candidate for a State Assembly seat, in the 1980s. Interview, Director of Cultural Affairs, Office of the President, Borough of Queens, April 17, 1991.

[27] For instance, there was talk of backing Rudolph Giuliani in the 1993 mayoral race, since David Dinkins was perceived to have slighted the Latino community. Or there are more general complaints: "We've spent the last fifteen years with the Democrats and haven't gotten anywhere." Meeting, Queens Hispanic Coalition, June 29, 1991.

Table 10. Party registration in Queens, 1991

	% Democrat	% Republican	% Independent	% other
New York City Council				
21st district (Corona)				
Latino	58	20	20	2
Non-Latino	71	13	14	2
25th district (Jackson Heights)				
Latino	55	23	20	2
Non-Latino	60	21	17	2
New York State Assembly				
30th district (Corona and Jackson Heights)				
Latino	55	23	21	1
Non-Latino	59	21	18	2

Source: Baca 1991.

their own clubs, but not in this area."[28] In fact, Latino Democratic clubs have been formed in the area in the past, but have not survived. The first attempt began during Jimmy Carter's first presidential campaign in 1976. "This club dissolved," one Ecuadorian activist said, "[in part] because there was a lot of pressure from the Democratic Party . . . which didn't want anything to exist outside the traditional clubs. They didn't see a need for a Latino Democratic club. [They asked] why didn't Latinos work within existing clubs?"[29] A second attempt in the early 1980s also collapsed. When Latinos do join the traditional clubs they often find the atmosphere unwelcoming: "The clubs have a 'closed' environment. . . . It's a *challenge* . . . [our people] feel the barrier . . . a bias which is difficult to define. Something very subtle. It's like they see one of us there and [they ask themselves] 'who is that person? Why are they here?' They don't think it's natural for us to be part of the group. There's an ambivalence. They want us there, and they don't want us there."[30] Political clubs in northwestern Queens tend to be overwhelmingly white, middle-class, and male.[31]

28 Conversation, August 5, 1991.

29 Interview (in Spanish), February 24, 1992.

30 Interview with Colombian activist (in Spanish; italic indicates English), November 4, 1991. A Puerto Rican told of being the first Hispanic on Community Board 3 in Jackson Heights: "Community board people are very political. OK? And I know that when I went on Board 3, and I was the first Hispanic on that board, that people resented it. But like a lot of people who are prejudiced and don't realize what they are saying, they said, 'I know you're Hispanic, but don't worry about it, you're not like them.' And I said, 'I *am* like them. I *am* Hispanic. . . . It hasn't changed. I think you people are putting up barriers to keep other Hispanics from coming aboard.'" Interview, April 24, 1991.

31 In 1975, typical club members in New York City were white (68%), male (62%), married (78%), and white-collar or professional (90%). Latinos were only 4% of the club membership

Table 11. Increase in rates of Queens voter registration in presidential election years, as a factor of registrations in previous non-election year

	1960	1964	1968	1972	1976	1980	1984	1988
Latino	9.4	3.4	2.3	2.8	6.8	3.8	5.1	5.4
Non-Latino	4.2	3.0	1.8	2.1	4.2	3.9	5.0	5.3

Source: Baca 1991. After election years, registration rates fell back to previous non-election year levels. However, the base levels of registration have been increasing incrementally from 1975, when Latinos represented less then 5% of new names on the voter rolls, to 1991, when Latinos accounted for slightly more than 18% of newly registered voters. Still, this is somewhat less than their 20% proportion of the borough's population, and much less than the growth rate of the Latino population, which is closer to 50%.

That Queens politicians seem to be making little or no effort to recruit new players into the electoral system confirms what Erie would predict. Given that the political machine in Queens is long established, and has only token competition, machine politicians have little interest in disrupting the status quo. Since electoral competition in the area dominated by an established, functioning machine is something of an oxymoron, Erie suggests that the mobilization of Italian and Jewish immigrant voters took place not because of competition but rather because of party mobilization during national campaigns (Erie 1988: 244).[32] This pattern is repeated on a smaller scale in contemporary Queens politics. Registration rates of both Hispanics and non-Hispanics go up sharply in presidential election years, when the race is contested at the national level and the local party machinery is expected to contribute to the national campaign effort (see Table 11). For example, in the presidential election year of 1988 five and a half times more Latinos registered as new voters than were registered during 1987. In general, the number of people registering to vote in presidential election years more than doubles the levels of preceding non-election years. This pattern continued in 1992 when, for the first time since 1973, voter rolls in New York City topped 3.2 million registered voters—613,181 voters having been added in the preceding year.[33] On the whole, then, ma-

(Adler and Blank, 1975: 64). At the meetings of three clubs in Queens (June 6, 1991, May 27, 1992, and June 11, 1992), the membership present was mostly male and almost all white. There are few Latino members.

[32] Of course, party mobilization during a presidential campaign explains only part of the upswing in voter registration. Among other things, voters are also likely to feel something is at stake in a presidential election and take more of an interest in the results. Voters often feel, mistakenly, that very little is at stake in local elections.

[33] "Voter Rolls Climb to Highest Since '73," *New York Times*, October 14, 1992, p. 87.

chine politics in north-central Queens tends to confirm Erie's hypothesis about noncompetitive party regimes.

Barriers to Participation

It would seem that Latin American immigrants in Queens would have good reason to seek alternatives to Democratic Party hegemony—turning to another party or challenging the party themselves. But if the political machine is indifferent to the incorporation of marginal actors, it is actively hostile to the mobilization of competition. In this it is abetted by New York City's political structure, which is designed to minimize the possible threat from the competition. It is difficult in the city to run against established incumbents, and hard to build up the necessary campaign infrastructure to challenge the state's arcane electoral rules. Possible routes for challengers—the community boards and the school boards—have [illegible] the borough's machine politicians. In sh[illegible] pay a high cost to gain [illegible]

The Power of Incum[illegible]

From 1961 Democrats have continuously filled the borough presidencies in Brooklyn, Queens, and Manhattan, and lost in the Bronx only from 1961 to 1965. Democrats have filled the comptroller's post through this period, and the City Council presidency for eight of nine terms, while also holding the overwhelming majority of the seats on the Council (Brecher and Horton 1993: 10). That Democrats have consistently held these elected positions may not, in and of itself, indicate an absence of competition within or outside the party. But less than half the Council contests between 1961 and 1989 involved a primary, and most of the general elections were not even close. In only 20 percent of elections was the margin of victory less than ten percentage points. A full 80 percent of the City Council races were not competitive. Competition for borough presidency varies across the city, reflecting the relative strength or weakness of the county party organization. In Queens, though, only one out of the last eight elections for borough president has been contested, and even that race was not close (ibid.: 60–75). Of all the major elected positions in the city, only the mayoralty has been consistently contested.

A good part of this record can be accounted for by the power of incumbency. No incumbent borough president from Queens, Brooklyn, or Manhattan, for instance, has ever lost his or her seat in an election (ibid.: 69). Rarely is a sitting City Council member defeated at the polls. Incumbency provides benefits that are extremely difficult for challengers to overcome. Among other things it gives candidates greater name recognition, opportunities for public exposure, and the possibility of using office to gain support (ibid.: 68; see also Mollenkopf 1995: 10).[34] It allows officeholders control over discretionary budget items, influence over appointments to community boards and other advisory committees, and a role in running the local Democratic clubs and party machinery, which has the attendant benefit of mobilizing a cadre of trained campaign volunteers. With low voting turnout in the city as a whole, and in local elections in particular, "the ability to deliver 200 or 300 votes in a single geographic pocket can be the deciding factor," as Councilmember Walter McCaffrey succinctly put it.[35] Incumbents have enough resources at their command—through appointments, budgetary items, and so on—to make it possible, in theory, to provide the margin of votes they need to win most elections.[36] As a result, even in a situation allowing for a larger than usual field of candidates, as happened with the expansion of the City Council in 1991, almost all those winning seats in the new Council had come up within the ranks of the Democratic party, and were running either as incumbents or with the party's blessing.[37]

[34] At the core of the Democratic political machine are the State Assembly districts. Their influence, contrary to expectation, may have waxed, not waned. "County party organizations have . . . become stronger in some respects since the 1950s. They generally continue to control access to the ballot. More important, they have turned legislative staff operations (both in district offices and in the assembly campaign committees) into the functional equivalent of the old machine, this time funded directly by the state. Some district organizations . . . have evolved into powerful campaign organizations. . . . From their position on the city's periphery, the regular Democratic organizations thus exercise considerable power in the Board of Estimate and state legislature and can constrain any Manhattan-based reform thrust" (Mollenkopf 1990: 80).

[35] "Low Turnout, Upset Predicted," *United Press International*, September 8, 1985; "Low Registration and Turnout Are a Continuing Embarrassment for Democracy," *New York Times*, editorial, November 18, 1985. Turnout in the historic 1991 Council elections, with the Council expanding from 35 seats to 51 and acquiring new legislative powers in city affairs, was still under 20%. Sam Roberts, "Council's New Era Takes Shape in New York Vote," *New York Times*, September 12, 1991, p. A1. Previous turnout in Council elections had ranged from 35% in 1985 to 40% in 1989. See Josh Barbanel, "New York Council Revision Fear Apathy," *New York Times*, September 11, 1991, p. A1. McCaffrey quoted in "New York's Council Primaries Test New Charter's Effect on Machine Politics," *New York Times*, September 8, 1991, p. 40.

[36] James McKinley "In a 4-Week Race for Council Seats, Money Is Talking Louder than Ever," *New York Times*, August 20, 1991, p. B6.

[37] Sam Roberts, "New York City Council Field: Fresh Faces, Traditional Mold," *New York Times*, August 11, 1991, p. 18; James McKinley, "New Voices to Mold Power Balance in the New City Council," *New York Times*, September 13, 1991; James McKinley, "New York City Council Results Show Ripples of Change," *New York Times*, November 6, 1991, p. B1. Even term limits passed by referendum in 1993 are uncertain; incumbents have proposed amendments that would gut the effect of the term limits law. See Steven Lee Meyers, "New York Council to Ask Voters to Postpone Limits on Its Terms," *New York Times*, April 17, 1996, pp. A1, B2.

Electoral Rules

The resources at the disposal of party-backed candidates are crucial for the manipulation of the state's electoral rules. Incumbency means access to campaign workers—through the party's clubs, or through the party's appointees to the community boards, antipoverty boards, or local development corporations, who form the organizational core of a run for office. This is true almost anywhere, but it is particularly true of New York City. A cadre of volunteers gives a candidate the organizational muscle to get on the ballot. This is no easy task in the state of New York. Just to run in the City Council elections one must collect nine hundred signatures.[38] Once signatures are collected they must survive expensive and time-consuming legal challenges by a candidate's opponents. Under New York State's intricate elections laws, candidates in the past have been knocked off the ballot for details as petty as having their petitions fastened together with a paper clip rather than a staple.[39] In the 1991 City Council races, for instance, three of five challengers in District 21 in Corona were knocked off the ballot by petition challenges. These challenges of often trivial details has become a full-time industry: half of all election litigation in the United States occurs in New York City. In spite of the general recognition that change is necessary, officeholders from both parties have dragged their feet on election reform, for obvious reasons: the rules heavily favor incumbents over challengers.

School Boards and Community Boards

Instead of engaging entrenched politicians in a frontal assault in the elections for City Council or State Assembly, new actors might choose instead to try to build a base first in the more accessible electoral arenas of school boards, or to win appointment to the community boards, and then use these as a springboard for broader office. The strategy is plausible; Dominican immigrants in Washington Heights, Manhattan, have used the strategy to good effect, capturing positions in the school boards, antipoverty boards, and community boards before going on to elect a candidate to the City Council.

38 Roberts, "Fresh Faces." To be placed on the Republican presidential primary ballot in 1996, a candidate had to collect a minimum of 1,250 signatures in each of the state's 31 congressional districts over a six-week period. See "Restrictive Republicans," *Wall Street Journal*, editorial, April 10, 1995.

39 Sam Howe Verhovek, "The Time May Finally Be at Hand for Election-law Revisions," *New York Times*, March 8, 1992, p. 38; "Changes Urged on Ballot Rules for New Yorkers," *New York Times*, August 22, 1985, p. A1; "Election Reform Hearings End," *United Press International*, August 19, 1986.

This strategy has the additional advantage that in New York City voters do not have to be citizens to vote in local school board elections, or to serve on community boards.

But there are problems with this strategy as well. The advantages that borough party organizations have in partisan elections also hold for school board elections. While technically nonpartisan, school board slates are informally backed by local politicians.[40] In elections with low turnout (school board elections rarely have turnout above 10 percent),[41] this backing provides crucial support in most elections. There are other similarities to the partisan elections held for other city offices: turnout is rarely actively encouraged by incumbents. Richard Perez, director of organizational development and voter participation for the Community Service Society, noted: "It's not in the interest of incumbents to do voter registration. Those in office have the winning number. New voters are like wild cards; no one knows how they will vote. They pose a threat to the status quo." There have been accusations that in some areas of the city, principals and other school employees have blocked distribution of voter registration materials to parents.[42] Even when all is working as it should, it is not easy for noncitizen parents to vote in school board elections. Registered voters can walk in and vote on the day of the election, but noncitizen parents must pick up registration material available at neighborhood schools and register as a "parent-voter" well in advance of the elections.[43]

The community board system allows even less room for challengers.[44] Members of the fifty-nine boards across the city are not elected; half are selected by the borough presidents, and the other half by local City Council members. As a proportion of their numbers, very few Latinos are ap-

[40] Matthew Purdy, "Web of Patronage in N.Y. Schools Grips Those Who Can Undo It," *New York Times*, May 14, 1996, p. A1.

[41] The 1989 turnout was 7.5%. The 1993 turnout of 12.5% was the highest since the first school board elections in 1970, when the school system was decentralized to give residents a greater voice in the operation of the schools. Turnout was more than triple the usual rate in some districts, due to confrontation between liberals and conservatives over the implementation of a multicultural curriculum. "Both Sides Garner Key School Board Seats in NYC Race," *The Washington Times*, May 25, 1993, p. A3. Even so, in Queens fewer than 16,000 people turned out to vote. Voter turnout in 1995 was again below 10%.

[42] Leonard Buder, "Charges of Corruption Spur School Vote Drive," *New York Times*, March 5, 1989, p. 42; Richard Perez quoted in ibid.

[43] "Who Is Eligible to Vote May 2," *New York Times*, March 5, 1989, p. 42.

[44] The community boards each have a maximum of 50 members. The 1975 charter revisions gave the boards three areas of responsibility: land use review, local budget priorities, and service monitoring. The charter provided that the boards receive funding for such operating expenses as rent, office supplies, and the salaries of a full-time district manager and board staff who serve at the pleasure of the board (Pecorella 1994: 128).

pointed to these boards. Those who are, together with other community board members, serve at the pleasure of the elected officials who direct the county party organization, and have very little real power of their own. The boards hardly constitute a threat to machine politicians. On the contrary, more often than not the boards function as yet another way of dispensing patronage and recruiting workers for the party. Both community boards and the boards of education exemplify how even reform impulses in New York City politics have been captured by the dominant party organizations and used for their own purposes.[45]

Latin American immigrants to Queens enter an environment that discourages participation in the formal political system. Though machine politics in Queens is in some ways unique, its passivity toward the needs of marginal political actors such as immigrants embodies the response of American political parties and the political system in general. Politics is assumed to be a matter for insiders. Not being an insider, a challenger has to pay high entrance costs—in organization, money and time—to be able to compete. It can safely be said that few challengers, and almost no new immigrants, can afford these costs.

Co-optation

The hegemonic party structure in Queens does not actively recruit new members, and does its best to discourage direct challengers. If a group or faction somehow succeeds in mobilizing itself, politicians attempt to enfold it within existing institutions (Verba et al. 1993: 306). In the weak one-party system that exists in the city, they do this very selectively, maximizing the limited resources at their disposal. Incentives for inclusion in the party's coalition remain more symbolic than material.

The party has been divided as to how to deal with the new immigrants. On the one hand they are a huge presence in Queens, and demographically there is every indication that they will one day become the dominant force in the borough. On the other hand, they have not succeeded in mobilizing themselves, so the party organization has no interest in expending more resources on them than they have to. The avenue taken so far—after much

[45] Indeed this was the case from the beginning: "Although the board system was a clear indication of the ascendance of post-reform politics, its formal structure pointed to the understandable hesitation in New York City about post-reform ideals. Indeed, commenting on the appointive system selected by the State Charter Revision Commission, one observer noted, 'In framing its proposals, the Charter Commission was primarily interested in "responsible government" not "participatory democracy"'" (Pecorella 1994: 134, citing Rich 1982: 11). "Responsible" government in the end meant little, if any, reform.

debate within the party leadership about whether anything should be done at all—has been the symbolic incorporation of a small number of ethnic elites into the party. In 1993 the executive committee of the borough's Democratic party finally recognized the existence of over 600,000 new immigrants from Latin America and Asia living in Queens by approving the appointment of six minority at-large district leaders—four Latinos and two Asians. These new district leaders were chosen by the party leadership from among current minority members of the Democratic clubs, so essentially they were already insiders. That one of the four Latinos—the only one with a position in the party—is assemblyman Joseph Crowley's Cuban brother-in-law gives some indication of how the party hopes to use these positions to co-opt "safe" minorities.[46]

Whose Responsibility?

Those who study immigrants and machine politics generally view the situation from the perspective of the machine, not that of the immigrant; Dahl, Wolfinger, and Erie all emphasize the machine's response to immigrants.[47] Their studies are about representation, not participation. The focus is on the principal decision makers in the political process, the elites who drive the machine. The concern with elites and representation can be traced back through Schumpeter, and reflects a long tradition of thought on a particular kind of liberal democratic theory. Here, "political participation is still seen as a necessary protective device, a cost that must be paid at least occasionally by some citizens, but ideally as seldom as possible; it is not an integral part of the individual citizen's life" (Pateman, [1980], 1989: 63). The responsiveness of elites is assured by the *potential* for activity by citizens, not their *actual* activity. Most citizens are assumed to be content with being apolitical (Dahl, 1961: 224–25).

The theoretical assumptions that political life is episodic, and that most people stay away from politics, help explain how Queens machine politicians easily blame immigrants themselves for not becoming participants in electoral politics, and how they see their own role not as one of encouraging participation, but primarily in terms of responding to the demands and

[46] Conversation, Queens borough president's office staff, October 24, 1992. See also Alison Mitchell, "New York's Political Parties View for Votes of Immigrants," *New York Times*, July 4, 1992, p. A1. For a historical perspective on this phenomenon, see Wolfinger 1965.

[47] Their historical methodology tends to draw them to institutions like political machines which leave a residue of recorded material, rather than to the perspective of the immigrant, who often leaves few traces of a passage through political life.

complaints of their constituents. Queens machine politicians have not only an instrumental interest in not seeing new players in the political system (an interest which Erie lays out), but an ideology that allows them to justify their inaction. Ironically enough, it is an ideology that draws from much the same tradition of democratic theory that Erie and his allies depend on. Thus, machine politicians constantly question why Latinos haven't mobilized and approached *them*, instead of talking about why they themselves haven't made the effort to involve Latinos. Politicians defend themselves based on the record of how they *respond*, as the City Council member for Jackson Heights did when defending himself to a Latino news reporter: "I always respond to invitations. If I receive an invitation I make every effort to be there. But I don't like to go where I am not invited."[48] Given this view of their mission, Queens politicians tend to respond best either to organized groups or those individuals who contact their offices directly. In both cases, these are people who have already mobilized on their own.[49] In neither case is the politician's goal to act as a mobilizing agent, but rather to channel or defuse existing mobilization. This view of politics is very distinct from that laid out by the one Hispanic judge in Queens:

> They will say Hispanics don't vote. Here we have to ask "What is the responsibility of a political party?" Is it to take care of their own interests, to cater to the needs of a small clique, or to look out for the public? Do they have the responsibility to develop leaders? Do they have the responsibility to encourage membership and participation? What efforts has the party taken? A party may exist to accumulate favors for "ourselves," but who is "ourselves"? They are being dishonest if they say they are representing the public.[50]

Questions about what responsibilities those in positions of power have to encourage democratic participation are not reflected in the theoretical concerns of political scientists such as Erie and Dahl, or in the practice of Queens politicians.

Immigrants are in a "catch-22" situation. The only avenue for incorporation that is recognized or permitted by the Democratic Party in Queens is within the party itself. The expectation is that groups on the margins of politics will mobilize themselves; only when mobilized will they receive the at-

[48] Conversation, City Council member, District 25, and *Impacto*, August 5, 1992.
[49] At the first public meeting of police and politicians at a Dominican club, a precinct captain said: "The 'squeaky wheel gets the oil' and that is why we are here, and why are you are here, because you've said 'we've had enough, and we want to work within the system.'" Meeting, Club Hermanos Unidos de Queens, September 18, 1991.
[50] Interview, July 1, 1992.

tention of politicians. Once groups are mobilized they receive the bulk of the attention politicians have to bestow. Those who are already mobilized then become the targets of mobilization by politicians, while those who are not remain on the margins. This makes sense from the tactical point of view of the individual politician or party, but not from the perspective of the polity as a whole.

5

Resistance from Within: The Myth of Return and the Community of Memory

There's a paradox in Latin American immigration to the United States. Many come to make the United States their permanent residence.[1] Contrary to popular belief, the return rates of the new immigrants are lower than those of immigrants in the past. Yet naturalization rates for these immigrants are also low; it often takes decades to make the decision to naturalize. Why is this? The first part of the answer, we've seen, is the consequence of external constraints—the logic of a machine politics that values the calculus of available resources over the incorporation of marginal players.

The second half of the answer is that, in part, the desire to stay is an acquired taste. Often people come to the United States with the hope (even if faint or obscure) of returning someday to their countries of origin. One recent observer astutely points out that no matter how much immigrants appreciate the United States, and even if they plan on staying, they always use the impersonal *"este país"*—"this country"—to speak of the United States, and emotional, possessive terms like *"mi patria," "mi tierra," "mi país"*—my land, my country—to refer to the country of their birth. There's always an emotional distance from the host society (Duany 1994: 33–34).

But these emotional ties to the home country are not enough in themselves to explain the hesitation to naturalize as American citizens. The explanation also lies with the costs immigrants encounter as they face the decision to naturalize. Even as immigrants shift their attachments and their lives to the United States, the costs of naturalization are simply too high for many of them to pay. American citizenship not only ends the romanticized

[1] Ninety-four % of Pachón and DeSipio's New York sample said they had "plans to make the U.S. their permanent residence" (1994: 177, table 8.31).

dreams of return, but also requires undivided loyalty, which immigrants are reluctant to give. More important, an immigrant's decision to acquire American citizenship may mean being disavowed or penalized by their compatriots and their countries of origin. Understandably, many postpone the decision.

Sojourners

Most Latin American immigrants come to New York City, as to other locations in the United States, for economic reasons.[2] Many say they want to return to their home countries, yet in the end most will not. Americans often find the idea of sojourner migration—in which migrants plan to stay for a limited time and return to their home country—to be odd at best and, at worst, suspect. One neighborhood organizer in Jackson Heights said: "The immigrants of old came into this country—my father, my grandfather, my wife's parents. They came here with the intention of making a better life for themselves. They were going to become Americans. The intention of the newer immigrants is not to stay."[3] A woman in Jackson Heights told me about her family's experience with immigration:

> My grandfather was a language teacher in Russia. . . . So when they got off the boat, my grandfather said, "My name is Herman Kuchuk" in perfect English, and they said, "Excuse me, are you sure you are getting off in the right place?" Yet I remember my grandmother speaking English with an accent, and I remember my aunt Ida who went to college here, she had an accent. But they all spoke English. They all read and write English. . . . You see that striving and wanting for their children to do better. But you don't see [new immigrants] necessarily . . . trying to make that point of entry, or whatever it is. To try and become a part of something larger.[4]

The old and new immigrations are seen by white ethnic Americans as fundamentally distinct, their telling requiring two different stories. The first is told through patriotic reminiscences of Americanization, the second in ac-

[2] Gurak and Kritz (1984) were surprised that while the most common answer to the question of why they had come to the U.S. was "to look for work and/or improve one's economic situation," less than a third of Colombian males gave this as their first response, and less than half of Dominican males. Nonetheless, economic factors played a major (if not always a primary) role in most migrants' decisions to come to this country.

[3] Interview, April 29, 1991.

[4] Interview, May 6, 1991.

cusatory tones of moral deficiency and failure. It's broadly implied that immigrants just aren't what they used to be.

Many native-born Americans are the children and grandchildren of immigrants, and therefore have reason to think that they know something of migration. The United States, Americans like to say, is a land of immigrants. This pronouncement assumes that migrants always come to the United States to stay. "Our image of migration tends to be very particular. In that image the migrant worker at his home makes a deliberate decision to move to some other place. The move is viewed as *permanent.* The migrant may indeed go back. But in the conventional view, to *go back* is to *change one's mind.* Often, in the conventional view, those who go back are spoken of as *failures*" (Piore 1979: 50). But this view is from the perspective of Americans *descended* from immigrants, that is to say, a view colored by the inherited memories of those immigrants who decided to *stay*—Americans don't hear the stories of those who went back. In fact, we can see from the return rates to the sending countries that earlier migrations to the United States were also, in large part, sojourner migrations. A congressional commission established in 1911 estimated that one-third of the migrants to the United States prior to World War I returned; many countries had an even higher rate of return. From 1908 to 1910, 2,297,338 immigrants were admitted, and 736,835 departed. The overall return rate was 32 percent. The return rate was 57 percent for Croatians and Slovaks, 63 percent for northern Italians, 56 percent for southern Italians, 65 percent for Magyars, 31 percent for Poles, 41 percent for Russians, 59 percent for Slovaks, and 51 percent for Spaniards (Piore, 1979: 150). Walaszek estimates even higher rates of return for Polish migrants before World War I—50 percent of the original emigration (1984: 214). Vietanen writes that the return rate for Finns, Swedes, and Danes emigrating in 1860–1930 was about 20 percent (75,000 of 380,000 Finnish migrants returned permanently to their home country), lower than the average return rate but hardly negligible (1984: 224).[5] Earlier immigration to the United States apparently has much more in common with today's immigration than one might guess.[6]

The migratory process is quite different when viewed from the perspective of the migrant. While from the point of view of citizens in the receiving

[5] Rates of return vary acro … ury migrations have lower retur … nd very low for Cuban émigrés

[6] Americans have always seen immigrants' return as shameful, opportunistic, or worse (Shumsky 1992); it has been easier for the descendants of the earlier immigrants to forget than to have to try to justify these rates of emigration in the face of the patriotic fervor of their fellows.

country returning is seen as a sign of poor adjustment to the new country, or perhaps an inability to assimilate, "the typical immigrant *plans* to spend only a short time in the industrial area; he then expects to return home. *Staying* represents a change of plans . . . to the extent that success and failure are useful terms of reference in analyzing the process, it is probably more accurate to say that it is the failures who stay on" (Piore, 1979: 50).

From the sojourners' point of view, migration is intended as a short interval in the long trajectory of their lives. Many migrants arrive with a "target" in mind—they only plan on staying long enough to save enough money to take back home (see Serra Santana 1984: 55). The fruits of their efforts are not meant to be enjoyed here in their host country. "Target" migrants plan to spend as little as possible here, saving their income and sending it home,[7] or accumulating enough to open a small business, buy land, or build a house upon their return.[8]

Many of the Latin American migrants to New York City exhibit a sojourner mentality. In their home countries, most of them were perched precariously on the edge of the middle class.[9] The income they earn here may be enough to bolster and secure their class status at home (Pessar 1987: 104; Bray 1984). To accumulate as much as possible, as quickly as possible, requires taking on work they would not normally consider in their home countries—as factory laborers, for instance. Because their interest is in short-term accumulation, finding a job—any job—is more important than job security or benefits.[10] It appears they have little interest in investing financially or emotionally in their situation here.

[7] Remittances of Mexican workers apprehended in the U.S. in the 1970s were about $170 a month from weekly earnings of $106. North and Houston, *The Characteristics and Role of Illegal Aliens in the U.S. Labor Market: An Exploratory Study* (Washington D.C.: Linton, 1976), pp. 84–86, cited in Piore 1979: 55.

[8] Astudillo and Cordero, writing acerbically on Ecuadorian immigrants to New York City, remark that "savings, the most important and fatal of migrants' obsessions, has obliged [Ecuadorian migrants] to lose themselves in the alleyways of the labyrinth, with the goal to get together the greatest amount of money for their return, or to convert their dollars little by little through slow remittances into an anthill of a house, a family car, home furnishings . . . " (1990: 29).

[9] According to the Díganos national survey in 1974 (Ugalde, Bean, and Cardenas 1979) and the Hispanic Settlement in New York Survey conducted by Gurak and Kritz in 1981, the Dominican migration stream, for example, is predominantly urban and middle class (Pessar, 1987: 105). See also Bray 1984; Portes and Guarnizo 1991; Grasmuck and Pessar 1991. The CCRP study (Cardona, Cruz, and Castaño 1980) cited by Mary Garcia Castro, indicates the same for Colombia: most migrants came from the middle class of the two principal urban areas (Garcia Castro 1982a: 24). My neighbors in Queens played up their middle-class background, telling me about family members who were doctors and lawyers and about how they had lived in the Dominican Republic (Author's fieldnotes, February 24, 1991).

[10] For further discussion, see Chapter 8.

Rates of Return

Every migration leaves behind permanent settlers no matter how impermanent the migration might seem to begin with. For example, in surveys of migrants to France and Sweden in the early 1980s, less than 5 percent of those migrating said they had intentions of staying permanently. However, 76 percent of those who had originally signaled their intent to leave in fact stayed (Rogers, 1984: 278, 281). In another survey conducted in the early 1970s, 11,024 migrants to Canada were asked soon after their arrival about their intention to stay and reside in the country: about a third indicated they were considering only a short stay. Contrary to their declared intentions, 77 percent of these were still in Canada five years later.[11] "The migrants' statements," Rogers writes, "proved poor predictors of their actual behavior; most stayed on far longer than they had thought they would, because it took them longer than they had expected to reach certain savings targets, because little changed in the economies of their own countries, and because their tastes and aspirations changed once they were abroad" (1984: 278). Their intentions notwithstanding, it seems clear that many sojourners to receiving countries do, in fact, stay.

Given that so many contemporary and historical migrants to the United States have been sojourners, it is striking how many remain. Between 80,000 and 95,000 people leave the United States every year to return to their countries of origin,[12] yet rates of return today are probably lower than before World War I. Accurate emigration data is not currently collected, but there are reasonable estimates (see Table 12). The estimated return rate for the period 1971–1990, when the most of the recent immigration has occurred, is around 24 percent, which is below the average from the period 1901–1990, and well below the figures for the last major wave of immigration, 1901–1930. One thing that distinguishes today's migration from immigration at the turn of the century is that the majority of current legal migrants from almost all sending countries are female. Prior to 1930, the annual sex ratios of new immigrants to the United States were almost always greater than 120 males for every 100 females (Salvo and Ortiz, 1992: 73). Two-thirds of the Finnish immigrants earlier in the century, for example, were men. Many were married and had left their families in their home coun-

[11] Only 7% of those who said they would stay left later (Rogers 1984: 282). The survey may have been done too soon after migrants' arrival. Vietanen found that if migrants returned, most did so in the first five years (1984: 227).

[12] Paul Gettner, "Amid Bitter Debate, Thousand of Immigrants Pack up to Leave Borders," *Los Angeles Times*, May 7, 1995, p. A36. Estimates are that between 130,000 and 195,000 people leave the United States every year; between 48,000 and 100,000 of them are native-born citizens, so the rest, one presumes, are foreign-born immigrants returning to their home countries. See "U.S. Emigration on the Rise," Associated Press, March 12, 1995.

Table 12. Comparison of U.S. immigration and emigration, 1901–1990 (in thousands)

Period	immigrants	emigrants	Net immigration	Ratio of emigrants to immigrants
1901–1910	8,795	3,008	5,787	0.34
1911–1920	5,736	2,157	3,579	0.38
1921–1930	4,107	1,685	2,422	0.41
1931–1940	528	649	−121	1.23
1941–1950	1,035	281	754	0.27
1951–1960	2,515	425	2,090	0.17
1961–1970	3,322	900	2,422	0.27
1971–1980	4,493	1,176	3,317	0.26
1981–1990	7,338	1,600	5,738	0.22
Total (1901–1990)	37,869	11,882	25,987	0.31

Sources: Figures for 1901–1980 are from Warren and Kraly, "The Elusive Exodus from the United States," Population Reference Bureau, 1985; figures for 1981–1990 are from the Census Bureau, U.S. Department of Commerce.

tries. These men were much more likely to return than their unmarried counterparts (Vietanen 1984: 225).[13] The emphasis on family reunification in American immigration law since 1965 clearly encourages the decision to stay. This may be why the numbers of immigrants staying in the United States appear as high as at any time in the last eighty years.

Naturalization in the United States

Despite the common assumption that once migrants decide to stay in this country naturalization is the automatic final step in the immigration process, legal migrants to the United States can have very low naturalization rates. For Latin Americans, naturalization rates are well below the average for all immigrants to this country. Of the three largest groups of Latin American immigrants arriving in New York City in the 1970s and '80s—Dominicans, Colombians, and Ecuadorians—only Colombians approximated the average rate for all immigrants (see Table 13).[14] These naturalization rates follow the historical pattern: Erie (1988: 95) notes that only "39% of

[13] This finding is reinforced by some findings from the current European immigration. A 1979 survey of Turkish immigrants in Berlin found that of those returning, 54% (as opposed to 20% of those who stayed) had a spouse in Turkey (Wolpert 1984: 101).

[14] The data collected by Portes and Curtis show similar results for the immigrant cohorts arriving in the United States in 1970 and 1971. After ten years of residence only 3% of Mexicans and 20% of Central and South Americans had naturalized. Latin American immigrants on the whole have very low naturalization rates in the first ten years compared with naturalization of immigrants from Asia, for instance (48%) (1987: 353).

Table 13. Naturalization rate of 1977 immigrant cohort, selected countries of birth, as of 1989

	% naturalized, U.S.	% naturalized, initial settlers, N.Y.C.	% naturalized, continuous residents, N.Y.C.
All countries	33.4	32.2	20.7
Dominican Republic	18.1	16.7	13.7
Colombia	31.3	26.6	16.2
Cuba	33.6	30.5	22.2
Ecuador	17.9	14.7	11.0
Peru	40.6	39.0	23.8
Honduras	34.6	37.3	29.7
El Salvador	33.6	30.5	22.2

Source: Unpublished INS data (1990), cited in Salvo and Ortiz 1992: 138, table 6-3, and 140, table 6-4.

New York City's Russian-born—more than three quarters of them Jewish—had become citizens by 1920 . . . [and] only 27% of the Italian born."[15] By 1910, only 11 percent of the 100,000 natives of Mexico living in the United States had naturalized (Pachón, 1987: 300).

Sojourner migrants to the United States not only have low naturalization rates overall, but what naturalization occurs takes place only after a relatively long period of residence. Again, this is particularly true of Latin American migrants (see Table 14). The median number of years of residence for Dominicans, Colombians, and Ecuadorians arriving in New York City—12, 10, and 11 years respectively—is well above the eight-year average for all immigrants to New York City. While over a third of those citizens from all three groups are naturalized within ten years, another third wait fifteen years or more (this is in marked contrast with Chinese and Korean immigrants to New York City, 75 percent of whom naturalize within ten years).

Even when Latin American sojourners say they plan to stay in the United States, and have positive feelings about naturalization, they are unlikely to immediately take the necessary steps to change their citizenship. Portes and Curtis, for instance, found that only 5 percent of their sample of approximately 440 Mexican immigrants had naturalized within six years of being in the United States, although slightly more than 70 percent signaled their intention to do so (1987: 356–65). Pachón and DeSipio found similar results in their report on the results of the National Latino Immigrant Survey: over

[15] Erie attributes the relatively low naturalization rates in part to the deliberate policies of the urban political machine. In Chicago, where the politics were still competitive, 45% of the city's Russian-born and 35% of the Italian-born were citizens by 1920, even though they were often more recent arrivals than in New York.

Table 14. Percent distribution of persons naturalized, by duration of residence prior to naturalization and selected countries of birth, New York City, 1982–1989

		Years of Residence				Median	Median age
	Total	0–4	5–9	10–14	15+	years	naturalized
Dominican Republic	27,581	1.8%	34.2%	24.6%	39.4%	12	33
Colombia	6,263	6.6	39.4	19.9	34.0	10	36
Cuba	4,408	.6	21.1	26.7	51.4	15	43
Ecuador	4,396	2.1	38.4	28.7	30.7	11	33
Peru	2,201	7.1	59.4	16.7	16.7	8	37
Honduras	1,953	6.8	52.5	16.5	24.0	8	35
El Salvador	1,396	6.6	60.7	20.8	11.7	8	34
China	25,009	5.4	74.8	11.7	8.9	6	34
Korea	6,186	5.1	75.6	16.6	2.5	7	34
All	229,681	3.7	57.4	19.3	19.5	8	35

Sources: Unpublished INS data (1990) U.S. Immigration and Naturalization Service, cited in Salvo and Ortiz 1992: 145, table 6-6. See also Portes and Mozo 1985, and Portes and Curtis 1987: 353 for similar data.

97 percent of their respondents from Mexico, the Dominican Republic, Central America, South America, and Cuba said they intended to make the United States their "permanent home," but less than a third (28 percent) had naturalized (1994: 144). Forty-one percent had never taken any steps at all to naturalize, while 31 percent had taken some initial steps (contacting the INS, filling out some of the preliminary forms, and so on) but never completed the process (ibid.: 153; see similar data in de la Garza et al. 1992). These studies indicate that having a favorable disposition toward long-term residency is significantly different from the going through the process for citizenship change. Permanent migrants may not choose to naturalize, and even when they feel they might, it may be years before they actually apply.

The Myth of Return

Why do some immigrants to the United States signal their wish to go back and then remain? Why, once they remain, do they shy away from becoming citizens? There are real contradictions here between what sojourner migrants say and what they do. These contradictions are only comprehensible if we keep in mind that these immigrants remain in some ways fundamentally and permanently undecided about their futures. If we think of these people coming here with their minds made up to stay, as American legend would have it, then their behavior makes less sense—why should they come, but not become citizens? Faced with this question, many observers have turned to structural explanations of discrimination and economic marginalization, and arguments for cultural deficiencies. But I think there is a simpler explanation.

As I noted before, sojourners often don't plan to stay long in the host country. They come to work and save enough money to return. Piore writes: "The temporary character of the migration flow appears to create a sharp distinction between work, on the one hand, and the social identity of the worker, on the other. The individual's social identity is located in the place of origin, in the home community. The migration to the industrial community and the work performed there is purely instrumental: a means to gather income, income that can be taken back to his or her role within *that* social structure" (1979: 54). Piore calls the initial migrant "a true economic man, probably the closest thing in real life to the *homo economicus* of economic theory" (ibid.). But this identity, divorced from a social setting, operating outside the constraints and inhibitions imposed in a social milieu, cannot be sustained. As people stay, there is a search for companionship, which gradually demands more time and resources. "People describe the development of community as a general encroachment, at first unconscious or at least unwilled upon the extreme asceticism that [migrant life] implies" (ibid.: 62). The development of social networks means that migrants work less than they planned and so earn less money. They spend more on consumption, so they have less money to send home, which means they have to stay longer to meet their initial target. As their stay continues, their need for community grows (ibid.). The maturation of an immigrant community and migrants' length of stay become a mutually reinforcing cycle. A Cuban immigrant noted that migrants in New York City say, "'I came here to solve my problems, and I want to be here four or five years and then go back to my country and live quietly there like it was before I left, and have my small business and peacefully retire,' but that illusion starts knocking against reality, and they get more and more entangled, and they have children."[16] As they continue in the host country migrants' lives get complicated. Return may be put off indefinitely, and they may de facto decide to stay.

Yet the ideology of return persists.[17] People talk about going back, year after year, even as they settle and develop roots in the receiving country.

[16] Interview, April 24, 1991. As John Lennon once sang: "Life is what happens while you're busy doing other things."

[17] "However settled [migrants] actually become," Piore writes, "they continue to see themselves in a certain sense as belonging to some other place and retain an idea, albeit increasingly vague and undefined, of returning 'home'" (1979: 65). Piore explores the consequences of this belief on migrants' attitudes toward work, but not on their political life. Georges (1984: 33–34)

"Even though people have integrated into the system," said one Uruguayan journalist, "they always have something which marks them forever, which is return, the idea of returning to their country."[18] A Colombian woman told me about her friends who had been living in the same cramped apartment for twenty years. She asked them why they hadn't bought a house now that their kids had grown up, and they told her they were still thinking of going back. "You've been thinking of going back ever since you got here," she told them. "That's the problem, that people dream about going back for years," she said. "I know a lot of people like that."[19] As many as two out of three Dominicans and half of all Colombians desire to return to their home country (Duany 1994: 38).[20] But only a minority will actually end up doing so; the longer they stay, the less likely they are to leave.

Consequences of the Myth

The myth of return can directly affect people's political involvement in the United States. The desire to return to one's country, one immigrant told me, "is an obstacle . . . it's the problem of immigrants everywhere. I'm Argentine, and my parents are Portuguese. . . . I got interested and was very active in Argentine politics. I would say something to my parents, or to the Italians, or the Poles. [And they would all say:] No, no, that's a problem for the Argentinians; we're foreigners. That's the problem in general with immigrants. Even after living here, and suffering all the same problems as the native, they don't assimilate."[21] "Why don't immigrants participate?" mused a woman from Ecuador.

> Because . . . they want to stay within their small group of friends. They come to work to save money. They don't see the possibilities of uniting to protect

develops some of the political consequences of the ideology of return in her work on Dominican immigrants in Washington Heights. See also Chaney 1980a: 292, and Hernández and Torres-Saillant 1994: 8.

[18] Interview (in Spanish), January 9, 1992.

[19] Conversation (in Spanish), September 8, 1992.

[20] In a poll done in 1991 for WXTV, respondents were asked what their future plans were: 52% of Colombians said they planned to return at some point to their home countries; only 27% indicated they planned to stay in the U.S. (Bendixen and Associates 1991). Pachón and DeSipio are more skeptical about the desire for return. In their survey, only 15.9% of respondents from New York said their "most important" reason for not naturalizing was their intention to return to their country of origin (1994: 182, table 8.39). Their data as presented, however, are not broken down to show how many think the possibility of return is *one* of the reasons they might not naturalize. See also U.S. Department of Labor 1996: 56, table 5A.

[21] Interview (in Spanish), February 24, 1992.

themselves . . . They always have their bags in their hand; they never form roots. They don't buy a house. They say "I'll do this, and I'm gone" and then they live very badly here. If they go, they spend it all, and then a year or two later come back again. Now many are becoming citizens, but only after being here fifteen years or more. And they've realized the time they've lost, and all they could have done.[22]

Another Ecuadorian commented on migrants' lack of interest in politics: "I'm not sure that Ecuadorians are looking to the electoral process. It requires an investment in time . . . to become involved, and then run, or support candidates, or whatever. If people are coming here with the idea of going back home, people don't want to make that kind of investment."[23]

Because people are unsure whether or not they will actually stay, they are reluctant to make a substantial investment in public life in the United States.

The myth of return has further implications for migrants' organizational and political life. Immigration is a disruptive experience, and immigrants frequently feel isolated and disoriented on arrival to New York City. Interviewees frequently spoke of the need for *"orientación"* in this country, literally help in getting one's bearings. One Colombian organizer remarked:

A recent immigrant leaves a circle in their country, a circle of friends, of acquaintances, in which they know the doctor, the lawyer, the architect, the musician. . . . That is to say, this is how you know yourself in your country, and coming here there is a completely different circle, with not even the people from the same country—the *paisanos*—not even they belong to the same circle you belong to. So there is an individuation, a person feels alone; you find yourself in a moment of nostalgia, of loneliness, let's say, of homesickness even, of thinking that you were better off in your home country, because it was easier. . . . This first stage after arriving is very difficult.[24]

In response to this sense of dislocation, organizations form to patch over the rupture left by the immigration process.[25] Initially, organizations attempt to

22 Interview (in Spanish), July 23, 1991.

23 Interview, August 28, 1991. "You must determine what legacy, what contribution, what role you want to play . . . you have to have an understanding of what you want to do with your time in this society. Too often we are betwixt and between—*me quedo, no me quedo, me voy*. I'll stay here for a little while and then I'll leave." Interview, Puerto Rican activist in Queens, August 12, 1991.

24 Interview (in Spanish), July 16, 1991.

25 See Chapter 6. For a limited discussion of this phenomenon see Sassen-Koob 1979. Her work draws on R. Anderson and G. Anderson, "Voluntary Associations and Urbanization: A Diachronic Analysis," *American Journal of Sociology* 65 (2) (1959): 265–73, and D. Parkin, "Urban Voluntary Associations as Institutions of Adaptation," *Man* 1 (1) (1966), among others. For a

rebuild or replicate networks disrupted by the migration process, and involve groups of people from the same home town, province, or region. This is as true of sports and occupational associations as of civic, social, and cultural organizations. Much of the sense of community among Latin American immigrant populations in New York City is built around the protection—and enforcement—of various homeland identities.

If in their personal lives immigrants begin to make allowances for being in another country, they make up for it in their organizational life. Descriptions of festivals and parades in the immigrant press lavishly praise native foods and music. There is a kind of jocular nostalgia peculiar to these descriptions: "We dream of going back to start our own business in the city where we were born. We never lose our loyalty to *frijoles*, nor to *cuchuco*, nor to *aguapanela*, nor to *mazamorra*, and even less to the traditional *arepa*, and what about those *papas criollas*, and *fritangas*, and that great drink *aguardiente*. We don't lose our accent either; on the contrary, it becomes more pronounced."[26]

It's as if through these events and organizations immigrants try to prove to themselves that they still are Colombians or Ecuadorians or Dominicans. To prove this, they maintain the fiction that their way of life remains unchanged—if not in their homes, at least in their public associations with compatriots. In these social circles the food doesn't change, nor the drinks, nor the accents. All this is perhaps meant to imply that their experiences as immigrants in the United States really haven't changed them or made them any different from those who stayed behind.

The ideology of return is intensified in immigrant organizations. While they exist to provide a social and cultural retreat for Latin American migrants, their official *raison d'être* is to raise money for charitable purposes in the home countries.[27] The recently established Club Social Cultural Salitre is typical. Its directors stated that the club was formed "with the sole end to promote social and cultural activities to raise funds with the goal to give humanitarian aid to poor children, senior citizens, and hospitals that need medicine and equipment, and so be able to give care to all the citizenry of our beloved Cantón Salitre, Urbina Jado, [in the province of] Guayas, Ecuador."[28]

---

counterview see Georges 1984: 7–8. She sees ethnic associations as a sign of adaptation to the U.S., rather than a simple continuation of patterns of organization from the home country.

[26] Orlando Gallo, "Colombianos Por El Mundo," *El Sol de Colombia*, April 16–30, 1992.

[27] Portes and Rumbaut note that "early . . . concerns of the foreign born . . . seldom have to do with matters American. Instead, they tend to center on issues and problems back home. This is especially true of sojourners" (1990: 109).

[28] "Ecuatorianos forman nueva entidad," *Diario/La Prensa*, July 24, 1991.

Organizations established by immigrants from other Latin American countries do the same. The Dominican club in Corona, for example, charters a plane every year to the Dominican Republic. They play in the softball championships, and raise money to buy gifts for some of the poor barrios of Santo Domingo. They keep picture-albums in the club, to show how they give away sports equipment, clothing, wheelchairs, and crutches.[29] Articles in the Spanish-language newspapers appealed for Argentinians to send aid to help with flood victims in Argentina.[30] The International Lions Club of Woodside, whose members are all first-generation immigrants from Latin America, has sent money to several countries in the region: Guatemala, El Salvador, Colombia, and Argentina. In 1991, for example, they sent two ambulances to Latin America; one to Argentina, and one to Peru.[31] Many of the social events in the Latin American immigrant community double as fundraisers for these causes. The amounts of money raised are not negligible; the Comité Cívico Ecuatoriano, together with the Ecuadorian consulate, gathered over $450,000 for flood relief for Ecuador in 1983 and 1987.[32] On the other hand, very little money is raised for charity or any other purpose to be used in New York City.[33] The many needs of the immigrant community in New York City—job referrals, housing, medical care—are only infrequently dealt with by the immigrant organizations, or are handled informally. This imbalance reflects the official ideology of many of these organizations: problems in New York City are temporary, but those in the home country are permanent.

The Cost of Naturalization

Acquiring American citizenship clearly generates tensions among immigrants. Some Latin American migrants see naturalization as U.S. citizens as

[29] Author's fieldnotes, Club Hermanos Unidos, December 6, 1991.

[30] "Argentinos de N.Y. Piden Solaridad con Compatriotas," *Noticias del Mundo,* July 27, 1992.

[31] Interview, former president, Lions Club (in Spanish), August 13, 1991. The International Lions Club of Sunnyside, which is also a Latin American immigrant club, sent eight to ten million doses of tetracycline to Peru to help combat the cholera epidemic, wheelchairs and other supplies to Ecuador and Argentina, and financial aid to Colombia, Mexico, and Puerto Rico to help with damage from natural disasters. "Personaje de la Quincena" and "'Contigo Peru' Es La Voz," *Imagen del Sur,* April 10, 1991.

[32] José Ramón Alvarez, "El Comité Cívico y las Telemaratones,"*Aquí Ecuador,* May, 1992.

[33] One of the very few instances I ran across was a marathon organized by the Woodside Interamerican Lions Club, to raise money for a school for deaf children, and for the Joseph Bulova School, both in Queens. More recently, in 1995 the Centro Cívico Colombiano held a meeting to protest the sale of Elmhurst Hospital. Other, more exceptional cases, such as the aid given following the Avianca crash in January, 1991, are discussed in Chapter 7.

a betrayal of country.[34] The language of betrayal pervades the Latin American immigrant discourse: "*vendepatrias*"—you've sold out your country, traitor. Georges, for example, quotes a Dominican club president who told her, "Dominicans still have a feeling of guilt, of fear in saying that they are U.S. citizens. Because we accuse them—I did too up until a couple of years ago—of being traitors" (1984: 35). A woman told me about a friend of hers who had become a citizen: "I know she felt very strongly the day she became an American citizen. She cried, she felt very strongly about it. Someone thought she had become so emotional because she had become an American citizen. No. It's because she felt she had betrayed her country."[35] Taken at face value, the language of betrayal may seem disproportionately fierce. However, while an immigrants' naturalization is unlikely to pose any significant harm to the home country, it is threatening to other immigrants because any immigrant's naturalization exposes the weaknesses of the myth of return. So the betrayal is really of the immigrant community, and is felt most strongly among them. The language of betrayal used by peers serves then to enforce the ideology of return.

Language enforces the myth in other ways. The oath required during the naturalization ceremony renouncing old allegiances and pledging allegiance to the United States is embroidered and circulated among immigrants as a kind of "urban legend" of desecration. At some point in the process of naturalizing, so the story goes, the judge will ask you to step or spit on your homeland's flag. This story appears in odd places: Joan Didion describes a conversation she had with a Mexican orchid grower around 1975 in which he told her that "he had never become a United States citizen because he had an image in his mind which he knew to be false but could not shake: the image was that of standing before a judge and stamping on the flag of Mexico" (1979: 221). The story appears again in Alvarez's interview with a Mexican immigrant who had become a citizen: "People talk about how difficult the process is, that one must step on the flag, but this is all false" (1987: 330; see also Moore 1984: 36). The story is repeated among immigrants in the Queens in the 1990s. A Colombian activist told it to explain why U.S. citizenship is a stigma among Colombians: "It started as an anecdote . . . that if you became an American citizen you had to renounce your country, and step on the Colombian flag. Of course no one has actually seen this. 'Look here's your country's flag [*la bandera de tu país*], stand on it and spit, or something!' . . . In the end, there are still people who be-

[34] In the pre-1995 version of the Ecuadorian constitution, treason and voluntary acquisition of another citizenship were associated—both were just cause for removal of citizenship. *Constitución Política del Ecuador*, Sección I, Artículo 10, cited in Hinojosa 1992.

[35] Interview, Colombian activist, August 29, 1991.

lieve that if you've become an American citizen, it's because at some time you stood on the flag."[36]

This story circulates widely among migrants. It's not necessary that the story be true, or even thought to be true among those who tell it. It serves to illuminate certain feelings about citizenship and the loss of homeland. The scenario juxtaposes the secular authority of the foreign state with the nationalist, almost religious symbolism of the home country's flag. The immigrant is asked to choose between desecrating the symbol and becoming an American, or staying an immigrant in a kind of martyrdom of marginality. The manner in which the story is told makes clear, of course, what the choice should be.[37]

The ultimate enforcer of the ideology of return lies in immigrants' fear that traveling back to their home country with an American passport means being treated as a foreigner or worse. In a meeting of Ecuadorian immigrants with a visiting legislator from Ecuador, a woman said that she had every intention and had *always* had every intention of going back to Ecuador. She owned a house and property in Ecuador, "always with the idea of going back," but she had become an American citizen. She resented the fact that when she returned her luggage was searched at the airport (to check for what she was bringing back from the United States), and that she had to get a visa if she was going to stay for more than thirty days. Another participant at the meeting said, "I resent that my country [*mi tierra*] treats me as a foreigner. I resent having to get visas for my children to travel to Ecuador."[38] Another Ecuadorian woman told me: "I have seen very sad cases of people who have changed nationalities and have come back to visit relatives and been very badly treated. People treat them very badly, saying, 'They are no longer one of ours.'"[39] This feeling is distilled in a letter sent by the Federacion de Entidades Ecuatorianas en el Exterior to the President of Ecuador in 1991, asking that those who had adopted another nationality not be treated as foreigners or worse, as if they had no country (*apátridas*) when they returned to Ecuador: "This [petition] has come about given that in certain sectors of the bureaucracy there are misunderstandings which lead

[36] Interview (in Spanish), August 14, 1991.

[37] In my own family we were told stories taking place in some ambiguous medieval past in which a Catholic believer would be captured by the infidels, and asked to step or spit on a cross. The believer would refuse, of course, and be martyred.

[38] Author's fieldnotes, August 23, 1991. This resentment is expressed by other nationalities as well. Mexicans in the U.S. have complained for years about the extortion, confiscation of property, and outright robbery they confront when they return to Mexico. See Patrick McDonnell, "Mexico Vows to Curb Abuses against Returning Citizens," *Los Angeles Times*, December 1, 1995, p. B3.

[39] Interview (in Spanish), April 17, 1991.

to abuse, discrimination, and their treatment like foreigners of their own brothers—who drown in their anxiousness to return to the country, to visit their relatives, and take with them donations or money to reinvest, won after much effort and sacrifice."[40]

The fear of being treated as a "foreigner in their own country" crops up repeatedly in conversations with immigrants, particularly those from countries who would automatically lose their nationality if they take on the nationality of another country. The loss of their original nationality, for many immigrants, substantially raises the cost of becoming a U.S. citizen. Even if they do not return, for many the closing of the *option* to return is unbearable.

The United States, like many other nations, demands an exclusivity of attachment. The oath immigrants take as they go through the naturalization ceremony asks that they "renounce and abjure absolutely and entirely all allegiance and fidelity to any foreign prince, potentate, state and sovereignty of whom or which the petitioner was before a subject or citizen." This oath is designed to take priority over all other pledges, and to place loyalty to the United States above all other loyalties (Levinson 1988: 93). This requirement has been demanded by immigrants' home countries in Latin America as well. The international norm has been that as soon as citizens abroad naturalize in another country, they automatically lose all claims to nationality in their countries of origin. Nations are, in Levinson's terms, "'greedy,' always seeking ways of making themselves the true center of attention" (ibid.: 114). They don't take divided loyalties lightly.

Immigrants, for their part, are loath to make a decision that requires them to break entirely with their home countries. There's a lot of hesitation in making the decision to become a citizen. Many more begin the process of naturalization than complete it. Being uncertain about their decision to become citizens, people proceed with constant second thoughts.[41] To become a U.S. citizen means to break with the myth of return, and with the ideological structure of immigrant organizational life. Even if immigrants decide to stay, pressures within the community keep them from advertising their identity as "American." For these reasons, many put off the decision to become citizens of the United States. The change of identity, the ultimate negation of the hope for eventual return, is too threatening to those who live inside the myth.

[40] Letter, September 11, 1991, quoted in Hinojosa 1992.

[41] Pachón and DeSipio 1994: 106–110. Some argue that the figures for uncompleted naturalization applications shows that there is something wrong with the procedure itself (ibid.; DeSipio and Pachón 1992). It is undoubtedly true that the procedure could be improved. But I would argue that failure to complete the process is also a sign of indecision.

III

LIMINAL POLITICS

6

In-between Identities: Race and Ethnicity in the American Context

Soon after arrival in the United States, immigrants find they are asked to choose between competing political spheres—one centered on their immediate surroundings, the other on their countries of origin. Each of these spheres demands fealty. Immigrants often refuse both. Instead, they seek alternatives, routes of escape, to alleviate or avoid these pressures. Many try to find this escape in the strategic manipulation of their own identities. Immigrants' adoption of a common identity with other immigrants gives them a sphere of their own in which to act, at least somewhat insulated from the political spheres that seek to claim them. But the identities immigrants adopt are not themselves unconstrained. In this chapter I describe how these, too, are structured by the two political spheres.

Is There a Common Latino Identity?

On arrival in this country Latin American immigrants are grouped together by the state—along with Mexican Americans and Puerto Ricans, some of whom have been here for generations—as "Hispanics" and labeled "minorities." This group identification is reflected in part in the language used by the immigrants themselves. People talk about *la comunidad latina* (the Latino community), or about being *hispano* or *Latinoamericano.* But it isn't clear what communalities really exist among Latinos beyond this language. Do Hispanic immigrants have an ethnic identity apart from that assigned to them by the state?

Many argue that they do not. Most of the work done on Latino or Hispanic identity in the United States assumes that self-identification with some pan-Hispanic label is instrumental, and does not credit these labels with evoking or describing any kind of substantial "content." Latinos accept the identity assigned by the state, expecting to reap the rewards, say, of affirmative action, political power, or some other material or nonmaterial benefit. The study of Latino identity reflects larger trends in the study of ethnicity. Most identities are now assumed to be instrumental in nature—a means to attain certain ends. Instrumental views of identity emerged in reaction to the earlier proposition that ethnicity was essentially "primordial," an underlying and fundamental set of characteristics that form a basis of collective sentiment and action (Shils 1957; Geertz, 1963; Isaacs 1975). As Geertz put it in his influential article on the role of ethnicity in new states, a primordial attachment is an "assumed given," a congruity of blood, speech, or custom which seem to have a coercive power in themselves. People are bound together, he believes, "*ipso facto*; as the result not merely of personal affection, practical necessity, common interest, or incurred moral obligation, but at least in great part by virtue of some unaccountable absolute import attributed to the very tie [of ethnicity] itself" (1963: 109).

This perspective has been repeatedly criticized for being overly deterministic and static, and for overemphasizing the involuntary and emotional elements of ethnic identity (McKay 1982: 396–98; Bonanich 1980: 9–12). The instrumentalist paradigm replacing the primordialist view of ethnicity emphasizes instead "change, contextuality, and competition among ethnic populations for scarce resources" (McKay 1982: 399; also Nagel and Olzak 1982: 127). The "primordial" content of ethnicity—language, religion, kin structures—is jettisoned or downplayed, while ethnic boundaries—those areas of contact and conflict between ethnic groups are highlighted (Horowitz 1977; Hechter 1971; Barth 1969).

The hegemony of instrumentalist theories of ethnic identity is now well established. These theories argue that ethnicity, formed in contact and conflict with other groups, is expressed in the maintenance and differentiation of borders among ethnicities (Barth 1969). There are two main strands to this work which I will discuss here: first, *state-sponsored* ethnicity, whose proponents contend that the parameters of ethnic identity are essentially constructed and defined by the state (Olzak 1983; Nagel and Olzak 1982; Enloe 1981); and second, a *situational* view of ethnic identity, centered on the strategic choices individuals make to take advantage of identifying themselves one way rather than another. While both emphasize the definition of group boundaries, the former focuses on their external imposition, and the second on their internal manipulation (Patterson 1975; Okamura 1981). These differing views can be, and often are, reconciled: situational choices

of ethnic identity are said to take place within the constraints imposed by the state (Vincent 1974; Yancey, Eriksen, and Juliani 1976).

In this chapter I argue that these instrumentalist theories of ethnic identity are incomplete. Current theories emphasize people's decisions in their present context, but people do not make decisions solely in the context of their immediate constraints. They also take into account past constraints, which may no longer even hold or apply in their present situation. The effects of these constraints continue long after people leave the original contexts. Once prior instrumental ethnic identities are internalized, they continue to shape choices, and thus politics. In the United States, ethnic identities—and certainly minority identities—*are* political identities. Politics becomes one of the principal arenas for the playing out of these identities.

In the first part of this chapter, I review present instrumentalist views of ethnic identity and their application to broader questions of Hispanic identity. Although some argue that a Hispanic identity does not exist at all, instrumentalists argue—I think convincingly—that state-offered incentives and the self-interested mobilization of various Latin American origin groups have encouraged, at the very least, the formation of a kind of Latino identity constructed around the ethnic label. In the second half of the chapter I maintain, however, that the state's decisions must be considered together with immigrants' own internalized constraints, which may reinforce or deflect the status assigned to them upon arrival in the United States. Drawing on Latin American immigrants' own views on their collective identity and on race, I assert that both are continuations of prior identity choices made in their countries of origin. In conclusion, I note that these prior instrumentalist choices, once made, cannot be so easily discarded; they have a certain inertia to them, which weighs on the choices that follow. Hispanic ethnicity is partly a construction of the state, but is also the continuity of identities from immigrants' home countries. It is, for Latin American immigrants, the unintended consequence of combining elements of both.

State-sponsored Identity

As I noted above, the instrumentalist paradigm has played out in two ways. In the first, the state plays a primary role in structuring the context of interaction among ethnic groups. The state can encourage the emergence or even the creation of ethnic groups.[1] But while state intervention can en-

[1] The literature on this subject has become extensive, with studies ranging from the role of British colonial administrators in constructing race categories in Malaya (Hirschman 1986), to the creation of ethnic-bloc parties in Guyana in the 1960s (Nagel 1986: 106–107), to mobilization of Native Americans in the United States along pan-Indian lines (Jarvenpa 1985; Nagel 1982).

courage people to identify and mobilize as an ethnic group, it can't actually make them do so. What the state does is set the parameters for ethnic mobilization. In her discussion of pan-Indian movements, Nagel writes that governments "specify the rules of access and allocation. The impetus from below determines *if* mobilization will occur. The impetus from above determines the *shape* the mobilization will take" (1982: 39). If ethnic mobilization occurs, the form it takes will not be an actual creation of the state, but a tactical reaction taking advantage of the policies set by the state.

It is still possible, however, for the state to establish conditions for artificial ethnic categories that are not representative of any "real" ethnic identity. The debate over the term "Hispanic" is a case in point. Widely used only since the 1970s, "Hispanic ethnicity" has been criticized as being an invention created for the purposes of outside actors.[2] The word "Hispanic" itself is a creation of the U.S. Census Bureau. In an interview with the *New York Times,* Jorge del Pinal, the chief of ethnic and Hispanic studies at the bureau, described discussions there in the 1970s about how best to describe this diverse group, which until then had been called "Spanish-speaking" or "Spanish-surnamed."[3] "Not all the people we considered Hispanic spoke Spanish," he said. "Not everyone had a Spanish surname." As a result, the final category came to be designated "Spanish/Hispanic Origin." Del Pinal noted that "it was really just a way to come up with a term to fit this amorphous group. . . . It really came right out of the dictionary."[4]

The perceived failure of "Hispanics" to unite in common action lies, some say, in the fact that those targeted by the term have nothing more in common than their designation as a group by an agency of the U.S. government. Gimenez, for example, contends that "the inclusion in the census of a self-identification question that forces . . . [national origin groups] to identify themselves as 'persons of Hispanic/Spanish origin' has resulted in the political and statistical construction of a new minority 'group,' a group

[2] Calderón notes that "[t]he categorizing of Chicano, Puerto Rican, Cuban, and other Latin American groups under the term 'Hispanic' seems to have arisen from external forces, including the use of the term by the media, the U.S. Census Bureau, and other government agencies, and politicians on the federal level, rather than from any cohesion of the groups themselves" (1992: 39; also 42–43).

[3] The 1970 census was the first in which the federal government tried to separate Hispanics from other ethnic groups. At that time, the census used several different definitions for the "Spanish heritage population." "In the southwestern states, those individuals who were Spanish-surnamed or who spoke Spanish were considered Hispanic. Puerto Rican birth or parentage was the criterion in the three mid-Atlantic states, while only Spanish language fluency was used in the remaining states" (Marín and VanOss Marín 1991: 20). "Hispanic" was first standardized for use in the 1980 census (U.S. Bureau of the Census 1979).

[4] David Gonzalez, "What's the Problem with 'Hispanic'? Just Ask a 'Latino,'" *New York Times,* November 5, 1992.

whose origins can be traced to statistical manipulation and the pursuit of immediate political advantage rather than to historical foundations" (1992: 10). When looking for a Hispanic identity, one finds there is (as Gertrude Stein supposedly once said about Oakland) "no there there." Hispanics, the argument goes, share neither a common culture nor a common history. The government's heavy-handed stereotyping denies different historical experiences among populations. For example, some have a common history of oppression and exploitation, and others have never been oppressed or exploited (ibid.: 8, 10; Hayes-Bautista 1980).[5] How then could there possibly be a sense of ethnicity based on this artificial identity?

Situational Identities

Instrumentalist views of ethnicity imply that if the state rewards certain kinds of ethnic identifications and associations, individuals will likely modify their ethnic identification to meet those expectations, if they can. Ethnicity in this view is, as Olzak argues, "at least partially chosen by individuals, based on a calculus of advantages and disadvantages . . . that a given ethnic boundary implies" (Olzak 1983: 362; see also Patterson 1975: 307, 311, and Bell 1975). This view assumes that individuals have a variety of group allegiances, and that they choose among them to maximize their economic and social status within the larger economic and political context that structures their choices (Patterson 1975: 305). Ethnicity in this view is volitional and strategic within the structural constraints imposed by the state (Nagel 1986: 95).

For an ethnic identity to exist, therefore, members in a group need not share any particular cultural history but, more important, must recognize each other and be recognized by others as an ethnic group (Vincent 1974: 376; Patterson 1975: 306). Within the parameters set by the state, ethnic boundaries remain flexible, fluid, and permeable (Nagel 1986: 95). Thus the affirmation of an ethnic identity shifts depending on the immediate social situation, each social situation making the display of some identities and cultural elements more relevant than others. Ethnic mobilization is, according to a number of theorists, "arbitrarily created and sustained for [its] pragmatic utility" (Vincent 1974: 377).

Some Latino theorists have begun to make a distinction between pan-Hispanic unity for the purposes of collective action on the one hand, and

[5] Hayes-Bautista argues, for example, that state labels should reflect what he thinks are the *real* commonalities of experience: discrimination based on Indian characteristics, and not Spanish descent. "The continued use of 'Hispanic' or 'Spanish origin' denies the very basis upon which discrimination has been based, and confuses the basis for civil rights and affirmative action efforts" (1980: 335).

the development of a historically distinct and separate ethnic identity on the other—claiming that it is possible to have one without the other (Padilla 1985; Calderón 1992: 43). In this case, even if there is no "true" pan-Hispanic identity, with communalities of cultural traits and historical experience, national coalitions of Latino leaders and activists could use the term "Hispanic" to symbolize communalities in issues and collective action. Herman Badillo, who was a congressman from New York City at the time, said that the move to adopt "Hispanic" was encouraged by leaders of various Latino groups, "who stood to gain more political representation and government services as a result of the designation."[6] In other words, Hispanic identification has been used to advance interests of individual national origin groups under the cover of an ethnic umbrella.

New York City: Puerto Ricans and Other Latinos

The instrumental use of Hispanic ethnic identification is readily apparent in the case of Latinos in New York City. Puerto Ricans were the first Latino group to enter city politics in any numbers and have dominated Hispanic politics since. They began building up political power through government-funded nonprofit organizations founded in the 1960s and then challenging Democratic incumbents in districts with heavily Puerto Rican populations.[7] Having built alternative electoral organizations and captured various political positions, Puerto Ricans have kept them ever since. Currently, Puerto Ricans hold two congressional seats and one borough presidency in the city.[8] Until very recently, Puerto Ricans were the only Hispanics elected to major positions at the city, state, and national levels from the New York City area.

Through the 1980s, Puerto Rican politics *were* Latino politics. All the while, Puerto Rican leaders benefited from the Hispanic label—pointing to the growing numbers of Latinos in the city to argue for increased benefits to the community while themselves occupying almost all the elected and appointed positions set aside for Hispanics. Today, however, the shifting de-

[6] Gonzalez, "Ask a 'Latino.'"

[7] Herman Badillo, for example, used the experience and connections gained in the nonprofit service organization ASPIRA to form his own political club in the Bronx as an alternative to the Democratic machine, and was elected Bronx borough president in 1966, and the first Puerto Rican to Congress in 1970 (Fuentes 1992: 28–29). Similarly, Ramon Velez, one-time City Council member and president of the Puerto Rican Day parade, has used antipoverty programs to gain control of jobs and funds which allow him to control his own patronage machinery and place candidates for office. David Gonzalez and Martin Gottlieb, "Power Built on Poverty: One Man's Odyssey," *New York Times,* May 14, 1993.

[8] Jose Serrano holds a congressional seat in the Bronx, and Nydia Velasquez one that lies primarily in Brooklyn. Fernando Ferrer, a former City Council member, is now Bronx borough president.

mographics of the Latino population have created something of a dilemma for Puerto Rican leaders. Puerto Ricans now constitute less than 50 percent of the Hispanic population in the city (though they are still the single largest Hispanic group). Puerto Rican political success, combined with the rapid growth of other Latin American groups, has led to considerable tensions among the various Latino groups.[9] There are accusations that Puerto Ricans have jealously guarded their position as gatekeepers to Hispanic politics in the city (Fuentes 1992: 32). The sense of injustice this belief provokes is only aggravated by the feeling that Puerto Ricans do not fully represent the views of other Latinos. Many of these Latinos, a good portion of whom cannot vote because they are not citizens, feel that Puerto Ricans, who are automatically citizens upon arrival, do not fully sympathize with the barrier that lack of citizenship poses to full political participation, and are not sensitive to the differences among the newer immigrants.[10] Colombian activists conducting a voter registration drive among recent immigrants in Queens, for example, had to throw out boxes of registration materials borrowed from a Puerto Rican organization, all of which were emblazoned with the Puerto Rican flag.[11] For their part, Puerto Rican leaders, echoing other New York politicians, say that they will deal with other Latinos as full partners only when they begin to vote in sizable numbers.[12]

This situation has begun to change as the wave of immigrants who arrived in the city in the 1960s and '70s begin to organize, naturalize as American citizens, and enter the political process. First Dominicans, then other groups, have begun to replicate or simply take over the organizations and networks built by the Puerto Ricans on their way to political representation and power (Fuentes 1992: 28). In 1991 Guillermo Linares, a Dominican, was elected to the New York City Council. For the first time, a Latino from another national group could claim to represent Hispanics in the city, and this has weakened Puerto Rican assertions (though not their desire) to be speaking for Latinos as a whole (Fuentes 1992: 31). To counter this shift,

[9] The relationship between Puerto Ricans and Dominicans is particularly edgy. Puerto Ricans call Dominicans *come platanos* ("banana-eaters," meaning uncultured hicks), and the Dominicans say Puerto Ricans have no country to call their own (*no tienen bandera*). Fuentes notes that Puerto Rican leaders have done little or nothing to defuse the tension, because they fear the possible competition from the nascent Dominican and other Latino leadership (1992: 32).

[10] One Ecuadorian activist noted that "we have two kinds of Hispanic communities everywhere, especially in the Northeast. One is the Puerto Rican community, and the other is the newer Latin American community. Our political views as well as our interests . . . as well as our situations are very different. . . . But of course Puerto Ricans are U.S. citizens. From the moment they arrive, they are U.S. citizens. So their political agenda is very different." Interview, April 17, 1991.

[11] Author's fieldnotes, July 13, 1991.

[12] Meeting of the Puerto Rican political leadership, Puerto Rican Legal Defense and Education Fund, January 23, 1992.

the Puerto Rican leadership has made emphatic use of the label "Puerto Rican/Latino" at events in which they present themselves as the spokespersons for Latinos in the city. This label sends the clear message, both to other Latinos and to non-Hispanic politicians around the city, that Puerto Ricans are still the key players in Latino politics. It succeeds in emphasizing communality and difference, precedence and subordination, all at the same time. Other Latinos often have the impression that Puerto Ricans are using the term "Latino" cynically, to leverage more power and inflate their numbers without being willing to share power. For the past several years, for example, there has been a "*Somos Uno*" ("We're All One") conference held in New York to set a statewide Latino political agenda. Every year there are complaints from non–Puerto Ricans. One Colombian complained to me that "everything there was about Puerto Ricans and Puerto Rican problems. Why do they call it *Somos Uno* if they are not going to include everyone?"[13] From the Puerto Rican point of view, however, this strategy makes perfect sense. Puerto Ricans may account for under 50 percent of the city's Latino population, but they make up a large majority of Hispanic voters—about 70 percent of those Latinos who voted in the last two mayoral elections were Puerto Rican. So although Puerto Rican and other leaders rhetorically emphasize the size of the Hispanic population as a whole, their focus tends to be on the Puerto Rican voter.

The rivalry and maneuvering between Puerto Ricans and other Latinos illustrates the way ethnic groups can manipulate identities in the political sphere to further their various interests as national groups within a government-sanctioned pan-Hispanic identity. This situation seems to confirm the usefulness of the instrumentalist approach to ethnic identification. It is also clear from this example, however, that choices about ethnic identification are not structured solely in the context of the United States. The Puerto Rican/Latino rivalry, for instance, reveals fault-lines in Hispanic identity along national-origin lines. Loyalties to national origins would seem to be superfluous in a context that values and rewards pan–Latin American identity; that they persist indicates some of the limitations of a narrow instrumentalist approach to minority identity in the United States. So what is the alternative?

Reinterpreting History

The persistence of nationalism points to other factors at work in constraining people's options for self-identification, and to the fact that these options

[13] Interview, August 22, 1991; author's fieldnotes, January 8, 1992.

are not only externally imposed but in some ways internal to the workings of various ethnic groups. To talk about these internalized constraints is to attempt to get at the *content* of ethnic identity (e.g. religion, race, culture, and so forth). Theorists have generally given up on the idea of describing the content of ethnicities: to describe content thoroughly requires keeping ethnicity in stasis; to describe the process of this content is to descend into definitional ambiguities or metaphors. Since Barth (1969), social scientists have generally limited themselves to talking about ethnic boundaries, while only rarely referring to what the boundaries enclose. Yet instrumental interpretations of ethnic identity implicitly depend on assumptions of content—that boundaries enclose *something*, and that it matters what they enclose. For most immigrants, ethnicity is not simply something one picks up and then drops at will. There must be more to instrumental ethnicity than meets the eye. To examine it more closely, however, I will look not at nationalism, but at its counterpart, pan-Americanism.

De la Garza et al., in their survey of three Latino groups in the United States, asked respondents to state their preferred ethnic identification. In all three groups—Mexican, Puerto Rican, and Cuban—large majorities preferred to be identified in terms evoking their national origin. Pan-ethnic labels, however, were the next most preferred set of identifiers. Over 10 percent of all three first-generation groups indicated they identified primarily pan-ethnically, as did about 20 percent of the native-born in the three groups. So for a small minority of respondents, labels such as "Latino" or "Hispanic" are the *primary* means of self-identification (de la Garza et al. 1992: 40). Left unexplored in the presentation of the data, however, is whether these labels play a secondary, though important, role in the self-identification of the other first- and subsequent-generation respondents. Do people identify in pan-ethnic terms *in addition to* self-identifying in national terms? It isn't clear. (Jones-Correa and Leal 1996 explore these questions further.)

However, in interviews with first-generation Latin American immigrants in New York, a strain of pan-American thought is constant. The theme of continental unity has never been completely absent in Latin American political or popular thought and rhetoric. Simón Bolívar, who fought in the South American wars of independence, is still seen as an inspiration for Latin American unity. People still refer to *el sueño de Bolívar*—Bolívar's dream—of a united Latin America.[14] This historical legacy is transferred to

[14] In 1815 Bolívar expressed the hope that the "universal link of love should bind together the children of Columbus' hemisphere" (Padilla 1990: 18). In 1818 he wrote a message to the Argentine people, urging that they join "into a single society, so that our motto may be Unity in South America." He wrote Juan Martín de Pueyrredon, an Argentine leader, to say that the "Americans should have only a single *patria* . . . for our part we shall hasten . . . to initiate the

the American context by Latino immigrants, and becomes a way of making sense of, a way of legitimizing, their "Hispanic" identity. Being Latino, as a Colombian activist defined it, is "originating, coming, from the same part of the world, of having roots there. Having a language in common, a pre-Columbian history. We've grown up saying to ourselves that we are *paises hermanos* [brother countries]. We have the *historia patria* [the history of our country], Simón Bolívar's struggle, the patriotic hymns, which all talk to us about the unity of these countries. Of a common brotherhood."[15]

But this pan–Latin American identity does not necessarily trump other identity choices, and nationalism continues unabated as well. A more cynical observer noted: "Language unites us. Culture brings us together. But our own nationalisms are prevalent, so here is where we clash. I think it is the old *sueño de Bolívar,* one Latin America, one country. That is the way I think it would have worked best. . . . There's that old saying 'divide to govern,' it's much easier. That's how they've governed us. And they've instilled in us this patriotism, this false pride for our own countries when really we're all one America. We should be living as one country."[16] *El sueño de Bolívar,* Simón Bolívar's dream of Latin America united, is invoked frequently by Latin American immigrants when the conversation turns to Hispanic unity in the United States. Some see the United States as an experiment, a place where the dream might become real. For others, the dream will remain just that, a dream.[17] As a Catholic priest noted wryly, "the dream of Simón Bolívar—they say he'll dream forever."[18]

A united Latin America is clearly *not* real, nor is it thought to be by those who refer to it, yet Bolívar's dream has been continually (though selectively) invoked for over a hundred and fifty years to express solidarity in the face of outsiders. First as a revolutionary sentiment, then as an anti-imperialist slogan, the idea of an indivisible Latin America has been useful in Latin Americans' dealing with foreigners. The idea is a kind of "invented tradition," as Eric Hobsbawm calls it, but nonetheless powerful for that. It is, in fact, an instrumental identity. There are two things I want to underline here: first, that pan-Americanism, like its counterpart nationalism, has reverberations among Latinos even in the United States, far removed from its origi-

---

American pact, which by forming a single body of our republics, will reveal America to the world in an aspect of majesty and greatness unequaled among older nations. . . . United in this way, America . . . will be able to call herself the queen of nations and the mother of republics" (ibid.).

[15] Interview (in Spanish), November 4, 1991.

[16] Interview, editor, *Noticiero Argentino-Uruguayo,* January 9, 1992.

[17] Interview, August 14, 1992.

[18] Interview, Father John Brogan, Queens Hispanic Ministry, February 26, 1992.

nal context. The second is that while there is a real continuity of Latin American historical traditions in the United States, it is also the case that nominal continuity can turn into something very different in the new context (Hobsbawm 1985: 5). It is ironic, for instance, that in the United States the anti-imperial tradition of *el sueño de Bolívar* is invoked to reinforce a state-defined Hispanic identity. But this reversal should not come as a surprise. As Hobsbawm notes, invented traditions are often "responses to novel situations which take the form of references to old situations" (ibid.: 2).

Latinos and Race

It seems clear that to get at the content of ethnicity for Latin American immigrants in the United States we must talk about continuities of identity from their countries of origin. But we cannot assume that these continuities will always be subsumed as neatly as *el sueño de Bolívar* is within Hispanic ethnicity. Race, for instance, plays a complicated and contradictory role in the formation of Latino identity in the United States. For Hispanics, to be defined as a minority in the United States is to be placed in a position analogous to that of African Americans. The state sees Hispanics as parallel to (and measures them against) American blacks. However, while African Americans see themselves and are seen by the state as a racial group, Latinos do not see themselves as a racial group per se. Nonetheless, the state does its best to fit them into its own racial categories.

In the United States, few choices of identity are more constrained than that of race. There is little room for ambiguity; attempts to escape rigid racial demarcations are simply categorized as another racial identity. In 1980 the Census Bureau, for instance, recoded all ambiguous Hispanic responses to the race question on its forms as "Spanish race"; in 1990 this was changed to "other race." People are expected to identify by race, and there is no place for those who wish to do otherwise. It is important to note, however, that once forced to choose among racial options, most Latin Americans prefer being labeled "white" rather than "black." In the 1990 Public Use Microdata Sample for Queens, for example, 47.9 percent of first-generation Latin American immigrants indicated that they regarded themselves as white, and 6.1 percent as black.[19] Denton and Massey report similar findings from the

[19] Data from the 5% 1990 Public Use Microdata Sample (PUMS), Census Bureau. In Table 15, much higher percentages of Dominicans and Cubans in Queens identify themselves as black. This difference might have something to do with the passing of ten years' time, with the particularities of New York City, or with some other sampling difference. Additional survey work is needed to know for certain.

1980 census for Caribbean Hispanics in general: about 58 percent of Caribbean Hispanics called themselves white, and only about 3 percent black (1989: 798). De la Garza et al.'s recent survey of Mexicans, Puerto Ricans, and Cubans from around the country found that very few first-generation immigrants, even those from countries with a substantial African heritage, such as Puerto Rico and Cuba, self-identified as black. Sixty-three percent of first-generation Puerto Ricans identified as white, as did 94 percent of foreign-born Cubans (1992: 23).

It makes sense instrumentally that, confronted with a rigid color line defined by the state, on one side of which lies the likelihood of discrimination and prejudice, Latin American immigrants choose to avoid self-identifying as black. There is probably little *objective* difference between some of those Hispanics identifying as "black" and those who were listed as white or "Spanish race" by the Census Bureau. The difference is not in skin color, but in the choice of identity. On the other hand it would be a mistake to think this choice has no roots in prior conceptualizations of race in immigrants' home countries. Race difference in Caribbean Latin America, say, does not have the rigidity of the race line in the United States—where one is either entirely white (or presumed to be) or else one is black—but there is a definite positive value to whiteness, and considerable disparagement to being black.

Denton and Massey note that "although racial prejudice may be denied, parents frequently urge their children to *adelantar la raza* (literally to 'advance the race' or marry whiter), make negative comments about Negroid hair ([*pelo malo*] 'bad hair') and lips . . . and discourage their sons and daughters from marrying blacks . . . to avoid 'spoiling the race' (1989: 792). Race prejudice in Latin America may be more subtle than in the United States, but it is no less pervasive or pernicious in its effects, leading to the concentration of power and prestige in the hands of the lighter-skinned. Latin Americans are well aware of this coincidence of color and social status. Denton and Massey point out that "the proportion of blacks has declined in successive Puerto Rican and Cuban censuses, reflecting social pressure[s] to identify as white whenever possible" (ibid.). It is not just that Latin American immigrants arrive in this country and are confronted with racism; it already exists in Latin America. It makes just as much sense to act instrumentally and distance themselves from "being black" in their home countries as it does in the United States. Latin Americans are predisposed, then, even before coming to the United States, to see race as a scale on which one shifts "upward" to become whiter, if one can.

In Latin America, however, the value of whiteness and the aspersions cast on blackness are often stated not solely in terms of race, but in terms of status. To put it another way, racial and status terms are bound together in the

Table 15. Self-identified race, first-generation immigrants, Queens, 1990

Country of origin	% white	% black	% other race
Colombia	54.4	1.2	43.6
Dominican Republic	31.9	17.1	49.9
Ecuador	42.9	1.0	55.5
Peru	44.2	1.8	53.0
Cuba	74.9	7.3	18.4
El Salvador	41.6	1.7	56.2
Mexico	39.4	4.1	54.2

Source: 1990 Census, Public Use Microdata Sample

language of race. It is clear, in this language, that being white is better than being black. But there are many different ways to present blackness and whiteness. A dark-skinned person in the Dominican Republic for instance, is a *prieto*, or in Cuba, a *mulato*. As social status rises, *trigueño* is substituted for *mulato*; to refer to someone of lower social class, *mulato* is replaced by *moreno*, which in many contexts has a pejorative connotation (Denton and Massey 1989: 792). What is significant is that Dominicans and other Latin Americans in New York City, when speaking in Spanish, consistently refer to American blacks as *morenos*, and reserve *prieto* and other terms to talk about mixed-race or black Hispanics. "There are blacks in Latin America," an Ecuadorian woman told me, "but *morenos* here are bad (*malucos*) and they have low habits (*habitos maniosos*)."[20]

But for many Latino immigrants, communalities of ethnic culture can trump race. For this reason, at least some Latin American immigrants reject the state's black/white racial dichotomy altogether. Asked to self-identify racially, more than a third of Puerto Ricans nationally and more than half of first-generation Mexicans give answers other than black or white (de la Garza et al. 1992: 23). First-generation immigrants in Queens give similar responses (see Table 15). Most respondents from every country but Cuba and Colombia preferred to self-identify as "other race" rather than black or white. Colombians narrowly preferred self-identifying as white. The rejection of strict racial categories can also be seen in Hispanic residential patterns. In New York City, Denton and Massey found that regardless of how they identify racially, Caribbean Latinos segregate themselves from American blacks and to a lesser extent are themselves segregated from white Americans. On the one hand, Latinos have no desire to reside with black Americans, but have no problem residing with racially mixed Hispan-

[20] Author's fieldnotes, August 27, 1991.

ics. American whites, on the other hand, don't mind sharing their neighborhoods with white Latinos, but don't care for mixed-race and black Hispanics. Hispanic immigrants' decisions to be in a neighborhood with other Latinos, regardless of their race, is *not* an instrumental choice given the racial code prevailing in the United States. White Hispanics are particularly disadvantaged by sharing residential space with black and mixed-race Hispanics—they are exposed to more white American prejudice than they might otherwise face. This is all to say that among Latin American immigrants, racial differences are sometimes eclipsed by ethnic commonalities.

The state, using its experience with African Americans as a template, has tried to create similar racial categories for other "minority groups." Latinos entering the United States see these attempts at racial classification for the most part as an opportunity to continue the practice initiated in their home countries of exchanging black identifiers for other labels. However, they do not fully buy into the racial classifications; while the categories bolster their own racial prejudices, immigrants draw cultural distinctions between American blacks and black Latinos. For many immigrants the value of the company of their ethnic compatriots more than outweighs the prejudice they may suffer for choosing to live in mixed-race neighborhoods. The tendency of many Latin American immigrants to blur racial lines in identifying themselves renders the state's attempts at a rigid classificatory system problematic at best.

If ethnic identity were simply a matter of choosing a means to an end, then a simple instrumental model would be sufficient. But even recognizing the constraints placed on ethnic options by the state and other outside actors, such a model does not explain enough. Ethnic choices are made not only on the basis of the immediate context, but also on the basis of previous contexts which may appear at first glance to be no longer relevant. This is particularly the case with immigrants. Latin American immigrants' ethnic identities are shaped not just by the choices they make in the United States, but also by the weight of identity choices made in the past. Previous constructions of identity have a kind of inertia to them; they become the raw materials for ethnic choices and ethnic politics in the United States. The continuity of previous constructions of identity explains, in part, the difficulties in forming political coalitions among Hispanics of various national origins in the United States, and the brittle quality of African-American/Latino alliances. These continuities, however, do not play out in any straightforward fashion: identities submerged in the home countries can resurface, and previous identities can take on a different significance in a new context. *El sueño de Bolívar*—the dream of a united Latin America—might yet unfold in the

United States. Hispanic identity here is something neither immigrants nor the state intended to begin with. That it takes the form it does is in many ways the sum of unintended consequences.

It is precisely because of the contingent nature of Latino identity that immigrants can retain significant autonomy and control in the expression of their identity. State-sponsored identities may be coercive, but their influence is far from complete. Historical continuities, for their part, are hardly hegemonic. In fact, as I will show in the next chapters, immigrants strategically manipulate the disjunctures among these competing identities to maximize their own autonomy. In spite of the structures that shape it, ethnic identity can therefore reflect individual choices in a way that highly institutionalized formal politics cannot. For this reason, Latin American immigrants turn to ethnic identity in order to escape the mutually incompatible alternatives posed by either "becoming American," or staying attached to the memory of their country of origin. Identity does not have to be exclusively tied or fixed to either Latin America or the United States. Multiple and changeable, it can apply to both contexts—and this is how Latin American immigrants use it.

7

The Politics of In-between: Avoiding Irreconcilable Demands, Keeping Loyalties

Latin American immigrant politics operates under constraints. Some of those constraints are external: to count as an actor in U.S. politics, one must become a U.S. citizen. Becoming a U.S. citizen means, for many immigrants, the loss of citizenship in their country of origin. Understandably, it matters to many immigrants that they are asked to repudiate their country of birth when they naturalize as citizens in another country, and this demand contributes to their indecisiveness about U.S. citizenship. It isn't that they are particularly attached to the formal politics of their country of origin, but rather that they do not wish to lose their identification and connection with their home country. Much of the political life of Latin American immigrants in Queens is a matter, then, of finding a balance between two mutually exclusive polities. The result is a politics in which they have a certain autonomy of action without making any irrevocable choices.

The commonly held belief is that low participation here must mean participation in the country of origin, but, as I show in this chapter, this is not the case for Latin American immigrants in the United States. Latino immigrants are likely to stay away from formal politics in both the country of origin *and* the United States, behavior that is consistent with an overall policy of avoiding partisanship and controversy—immigrants try not to pick sides. Instead, Latin American immigrants use the space opened by public events to express multiple (and conflicting) identities, without being forced to make choices among them. Those moments when immigrants do move decisively into the public sphere draw from a Latin American repertoire, but only succeed if they coincide with the desire to avoid irreconcilable commitments. From the point of view of American politicians, immigrant mobilization appears to be sporadic or episodic, but is in fact consistent within a framework of a politics of in-between.

Staying away from Electoral Politics

One frequently offered explanation of Latin American immigrants' low levels of participation in formal politics in the United States is simply that they are absorbed by the politics in their countries of origin (Dwyer 1991: 68).[1] A Puerto Rican activist in Queens expressed this view succinctly: "I believe the Latino community in Queens is more of the social, civic organizations. Most people are not involved in politics. Now that could be for several reasons. One is—and this is the big one as far as I am concerned—that they are super-involved in the politics of their own country. *Están llegando mas allá y menos acá* [they're putting more effort there than here]."[2] But there is little evidence that immigrants' efforts are so focused on Latin America that they have neither the time nor the inclination for politics in the United States. Very few Latin American immigrants are actively involved in the electoral politics of their home countries.

The most striking example is Colombians in the United States. Colombia is the only Latin American country to provide the opportunity for its nationals living overseas to vote in presidential elections from abroad.[3] Voting is relatively easy. Colombian immigrants have only to go to the Colombian consulate in Manhattan to register, and then return there, or to one of the polling stations set up by the consulate in Queens, to cast their ballots. Yet in the last elections, in 1990, only slightly more than 3,000 did so, out of the approximately 200,000 Colombians residing in the metropolitan area.[4] If anything, participation in the home country has declined. In 1970, with a

[1] Jennings (1988) makes a similar argument for Puerto Ricans in New York City.

[2] Interview, June 10, 1991. See also Hardy-Fanta 1993: 176, n. 219–20.

[3] See Chapter 8 for more details on immigrant campaigns for dual citizenship.

[4] The Colombian consulate in New York City indicated that 3,012 Colombian nationals voted in the 1990 presidential elections, out of an estimated 200,000 in the metropolitan region. Written communication, Colombian consulate, New York City, March 23, 1992. Also author's fieldnotes, Federación de Organizaciones Colombianas meeting, July 11, 1991. "La Colombia de Jackson Heights," *El Diario/La Prensa*, July 18, 1991, p. 21. Colombians are not the only ones to encourage voting by their residents abroad: Poles can vote in their national elections at their consulates as well, and of course Americans abroad can send in absentee ballots to record their vote.

Colombian population in New York City one-third the size of today's, 3,700 Colombians voted in their national elections.[5]

Not only does participation in the home country involve a minuscule proportion of immigrants, but Latin American immigrants often have strong negative views of politics and politicians in general. For many immigrants politics is, as one Colombian put it, "a necessary evil."[6] Even activists believe, as one Colombian woman indicated, that "politics is dirty. Unfortunately one has to be involved in politics to do something for the community."[7] For most, it is something best avoided. A Colombian woman active in the community noted that "political topics are not interesting to most people . . . if things turn to political topics, they leave quickly."[8] An Ecuadorian noted that "of Ecuadorians [who are] citizens, there aren't too many who participate in electoral politics. . . If they are first-generation immigrants, participation in Ecuadorian politics is not that high either."[9]

A look at electoral participation in the three Latin American countries providing the largest flow of immigrants to New York City—Colombia, Ecuador, and the Dominican Republic—reveals substantial gaps in electorial participation. Colombia, for instance, has some of the highest abstention rates in the region, reaching as high as 60% in 1966 and 1978, and 44% in 1986 (see Table 16). While this may not seem abnormally high by American standards, it is unusual for Latin America. However, these figures have to taken in the context of *La Violencia*, an intraparty civil war which lasted from 1946 to 1956, costing at least 200,000 lives and continuing guerrilla and drug violence ever since. As Kline notes, an entire generation of Colombians "grew up thinking that violence was the *normal* way of life" (1985: 257). The mistrust of politics has carried over to the present. In a recent Colombian poll, for instance, the majority of respondents reported confidence in the institutions of the family, private enterprise, and the Catholic church, but indicated a great deal of mistrust for the police, military, and government authorities.[10] Low participation rates continue as well.

[5] *New York Times*, February 13, 1974, cited in Reimers 1992: 143. The Mexican government, under pressure from opposition parties (particularly the Partido Revolucionario Democrático) has dropped hints that it might also consider some form of voting from its consulates abroad. This has led to speculation about the huge numbers of Mexican nationals who might participate in their home country elections, and the potentially significant impact they might have. If the Colombian case is any indication, this impact is widely exaggerated.

[6] Interview (in Spanish), August 31, 1991.

[7] Conversation (in Spanish), October 21, 1991.

[8] Author's fieldnotes, April 18, 1991.

[9] Interview, August 28, 1991.

[10] Results of a survey conducted in October and November 1990 by Centrum, Ogilvy, and Mather of 744 middle-class men and women in the cities of Bogotá, Cali, Medellín, and

Table 16. Electoral participation in Colombian presidential elections, 1958–1986

Year	% voting
1958	58
1962	49
1966	40
1970	53
1974	58
1978	40
1982	50
1986	56

Sources: Belasario Betancur, "Abstención y Participación," in *La Abstención* (Bogota, Colombia: Editorial Presencia), 1980, p. 158; *Estadisticas de la Registraduría Nacional del Estado Civil*, cited in Hernández 1986: 135, note 16. Pachón and DeSipio asked a sample of Latin American immigrants in New York State about their participation in events in their home country. Less than 5% of those who migrated as adults said that they had voted in their home country before immigrating. Although this agrees with the general point I would like to make, it also seems suspiciously low. A much higher percentage (62%) said they had taken part in political rallies and marches (Pachón and DeSipio 1994: 174, table 8.29).

In a survey of young people aged 16–27 in Medillín, Colombia, 65 percent said they had never been active politically, 75.8 percent indicated they had never voted, and 59 percent indicated they did not believe in the electoral system.[11]

Colombia has had elections continually throughout the century, with only one interruption from 1953 to 1957. Ecuador, on the other hand, had military governments from 1963 to 1966, and again from 1972 to 1978, and during those periods when there were elections, a sizable portion of the

---

Barranquilla, reported in *El País* (Cali, Colombia), March 19, 1991, p. A3 and compiled in the Foreign Broadcast Information Service, *Latin American Report*, April 25, 1991, p. 26. These findings are supported by other surveys. A nationwide poll of over 4,500 respondents taken by the Liberal Party found that large majorities had negative views of almost every governmental institution (*El Tiempo* [Bogotá, Colombia], March 11, 1993, p. 7A, compiled in FBIS, March 17, 1993). Finally, a 1989 poll of residents of Bogotá, Medellín, Cali, Baranquilla, and Bucaramanga found that 68% of respondents had a negative view of the judicial system, and 61% felt the same about Congress. *El Tiempo* (Bogotá, Colombia), June 2, 1989, p. A1, compiled in FBIS, July 14, 1989.

[11] The survey, undertaken by the Center for Political and Economic Studies (CEPE) together with the University of Medillín, surveyed 1,000 people over three months in 1989. Results were reported in *El Colombiano* (Medillín, Colombia), June 19, 1989, p. A6, and compiled in FBIS, *Latin American Report*, August 7, 1989.

population was disenfranchised by literacy requirements until after 1978. After the return to democracy and the liberalization of the constitution in the late 1970s, it took some years for registration rates to reflect the full voting population. In 1978 there were about two million people registered out of a population of eight million; by the 1980 municipal elections there were almost 2.8 million. In 1984, in the second presidential election since the end of military government, about 2.85 million people were registered, and by the 1986 congressional elections there were 4.25 million registered voters (Mena 1986: 99–100). It is clear that before the most recent period of democratization in Ecuador a significant number of the population were outside the electoral system.

Polls indicate that many Ecuadorians are skeptical about the political system, in spite of the most recent transition to democracy. In response to the question whether political parties were concerned with the problems of ordinary people, 87 percent of those polled in a 1991 survey answered "no." In addition, respondents believed democratic governments and dictatorships were equally corrupt. These results, noted a commentator in Ecuador, indicate that "the great majority of the Ecuadorian people have come to the . . . conclusion [that] all . . . leaders are corrupt, self-centered liars. . . . Common and ordinary citizens regard political life as a spectacle in which they do not participate. They feel that political parties and politicians are increasingly concentrating their attention on resolving personal quarrels and dividing the crumbs of power, while they are less interested in resolving the people's problems."[12]

The Dominican Republic, which since the 1970s has been the single largest sender of immigrants to New York City, has had, like Colombia and Ecuador, a checkered electoral history. Rafael Trujillo's despotic regime lasted from 1930 to his assassination in 1961. Juan Bosch's election and subsequent deposition led eventually to U.S. intervention in 1965 and rule by Joaquín Balaguer from 1966 to 1978. Only in 1978 did regular constitu-

[12] Jaime Durán Barba, *La Otra* (Guayaquil, Ecuador), July 11, 1991, pp. 22–23. The poll was conducted by the Institute of Studies of Public Opinion on June 21, 1991, with a sample of 400 respondents in the cities of Quito and Guayaquil, and compiled in FBIS, *Latin American Report*, August 16, 1991.

Extensive opinion polling in Latin America is a relatively new phenomenon, and these polls are only imperfectly collected in the U.S. Some countries seem to have a wealth of polling data available here, while others have almost nothing. There is little available on the Dominican Republic, for instance, but a great deal on Peru. I focus on Colombians, Ecuadorians, and Dominicans because of their importance to the migrant streams into Queens. Polling data for Peru show results similar to those for Colombia and Ecuador. See *Peru Economico* (Lima, Peru), October 1991, p. 15, compiled in FBIS, November 10, 1991; and *Expreso* (Lima, Peru), September 15, 1991, p. A14, compiled in FBIS, October 24, 1991.

tionally guaranteed elections resume (Wiarda 1985: 587–91; Brea 1986: 258), although Balaguer essentially remained in power for another fifteen years even so. As in Colombia and Ecuador, the closure of the political system in the Dominican Republic led to disillusionment with formal politics. This period of disillusionment was crucial to the development of the Dominican community in New York.[13]

It seems plausible that Latin American immigrants' mistrust of government and their experience with the electoral process in their countries of origin contributes to their disconnection from formal political participation, both there *and* in the United States.[14] One Colombian noted: "A lot of people are predisposed against [becoming involved in electoral politics]. They don't want to do it, because let's suppose they come from countries in which the electoral processes in particular are a charade, a farce. Then they come here with an incredible cynicism."[15] The president of the Colombian Liberal Party in New York agreed:

> Yes, it's true. Because most of our compatriots have the same experience . . . that the state has been inefficient and irresponsible, and it hasn't responded to the demands of its people. And the people have had to leave the country where they have all their feelings, their values . . . their lives . . . they have to go in search of new horizons. So possibly they are a little resentful. People [look down] on politicians. . . . And so this is the attitude not only of Colombians but of other communities as well. . . . So they come here and they say "I'm not going to get involved in politics" [*no voy a vivir lo político*—literally "I'm not going to live the political"].[16]

This mistrust and cynicism lead many observers to the conclusion that Latin American immigrants live outside politics entirely.[17]

[13] The period 1961–78 was especially critical. Unlike Colombia and Ecuador, Balaguer encouraged the migration (rather, the de facto exile) of political dissidents, many of whom went to New York. These politically motivated migrants, says Georges, reconstituted Dominican opposition parties here, which in turn lay the foundation for grassroots organizations that increasingly focused their attention on the conditions of Dominicans in the city, particularly in Washington Heights (Georges 1984: 23, 37–46; Hernández and Torres-Saillant 1994: 9–10).

[14] For a contrary view, see Hardy-Fanta 1993: 179–84.

[15] Interview (in Spanish), August 14, 1991.

[16] Interview (in Spanish), August 9, 1991.

[17] A certain amount of fear and caution toward the state may even keep people from taking advantage of social services. An Ecuadorian woman described how she served as an intermediary between her Latin American neighbors and the police. "They don't know how to call. A lot of people call 911, O.K. But they are afraid to give their names. They are afraid to give their address. They give a false address." Interview (in Spanish), May 1, 1991.

Avoiding Partisanship and Controversy

At first glance, immigrant associations seem to confirm this impression. The vast majority of immigrant organizations in Queens go out of their way to advertise their nonpolitical nature. Dominican social clubs, for instance, state that their goal is to promote a "family atmosphere" (*un ambiente familiar*) for immigrants to gather and socialize, not for any potentially controversial purpose.[18] Likewise, the president of the Centro Cívico Colombiano pointed out that the purpose of his organization was to "bolster Colombian patriotism and pride. . . . There are so many negative [stereotypes] which affect a person of Colombian origin. So that's what we try and do; so that the Colombian here doesn't feel isolated and think there aren't organizations which represent them in the cultural sphere. We aren't politicians and we aren't involved in politics [*no estamos metidos en la política*]."[19]

Immigrant organizations in Queens, then, tend to bill themselves as solely social, cultural, or occupational groups, neither explicitly political nor oriented toward the United States.[20] Pachón and DeSipio's sample of first-generation immigrants in New York (1994) illustrates the composition of organizational membership (see Table 17). The numbers have, if anything, understated the tilt away from formal political involvement. Membership in social and cultural organizations has a multiplier effect: at social events like dances, concerts, or festivals every member brings family and friends. The weekly dances at the club Hermanos Unidos, a Dominican social club in Corona, brought in a packed house far outnumbering the formal members of the organization. A study of Dominican social clubs in Washington Heights found that just eighteen associations reached approximately 20,000 Dominicans in the area through activities which brought in and involved extended social networks (Sainz 1990).

The attitude prevalent in immigrant associations is not surprising given the mistrust of politicians and politics among the immigrant population as a whole. What is interesting is the manner in which immigrant activists set aside a whole range of collective activities from what they wish to consider "political." The president of the Comité Cívico Ecuatoriano explained that

[18] Author's fieldnotes, February 15, 1991; various handbills and flyers, 1991.

[19] Interview (in Spanish), April 12, 1991.

[20] The exceptions are Latin American political party organizations—the Colombian Liberal Party has a permanent office in Queens, as does the M-19. The Dominican Movimiento Partido Popular also has an office in Queens, but it is rarely active. Note again that the absence of organized political activity is in marked contrast to the situation Georges describes among Dominicans in Washington Heights, in large part due to the arrival of highly politicized activists after Trujillo's death in 1961 (1984: 16–20). There were also two attempts to form Latino Democratic clubs in the 1970s, both of which failed (see Chapter 3).

Table 17. Participation of Latin American immigrants in community organizations, New York State

Type of organization	% indicating participation
Church	61.9
Parent-teacher's association	21.7
Social club	14.5
Sports club	13.4
National origin club	12.2
Union	5.3
Fraternal club	4.2
Senior citizens group	3.1
Political club	2.0

Source: Adapted from Pachón and DeSipio 1994: 171, table 8.23.

his organization was an institution formed by the various Ecuadorian organizations, each of differing natures—social, cultural, athletic, and civic—but not, he was careful to specify, political or religious. "All those things in which the Comite Cívico is involved," he said, "are events which have to do with Ecuador. These events, I repeat, are apolitical. There is something, for example, that we also uphold as an aspiration. This could be called political, but you really can't call it that because it isn't proselytizing. It's an old aspiration, which is to get the right for Ecuadorians overseas to be able to vote for president and vice president [in Ecuador]. But since it's so generic, it can't be proselytism because it's not in favor of one candidate or another, but for whichever candidate it happens to be."[21]

This kind of scholastic reasoning essentially guts the common definition of "politics," equating it with proselytizing for partisan purposes. Using this rationale, organizations freely advocate "patriotic" causes and symbolic nationalism without thinking twice about whether or not they are "political." Immigrant associations can advocate allowing nationals to vote in elections in their home countries (Ecuador, Dominican Republic, Mexico), push for dual citizenship in the home country for immigrants and their children who have become American citizens (Colombia, Ecuador, Honduras, Mexico, and the Dominican Republic),[22] and invite prominent home country politicians as guests of honor at local immigrant events (all nationalities). But these entanglements in the formal politics of the home country fall under "cultural" or "civic" activities.

[21] Interview (in Spanish), May 10, 1991.

[22] In some countries dual citizenship is a constitutional guarantee protecting an individual's rights as a national in the country of birth regardless of whatever other citizenship may be adopted. These measures are now in place in Colombia, Ecuador, Uruguay, El Salvador, Panama, the Dominican Republic, and Mexico. For further discussion, see Chapter 8.

The flip side of disguising much of the commonly understood meaning of "the political" under civic or cultural labels is that civic and cultural activities become increasingly politicized. They do so not just by the inclusion of political personalities and issues, but by the infusion of national symbols into every aspect of organizational activity. Thus when the Comite Cívico Ecuatoriano opened its new offices in Astoria it was taken for granted that the Ecuadorian consul would be invited, that Ecuadorian flags would be hung, that the Ecuadorian national anthem would be sung (while the U.S. anthem was played people stood by silently), and finally, that a Roman Catholic priest from Ecuador would bless the space with holy water.[23] All of these acts and rituals point to ties with state, religion, and nation, but none would be considered political; rather, they are symbolic, nonpartisan, and hence uncontroversial.

However, while immigrant associations are glad to associate and be associated with their home countries' symbols, and to an extent accept their authority, that authority is compromised by immigrants' unwillingness to participate in formal partisan politics. Being partisan requires picking a side. As immigrants, picking a side and accepting the full authority of nation and state would be to take on undivided loyalties and an uncompromised citizenship. After choosing to live, sometimes for years, as immigrants in another country, this is often unacceptable. Partisanship is divisive because it asks for a clarification of status, the making of a final, irreconcilable choice. Not only is formal politics something Latino immigrants mistrust through experience in their home countries, but this mistrust is compounded by the demands formal politics lays on them to make this choice.

Identity Politics: Organizations and Parades

Latin American immigrant organizations in Queens provide an alternative to these mutually incompatible commitments through what I call the "politics of in-between." Even though most first-generation immigrant organizations are oriented toward the home country, the autonomous space they create here lends itself (perhaps unintentionally) to the expression of multiple identities that allow them to avoid the closure demanded by formal politics. Movement from one identity to another—from regional affiliations to national pride, and from national pride to an awareness of communalities with other Latinos in the United States—is accomplished with tension and ambivalence, perhaps, but without confronting stark choices.

[23] Author's fieldnotes, 1992.

As I mentioned in Chapter 5, Latin American immigrant organizations tend to be regionally or nationally based. Each of the major national groups has its own cluster of regional organizations. Ecuadorian social and cultural organizations, for instance, are regionally based by province. There are organizations for Biblián, Manabí, Chimborazo, Guayas, Tunguragua, and Guayaquil, among others, but membership is not limited to individuals from those areas. Sports teams, for instance, are often organized around regional or national lines, but the actual players may be drawn from any number of Latin American countries. Likewise, while the Centro Cívico Colombiano and the Escuela Simón Bolivar offer classes in Latin American history and Spanish for Colombians, and the Escuela José Pedro Varela for Uruguayans, these institutions actually provide services to a range of Latin American children.[24] Occupational associations are grouped around nationality or around a Latino identity—as are FEDECOP, the Colombian professional association, and PROECUA, its Ecuadorian counterpart. Regional and occupational organizations are then grouped under citywide umbrella organizations such as the Comité Cívico Ecuatoriano or the Federación de Organizaciones Colombianas, or brought together by a national congress.[25] Each immigrant nationality also generates a market for newspapers, radio shows, and cable programs targeted at the particular population, which are inserted in the larger arena of Latino media. For example, various national groups have radio programs at different times of the day on Radio WADO, have pages in the city's Spanish-language dailies devoted to the concerns of specific national groups, and cable channels showing material from each Latin American country.[26] In short, while an organization may draw most of its members from a particular region or nationality, their interactions are rarely limited to members of that particular subgroup. Affiliations are "nested," one within another (not necessarily in a hierarchical

[24] Interview (in Spanish), president, Comité Cívico Ecuatoriano, May 10, 1991. See also George Ferreira, "Escuela Uruguaya José Pedro Varela," *Noticias del Mundo*, March 3, 1994, p. 8A.

[25] There are similar umbrella organizations for Dominican and Peruvian groups. In addition, Colombians, Ecuadorians, and Peruvians each have a national congress which meets once a year in different part of the United States, bringing together immigrant groups from around the country. The Ecuadorian congress was established in 1985; the Peruvian in 1984. "Congreso de Ecuatorianos Residentes en EE.UU.," *El Universo* (Guayaquil, Ecuador), December 20, 1991; for a more detailed description of the Peruvian national congresses see Altamirano 1990 and Altamirano 1992.

[26] Weekly newspapers are primarily targeted to a particular national group, but even they also incorporate wire stories that would appeal to a broader Latin American audience. Interviews, editor, *Noticiero Argentino-Uruguayo*, January 9, 1992, and editor, *Noticiero Colombiano*, February 24, 1992.

fashion), so that each national group has a variety of linkages with other regional, national, and Latino associations.

Rituals such as parades and festivals are occasions to display the politics of identity (see Kasinitz and Freidenberg-Herbstein 1987). Here, Latin American immigrants manage a number of identities simultaneously. In late July and early August there are huge all-day gatherings in Flushing Meadows Park organized by Colombian and Ecuadorian groups, as well as an overall Hispanic festival. Hundreds of thousands of people come to spend the day with their families, eating ethnic food at the booths and listening to music and speeches. These events privilege national identities, but they include symbols alluding to other identities as well. The Ecuadorian parade, for example—one of three annual Latin American immigrant parades on 37th Avenue in Queens—is an explicitly Ecuadorian celebration,[27] but other associated identities are evident throughout, as was clear from the 1992 parade.

As was to be expected, this parade was rife with symbolic references to Ecuadorian nationality. The guests of honor, the Ecuadorian consul in New York and the mayors of Quito and Cuenca, two of Ecuador's largest cities, marched at the front of the parade. The beauty queens from various Ecuadorian expatriate organizations (the queens of the Comité Cívico, Guayaquil '85, the Sol y Mar Club, the Club Dinosaurio, and San Anselmo from the Bronx) were present together with Miss Ecuador 1992 and the beauty queens from Quito, Guayaquil, and Ambato.[28] In addition to floats from metropolitan sports organizations (Daulis Soccer Club "Deporte sí, Drogas no"; the Asociación de Peloteros Ecuatorianos; and the Ecuador Sporting Club) and social organizations (Club San Luis de Grasuntes of Stamford, Connecticut, and the Metropolitan Lions Club), there were floats from Ecuadorian businesses: airlines (Saeta, "The Airline of Ecuador," and Ecuatoriana, "The Airline of All the Americas"), travel agencies (Ecuadorian Line/Galo Travel, Murillo Travel, and Ecuador Travel), and remittance offices (Empresa Ecuatoriana de Envios de Valores y Encomiendas). Tucked away in the middle of the procession was a van with a "Unidad Nacional Independiente, 1992/Sixto for President" campaign poster to celebrate the recent electoral victory of the Conservative Party in Ecuador.

References to the larger Latino population in New York and the United States included floats sponsored by the big ethnic food companies (Goya

[27] The Ecuadoran parade first started in 1984. There are also Argentine and Hispanic parades.
[28] These beauty pageants are widespread in Latin America as well as in Queens, and are exceptionally popular events: see David Marcus, "Miss (You Name It!)," *New York Times*, Style section, April 18, 1993, which describes the widespread beauty pageant phenomenon in Colombia.

Foods, Bonita Bananas, Cafe Tampico) and American companies (Miller Beer), which underscored the significance of Latinos as a market. These floats appear at every Latino parade or festival. *El Diario/La Prensa* sponsored a float as well—*El campeón de los hispanos* [Champion of Hispanics]. Interviewers and cameramen from Tele-Amazonas were there; one cameraman said the producers would try broadcast coverage of the parade not only in Ecuador, but all over South and Central America as well—Ecuadorians being part of a larger Latino media market.

Finally, there were references to immigrants' relation to the United States. The parade was led by flag-bearers with the Ecuadorian and American flags—an acknowledgment of ties to both countries. The men in the parade belonged to soccer leagues (each team organized by country, and at times by town or province), and the children marched with their Little League softball teams (sponsored by American businesses, or professional sports teams like the Mets). One of the bands from Catholic high schools played, interspersed with salsa and Andean music groups, the U.S. Marine Corps anthem ("From the Halls of Montezuma/To the Shores of Tripoli . . .") on the xylophone. The juxtaposition of the music might seem odd, until one takes into account that in the 1991 parade two Ecuadorian soldiers who had fought in the U.S. military during the Gulf War were guests of honor. And although there were Ecuadorian beauty queens and politicians there, the biggest attraction of the 1992 parade was "Geraldo," an Ecuadorian rap singer who had flown in from Los Angeles.[29] Nor were American politicians entirely absent from these kinds of events. Mayor Koch was present at the Colombian festival in 1988 and 1989, Mayor Dinkins appeared at the Ecuadorian festival in 1992, and Mayor Giuliani marched with the parade in 1996. On these occasions American elected officials played much the same role as Latin American officials do—symbolizing ties without demanding any commitments.

The Ecuadorian parade and others like it give some indication of the complexity of identity for Latin American immigrants in this country. Even while the emphasis is clearly on the country of origin, there is an implicit acknowledgment of separation as well. It is no accident that the major immigrant-owned businesses sponsoring these public events are airlines, travel agencies, and remittance offices. They, together with immigrant organizations themselves, exist *because* of the distance between immigrants and their countries of birth, while simultaneously benefiting by reminding immigrants of the ties that bind them to their home country. Thus the sym-

[29] Author's fieldnotes, Desfile Ecuatoriano de Queens, August 2, 1992.

bolic display of immigrants' relationship to the United States, and their identity here, is often the most ambivalent and ambiguous of all. While they may be invisible or veiled in the official program, references to immigrants' relationship to the United States are present nonetheless.

Politics by Other Means: The Caravan

The moments at which Latin American immigrants have gone beyond organizing celebratory events to mobilize in other ways also demonstrate the hybrid nature of immigrant politics. The forms of mobilization immigrants choose are almost ritualistic in nature. Like others mobilizing collectively, immigrants are not calculating tacticians who seize every available opportunity to act; instead, they choose the form and timing of their collective action from a narrow repertoire. A repertoire, writes Charles Tilly, "implies that the standard forms are learned, limited in number and scope, slowly changing, and peculiarly adapted to their settings. Pressed by a grievance, interest, or aspiration and confronted with an opportunity to act, groups of people who have the capacity to act collectively choose among forms of action in their limited repertoire" (Tilly, 1979: 131; see also Tilly 1985; Tilly 1978). Forms of collective action are rooted in their context and history. Forms of contention are regularized and routinized over time. The current repertoire of collective action in the United States might include, for example, striking, petitioning, and the organization of pressure groups, among others. Americans' repertoire would probably not extend to hijacking, machine-breaking, mutiny, violent tax rebellions, self-immolation, lynching, and the vendetta (1979: 152). Protests marches are common, protest caravans are rarer, and electoral caravans almost unknown.[30]

Among Latin American immigrants in Queens, however, automobile caravans, which are a common tactic for popular political expression in Latin

[30] Protest caravans do occur with some frequency. Consider, for example, the massive rally by 3,000 livery cabs in New York City to protest working conditions (Keith Greenberg, "In the Danger Zone: New York City Cabbies Live in Fear," *USA Today*, October 27, 1993, p. 11A) and a similar one to protest proposals by the Taxi and Limousine Commission ("Medallion Cabbies Stage Rolling Protest," UPI, January 23, 1992); and the protest by southern African-American farmers against farm foreclosures (Susan Laccetti, "Black Farmers Seeking to Put Plight on National Agenda," *The Atlanta Journal and Constitution*, March 9, 1992). Through Nexis-Lexis I found about twenty references to protest caravans in the United States in the last ten years.

I found only one reference to a popular electoral caravan in the U.S. The article itself points out the rarity of this form of collective action: "Taking an unconventional tack, Perot supporters are scheduled to have a car caravan on the Sunday before the election." Mike Oliver and Mary Shanklin, "Workers Set for Stretch Run in Presidential Campaign," *Orlando Sentinel Tribune*, October 26, 1992, p. B1.

America, are a common choice from the collective repertoire. The caravan in Latin America has both a particular style and recognizable form: lines of vehicles, honking their horns in unison, often with placards hanging from the sides and national or party colors being waved from the windows. The popular caravan is distinct from the presidential caravan, assembled for campaigning through the country. The official caravan is clearly hierarchical and self-enclosed, and it reinforces distinctions between patrons and passive recipients.[31] Popular caravans are essentially open, participatory, and democratic. Though participation depends on having access to an automobile, nonetheless the tactic appeals across classes and ideologies.[32]

The popular caravan has two variations. In the first, used at election time, it signals support for one candidate over another. A 1990 news story described its use in the Costa Rican national elections: "While election year activities have been subdued here, a decades-old tradition has not been forgotten. Party faithful have snarled San Jose's narrow streets with caravans of horn-blaring cars flying the green-and-white banner of the Liberation Party and the red and blue colors of the Unity."[33]

Another article noted that "rival supporters blasted each other with horns, beeped in unison to the rhythm of their candidates' name. Hour after hour, wave by pounding wave, the strident battle swept across San Jose."[34] Color and sound in the caravan are emblems of allegiance to a candidate. A Costa Rican listening to drivers beating a tattoo on their car horns would immediately know which candidate they were supporting. Two short blasts followed by one long, for example, might indicate support for Rafael Calderón, of the Social Christian Unity Party: *Cal-de-rón, Cal-de-rón.*

Second, the caravan is used for political protest. Because automobiles are ubiquitous in urban centers, bans on caravans are not easy to enforce. Dur-

[31] The official caravan is common in both the United States and Latin America. An example is Clinton and Gore's bus caravan in the 1992 election (Brian Dickinson, "Democratic Boys Keep to the Middle of the Road," *Houston Chronicle*, July 26, 1992, p. 1). For a vivid if fictional account of the official caravan in Latin America, see Gabriel Garcia Marquez, *The Autumn of the Patriarch* (New York: Harper and Row, 1976).

[32] The dependence on automobiles gives this form of protest a distinctly middle-class tinge (underlining again the middle-class character of the Latin American population in Queens). In Panama, for instance, General Noriega mocked the opposition as the "BMW protesters" because of the cars they drove in the opposition caravans. Some of these same BMWs and Mercedes turned out in the streets to protest U.S. sanctions later on. *New York Newsday*, February 22, 1989. In Argentina, caravans drove past the U.S. Embassy to protest U.S. backing of Great Britain during the Malvinas War. Carl Migdail, "For Argentina, Troubles Are Just Beginning," *U.S. News and World Report*, May 17, 1982, p. 29.

[33] Emma Daly, "Centrists Vie for Presidency in Costa Rican Elections," Reuters, January 31, 1990.

[34] "Son of Ex-president of Costa Rica Claims Victory in National Vote," *New York Times*, January 5, 1992, p. A2.

ing the increasing confrontation between General Manuel Noriega and the opposition in Panama, many Panamanians resorted to the caravan as a form of protest. Caravans would appear twice a day—at noon and at six p.m.—in the downtown areas, their drivers waving white handkerchiefs from the window to indicate their support for the opposition, and honking their horns.[35] Panamanian authorities issued decrees attempting to ban these protests at least twice, in 1987 and 1989. The proclamations prohibited "marches, meetings, public demonstrations, and caravans of vehicles."[36] These decrees by Panamanian authorities were in themselves a recognition that caravans were a regular option for popular collective action, and part of the repertoire of the political opposition.[37]

In its haphazard way, the international press occasionally documents the use of the caravan as a regular part of the repertoire for collective action across Latin America. I found references to electoral and protest caravans in Argentina,[38] Brazil,[39] Chile,[40] the Dominican Republic, Ecuador, El Salvador, Mexico, Paraguay, Puerto Rico,[41] and Venezuela.[42] It should not be surprising that such a widespread practice would also be found in much the same form among Latin American immigrants in New York City. Tilly suggests that under new circumstances people adapt existing forms of action to new interests and opportunities, rather than inventing new forms that

[35] "Panamanian Protestors Take a Work Break; Leaders Skip Rally for a Work Fair," *Washington Post*, March 13, 1988; "Panamanian Tightens Ship," *Washington Post*, October 18, 1987.

[36] "Noriega Defies Ban," *New York Newsday*, May 21, 1989. "Panama City mayor bans public demonstrations and gatherings; banning of White [opposition] rally scheduled . . . and of all caravans and any other type of activity that will affect the public order." BBC, August 7, 1987.

[37] Proving once again that imitation is the sincerest form of flattery, before banning car caravans outright "the Panamanian government also imitated the opposition's protest style by sending its own supporters out in caravans to honk car horns for support." Dan Williams, "Panama Government Bans All Demonstrations," *Los Angeles Times*, July 8, 1987, p. 11.

[38] "Argentine Vote Keeps Alfonsín at the Helm," *Chicago Tribune*, November 4, 1985, p. 5. Jackson Diehl, "Argentine Voters, Fearing Anarchy, Face Key Election," *The Washington Post*, October 27, 1983, p. 29.

[39] *New York Times*, December 18, 1989, p. A3, and November 16, 1989, p. A16. James Nelson Goodsell, "Brazil, Emerging Power," *Christian Science Monitor*, November 15, 1982.

[40] Tina Rosenberg, "Fall of the Patriarch: Pinochet Gives Way Ungracefully," *New Republic*, December 13, 1989, p. 20. Barbara Durr, "U.S. Grape Embargo Angers Chileans," *Chicago Tribune*, March 17, 1989, p. 4. Eugene Robinson, "Chile's Opposition Seeks to Consolidate Victory; Pinochet Resists Accelerating Power Shift," *Washington Post*, October 11, 1988, p. A15.

[41] "Puerto Ricans Vote on Future: Status Quo, Statehood, or Independence," *Cleveland Plain Dealer*, November 14, 1993, p. A3. "Puerto Rico Debates Status as Vote Nears," *Chicago Tribune*, December 28, 1991.

[42] "Fears of Violence, Coup Clouds Venezuelan Elections," *Agence France Press*, November 29, 1993. Joe Mann, "Voices Stilled in Venezuela's Strident Poll Campaign," *Financial Times*, December 3, 1988, p. A3.

might be more effective under the circumstances (1979: 152). This is perhaps especially true for immigrants, who abruptly find themselves in a different setting with little, if any, transition.

The clearest instance of this transfer of patterns of collective action followed the crash of Avianca flight 052 on January 25, 1990, en route from Bogotá to New York City. Immediately after the accident—which killed seventy-three passengers and injured another eighty-five, most of them Colombians—Latin Americans in the metropolitan area began to organize to protest what they felt was blatant discrimination by American airport authorities. Many believed that the plane had been prevented from landing because authorities did not want passengers on a plane from Colombia to disembark without a search for drugs. Fernando Oliver, a Colombian-American lawyer involved in the case, expressed a common sentiment: "Simply out of fear for drugs, people died."[43] A month to the day after the disaster, about a thousand vehicles assembled in the parking lot of Shea Stadium in Queens to drive over to Kennedy Airport in protest. The caravan drove down the freeway to the airport with headlights on, led by a hearse, in a kind of mock funeral. The first seventy-three cars carried the names of those killed. The vehicles following had placards with slogans—"Discrimination against Colombians"—and Colombian flags hanging from the sides, while the Colombian national anthem played on the car stereos.[44]

The organizers of the caravan assembled in Queens to protest the crash of flight 052 took a Latin American formula for political protest and transferred it to a new context. The protest caravan kept its populist, open quality, and retained its manipulation of sight and sound to carry symbolic meaning. On the other hand, its focus and purpose had shifted slightly. From being a challenge initiated by members within a polity, the caravan had become a way for outsiders to protest their marginality. The Colombian flags and national anthem underscored protesters sense of otherness as immigrants, even as they objected to being treated as outsiders.

The caravan to Kennedy Airport mobilized a great number of Colombian and other Latin American immigrants, and attracted considerable attention—from the media, and from the air traffic authorities.[45] But it was also seen by everyone involved as an extraordinary response to a catastrophic event, not a normal tactic for expression of collective sentiment. The pro-

[43] "Trying to Heal Scars of Jet Crash," *New York Newsday*, July 19, 1990.

[44] Jason deParle, "Caravan of Cars Enters Kennedy to Protest Crash," *New York Times*, February 26, 1990, p. B4; "Kin Blame Racism in Air Crash," *New York Newsday*, February 26, 1990.

[45] The protest was acknowledged in the industry's trade publication, *Airports* (March 6, 1990, p. 107).

test was not seen particularly as having political meaning, especially by Queens politicians, who for the most part remained oblivious or indifferent to its occurrence.

The electoral caravan, on the other hand, proved much more difficult to translate to a new setting in Queens. In 1988 a group of Latin Americans active in the Democratic Party approached the Dukakis campaign's New York City headquarters to ask for permission to organize a caravan through the neighborhoods of Jackson Heights, Elmhurst, and Corona. After some hesitation, the campaign was persuaded to lend them posters and literature for the event. The caravan had many of the elements of those in Latin America—flags, loudspeakers, banners, and placards (many of them in Spanish). A couple of dozen cars toured the neighborhoods, distributing literature throughout the predominantly immigrant area. But as a political act the caravan was not read in Queens as it would have been in Latin America. Most Latin American immigrants probably recognized it as part of their political repertoire, even in the different context, but they did not actively support it. The turnout was small compared to the massive election rallies in Latin America. The purpose behind the caravan—to encourage participation in American politics—was not one that most immigrants were prepared to fully endorse. Queens politicians, for their part, were skeptical of the idea of the caravan, which was not part of *their* political repertoire. In 1991, when Latino activists approached the campaign of an American politician running for City Council with the idea of organizing another caravan, their proposal was rejected outright by the candidate's campaign managers. The Latin American organizers interpreted this rejection as the campaign's desire to relegate Latinos in the campaign to a back seat, so as not to alienate the politician's core support of older white voters, who would be offended by the cacophony and visibility of the demonstration.[46] However, it is equally plausible that the campaign management simply did not recognize the caravan as a viable political tool.[47]

Thus far the electoral caravan has failed to take hold in its new setting, in part because of resistance on the part of skeptical American political man-

[46] Conversation, September 11, 1991.

[47] The following passage from the political trade magazine *Campaigns and Elections* gives an idea of why the electoral caravan is rare in U.S. politics: "Where legal, get roving vehicles with loudspeakers to travel through targeted precincts . . . some campaigns have caravans of colorful cars with signs and balloons that drive around raising attention for the campaign. But be careful that visibility projects do not anger people. If a voter misses an appointment because she is stuck behind your candidate's car caravan, you may lose a vote." Cathy Allen, "Campaign and Elections' Grassroots Blueprint for Success on Election Day," *Campaigns and Elections*, October/November, 1990.

agers. But more important, the electoral caravan—though recognizably Latin American in form—did not resonate with most Latin American immigrants in Queens. The Latino activists who organized the caravans attempted to translate the Latin American repertoire literally, without taking into consideration the difference of immigrants' position in the United States. The electoral caravan functions, of course, within the framework of formal politics, but for most Latin American immigrants participation in an American setting would mean entering this country's political system. And this they were not prepared to do.

Both the protest and the electoral caravans point to the difficulties of expecting previous repertoires of action to translate neatly into new contexts. In Queens, the old repertoires succeeded only when they resonated with Latin American immigrants' own understanding of their position. The caravan to Kennedy airport succeeded in part because it allowed immigrants to maintain their precarious balance between two worlds. Participation in the electoral caravan, for its part, simply asked too much of them—it would have meant upsetting that balance.

Episodic Politics: Friction and Confrontation

As a result of immigrants' distance from formal politics, American politicians and activists continue to assume that Latin American immigrants are by and large apolitical. Certainly they are less involved in the kind of electoral politics that Americans talk about when they refer to "politics," but it is clear from the above cases that Latin American immigrants are nonetheless involved in a *kind* of politics, with a distinct style of collective action and a distinct focus. Only occasionally do the American and Latin American views of politics converge. This happens when the cultural sphere immigrants are trying to nurture is threatened from outside. In these situations, immigrants mobilize to counter the perceived threat.

Simple misunderstanding can result in confrontation between American authorities and Latin American immigrants. On June 19, 1990, Colombia won a crucial match in the playoffs for the World Cup in soccer, with just seconds to spare. There was immediately, as one press report put it, an impromptu party: "Fans poured out of homes and shouted from windows, and motorists drove around honking their horns and flying the Colombian flag within minutes of the dramatic whistle-beating goal."[48] The immigrant re-

[48] Joseph Queen, "Colombia Soccer Win Stops Queens Traffic," *New York Newsday*, June 20, 1990.

action to the Colombian soccer victory was essentially a spontaneous celebratory caravan, with about a thousand revelers on Roosevelt Avenue stopping traffic for about an hour.[49] When New York police arrived at the scene, however, they arrested people for disorderly conduct and blocking traffic. The incident led to two large community meetings at which Colombian residents, police, and American politicians discussed ways to better cultural understanding. "We explained to them why there was such an explosion of celebration," said one Colombian who participated in these encounters. "And they talked to us about why they had to keep the public order and whatnot . . . that there were norms which had to be enforced which prohibited people from walking in the middle of the street. . . . Something happened because of lack of contact, of communication."[50] Confrontation and mobilization after the soccer riots was only momentary. All that was needed were explanations and apologies. No further negotiation was necessary.

But there have been times when friction has meant the need for more prolonged negotiation. The Latin American parades that make their way down 37th Avenue, for instance, go through the middle of the co-op residential area of Jackson Heights, which is inhabited by mostly white residents—who have habitually complained about the noise and trash produced by the parade. A white businessman, resident for many years in the neighborhood, offered this interpretation: "Some of the people resent [the parades] because they come down 37th Avenue. . . . The old-timers don't want to see the area going over to the Spanish or Hispanics, even though they are not offensive parades."[51] All the complaints, whatever the specifics, revolve around the use of public space and the disruption to the neighborhood—which, it is implied, comes as a result of the influx of immigrants. Several years ago there was an attempt by the community board and homeowner's association in the area to put a stop to the parades. A Puerto Rican organizer recalled: "They were all anti-parade, they wanted the parade to be stopped and all these parades to go. It was a big issue they were making about it. . . . So we went . . . and we met, we met, we worked at this big massive meeting. And all these people who perhaps behind our back were saying 'We'll get rid of their parade,' when they went . . . they didn't say anything in front of us. 'Oh, no, we don't mean you; we don't mean *your* parade.' Maybe they didn't. Maybe they were telling the truth."[52] Partly as a result of the intervention of city officials, negotiations were held among local politi-

[49] Raymond Hernandez, "National Passions at Fore for Games," *New York Times*, July 23, 1995.
[50] Interview (in Spanish), August 9, 1991.
[51] Interview, April 13, 1991.
[52] Interview, August 29, 1991.

cians, white ethnic residents, and Latino organizers. The brief mobilization by immigrant organizations seemed to work.

In 1993, however, the community board intervened again, this time not to ban the parades outright but to restrict their route through the residential area of Jackson Heights. In response, for the first time, the Latin American parade committee, together with a new organization, the Latin American Cultural Center of Queens, have stated they will band together permanently to lobby for the parades to be allowed to march as they have in years past.[53] At least some members, then, of the new immigrant communities are willing to challenge their neighbors on the definition and use of public space.[54] It isn't clear what consequences, if any, this will have on the interactions between the immigrant community and the city's managers and politicians.

Perceived threats to the immigrant community, or to the home country itself, can also spur mobilization within immigrant communities. Disasters or needs in the home country can stimulate organizational efforts, as can disasters and tragedies in the immigrant community itself. Disasters affecting the home country can lead to the mobilization of aid efforts that have long-term organizational consequences in the immigrant community. Disasters affecting the immigrant group itself are both a continuation and a discontinuation of pre-immigration patterns: a continuation in the sense that the driving force is still mutual aid to one's compatriots; a discontinuity in the sense that this help is the result of the realization that if the mobilization of aid does not come from immigrants themselves, there will be no assistance at all—from either the home country or the receiving country.

The Honduran community has been active in the city for decades, especially within the Club de Honduras since 1957. There was a great deal of activity among Honduran groups in response to Honduras's "Soccer War" with El Salvador in 1974, when a soccer match between the countries' teams led first to riots and then bloody border warfare before a cease-fire could be negotiated. But the club's history has mostly been punctuated by internal disputes and divisions. In 1990 the Happy Land social club burned down in the Bronx, killing eighty-seven people, seventy-nine of whom were Hon-

[53] Conversation with Ecuadorian activist, June 2, 1994.

[54] Hernández and Torres-Saillant note another way in which claims for public space are made: in Northern Manhattan, where the Dominican immigrant population is largely concentrated, parents made demands to have schools renamed after major figures in Dominican history. This resulted in the renaming of three schools: the Juan Pablo Duarte School, after the founding father of the Dominican Republic, the Salomé Ureña School, after a 19th-century poet laureate, and Gregorio Luperón School, after a patriotic hero who fought to liberate the country from attempts at foreign annexation (1994: 11).

duran. The victims' deaths were a shock to Hondurans in the city. "The Honduran community [*el pueblo hondureño*] is not used to this," one activist said. "It's the first tragedy the community has suffered in the sixty years they have been here."[55] The Federation of Honduran Entities in New York (FEDEHONY), an umbrella organization of Honduran groups, and the result of the first real attempt to put together a unified pressure group, was formed as a direct response to the Happy Land fire. "We had community organizations, but there were no organizations *representing* the Honduran community itself. So a week or two after [the Happy Land fire] . . . we met in a church . . . and decided to organize a federation," noted one member of the FEDEHONY board. The federation served to coordinate aid to the families of survivors and victims, accompanying them to court and speaking in their behalf. This continued for two years after the fire. By then the federation was negotiating with city to open a permanent Centro Hondureño on city-owned property.[56]

Colombian organizations have also existed for decades in New York, although the Centro Cívico Colombiano, the first organization to own its premises, was opened only in 1980. Several large-scale fund drives have been organized in the immigrant community in response to events in Colombia. In 1985 there was a large collection of donations for the victims of the mudslide that buried the town of Armero, and in 1990 the crash of Avianca flight 052, in addition to sparking the thousand-vehicle protest caravan to Kennedy Airport, also led the Colombian community to organize a huge blood drive. The organizational effort in response to the airline crash ended up spinning off at least three organizations: Colombianos con Amor, a survivor's organization; Colombianos Unidos, which became a general service organization; and the Alianza Iberoamericana. The Federation of Colombian Organizations (FEDOCOL) was formed in 1990 partly in response to the crash, and partly in response to the murder of Pedro Mendez, a functionary in the Colombian Liberal Party in New York City. As the president of FEDOCOL noted, "We thought, why wait to get together only in times of crisis? Why not always work together? . . . The idea was to present [courses of action] to the Colombian community in the different situations that could affect us as Colombians."[57] FEDOCOL has gone on to promote the involvement of Colombians in the politics of the United States, and has sponsored citizenship drives among immigrants.

[55] Author's fieldnotes, Federación de Hondureños en Nueva York meeting, August 8, 1991.
[56] Interview (in Spanish), April 3, 1991. Coalición de Personas Hondureñas, another Honduran service organization, was also formed in response to the Happy Land tragedy. See also Edna Negrón, "Club Tragedy an Awakening for Garifuna," *New York Newsday*, August 18, 1991, p. 23.
[57] Interview (in Spanish); April 12, 1991.

Both the Colombian and Honduran disasters were followed by the formation of umbrella organizations.[58] These serve two purposes: to coordinate the response to the disasters themselves, and to establish a mechanism to respond more effectively to future threats to the immigrant communities. But the formation of these umbrella organizations has made it difficult for the older leadership to sustain organizational focus on the home country. New insurgent leadership used the disasters as an argument for a redirection of efforts toward the problems and needs of Latin American immigrants in New York City. The conflict over the course of immigrant organizations is still underway, and has yet to be resolved.[59]

Mobilization in response to tragedy not only has organizational effects on immigrant groups, but can draw recognition from the American political establishment as well. A rally of five hundred people organized to protest the death of a local Dominican businessman in Corona led in 1991 to the first meeting ever between the New York City Council member for the district and the presidents of the Dominican social clubs in the area. A week after the rally there was an open meeting at one of these clubs, with police precinct captains and the council member in attendance.[60] The meeting was the first sign of any American politician's recognition of the Dominican community in Queens. The eight-hundred-person funerary procession down Roosevelt Avenue in Jackson Heights for Manuel de Dios Unanue, a Cuban journalist assassinated for writing on drug issues, also drew the New York City City Council members from the surrounding districts as well as various police officials.[61] These communal tragedies indicate the potential for mobilization latent among immigrants, and serve, however briefly, to bring this potential to the notice of American politicians.

There is some question whether these mobilizing efforts have any lasting impact. Most organizers believe that the effects from disasters tend to be short-term for the group as whole. On the effects of the 1990 Avianca crash one leader commented: "The accident was like a blow. . . . It had a large impact on the Colombian community. The proof is in the blood drive we had,

[58] The Ecuadorian community, which has had no comparable disaster affecting immigrants here, organized an umbrella organization in 1980 as the result of border skirmishes between Ecuador and Peru, and provided a framework for flood relief for Ecuador soon after. Conversation, Ecuadorian activist, September 10, 1992.

[59] The conflict is not only about focus of but also about organizational turf battles among leadership factions. Conversation, president of FEDOCOL, August 6, 1991; conversation, Tim Golden, reporter, *New York Times*, April 1, 1991.

[60] Author's fieldnotes, meeting at the Club Hermanos Unidos de Queens, September 18, 1991.

[61] Author's fieldnotes, mass for Manuel de Dios Unanue, March 27, 1992. See also Ian Fisher, "Slain Editor Honored at Mass as Fearless Warrior," *New York Times*, March 19, 1992, p. B3.

which was a great success. . . . But I don't believe [it had a long term effect]."[62] On the other hand, an Ecuadorian activist commented that the tragedy had made people aware that there was a substantial Colombian community here, and that "it's not a community that can be ignored. . . . And maybe there was the realization that they are still seen as 'immigrants.' They don't have political power, or a strong voice."[63] While disasters may shift the patterns of immigrant organizations, they do not completely resocialize immigrants by themselves. Resocialization from these communal tragedies is marginal compared to the scale of the socialization effects shown, say, for American adolescents growing up during the years of antiwar and civil rights protests in the 1960s. However, there may be more focused effects among activists. Studies have shown that former activists continue to display an orientation distinct from the rest of their generational cohort, and that activism seems to foster a lasting political consciousness and broad interest in social issues (McAdam 1989; DeMartini 1983; see also Fendrich 1977). It may be that those who are involved in active roles in these local disaster efforts, or those who directly experienced the disasters themselves, then become socialized to participate more actively in other organizational, particularly political, arenas. Organizations or coalitions founded by individuals in response to specific threats to the community persist beyond the duration of the threat, and often turn their energies to broader needs and concerns of the immigrant population in the receiving country.

In retrospect, it is easy to see why there is such misunderstanding between Latino immigrants and American politicians. Contact between Latin American immigrant social, cultural, and civic associations and the American political system in Queens is almost always brief and episodic. From the point of view of most of those involved in these Latino groups, the purpose of such contact is only to defuse the problem or crisis at hand, not to establish permanent links. Likewise for American politicians, immigrant organizations seem to surface when there is trouble and then to disappear again. The City Council member for the district said he often wondered if there were any immigrant organizations out there at all. "I know hundreds of people," he said, "and none of them know of any Latino groups holding regular meetings."[64] There are in fact dozens of institutionalized immigrant organizations, but none that are what local politicians are looking for—an

[62] Interview (in Spanish), president, Centro Cívico Colombiano, April 1, 1991.
[63] Interview (in Spanish), February 24, 1992.
[64] Conversation, March 30, 1992.

organization that can be co-opted to play an advocacy role for immigrants, mediating for them in the American political system. If such a group appeared, Hispanic immigrants could then be treated as just another interest group with easily recognizable, coherent demands. Latin American immigrant organizations have refused, thus far, to play this role. They have kept their distance, avoiding getting too involved or making irrevocable commitments in the United States.

Latin American immigrant organizations choose to maintain their position as outsiders as a way of preserving a certain amount of autonomy from the demands of both the United States and their countries of origin. This autonomy is expressed through a "politics of in-between," the goal of which is to simultaneously maintain distance and ties to both polities through the manipulation of immigrants' multiple identities, drawing on continuities from their countries of origin, but tailoring action to their situation as immigrants in this country. The "politics of in-between," expressed through the organizational and group life of immigrants, shapes how they mobilize collectively, and the timing of this mobilization. In this sense, immigrant politics are not simply irregular, sporadic mobilizations, as it might seem if viewed from the outside. Rather, these mobilizations are like ocean islands—occasionally breaking the surface of the water, but as part of a continuous organizational life that sustains these startling appearances in the larger public space.

IV

BREAKING THE IMPASSE

8

Wanting It Both Ways: The Quest for Dual Citizenship

The swells of immigrant political mobilization are based on a substratum of first-generation immigrant organizations which encompass a range of religious, professional, and social groups. These institutions are often constructed to maintain a link between immigrants and their countries of origin, but they must also resolve the dilemma confronting all Latin American immigrants in the city: how to reconcile the demands pulling them in seemingly irreconcilable directions? How to recognize connections to their home countries while accepting the realities of settlement?

The fundamental logic to their responses differs according to gender. Men undergo not only the disruption of the immigration experience, and with it the rupture of family and social networks, but also a relative loss of status as they negotiate entry into the economic sphere of the receiving country. Well-educated and comparatively middle-class in their countries of origin, Latin American immigrant men initially take jobs in the receiving country with status and class positions well below those they held before immigrating. The immigrant organizations they form compensate for the loss of status by providing a social arena where a migrant's previous status is recognized and bolstered. This is particularly true of those seeking organizational or leadership roles.

Women, on the other hand, usually enter the labor market with less previous work experience, so although they may hold low-status jobs, they experience less downward mobilization in the job market and suffer less loss of status. In fact, women working for pay gain a greater say in the household, which gives them an increased incentive to stay in the United States. Moreover, through their children, women come into contact with a much broader range of public institutions than men. Immigrant organizations generally deny leadership positions to women, so women's contact with American governmental institutions provides them with an alternative route to mobilization. The structuring of social and economic experiences in the United States leads to very different kinds of organizational incentives for immigrant women and men.

Men and women respond very differently to the conflicting pressures of home country and receiving nation. While immigrant Latino men are more likely to favor continuity in patterns of socialization and organization, immigrant Latinas are more likely to favor change. This difference in emphasis leads to corresponding differences in strategy for resolving their ambiguous position as immigrants between two nations. In this chapter, I lay out the organizational strategies of the largely male-dominated first-generation immigrant organizations. In Chapter 9, I discuss the political pathway followed by first-generation activist women.

Men's Organizational Logic

Mainstream first-generation immigrant organizations, dominated by a male leadership, are likely to be concerned with keeping ties to the home country intact. But even those organizations committed to an ideology of return begin to feel the pressures from competing loyalties. Confronted with a choice between mutually irreconcilable polities, Latin American immigrants in Queens often try to negotiate a space in between that allows them to avoid making irrevocable decisions. However, this in-between politics is inherently unstable. The passage of time, the increasing permanence of the settlement, and the growth of the second generation all increase the pressure on first-generation immigrants to find some way to resolve the dilemma. If they continue to do nothing, simply living in the in-between, then they are adrift—at the mercy of other forces. Faced with high costs in choosing full membership and participation in the United States, immigrants choose other strategies. Instead of directly trying to surmount the obstacles keeping them from full membership and participation, immigrants choose instead to detour around them.

Latin American immigrant men, working within organizations that are largely oriented toward the countries of origin, seek to defuse the pressure of dual loyalties in the way they know best—by appealing to their home countries—lobbying for dual citizenship so they can lower the costs of participation and membership in the two states in which they have ties. Here the contributions immigrants make in terms of remittances and campaign funds directed at their countries of origin give them leverage to demand, and largely receive, a clarification of their status as citizens. By attempting to secure permanent status as nationals in their home countries, immigrants are paradoxically affirming their attachment to the United States, for dual citizenship lowers the costs of naturalization and participation in the American polity.

Downward Male Mobility

Studies of immigrant earnings have shown that immigrants usually experience a decline in income and occupational status after arriving in the United States. This is particularly true for Latin American immigrant men in Queens, who often immigrate to the United States with an education, training, and a set of skills which would place them within the middle class in their home countries. Chiswick's study of male immigrants entering the United States in the late 1960s and early '70s shows earnings at the time of entry on average 15 percent below that of native-born men with the same demographic characteristics—education, age, numbers of weeks worked, and so forth. Schooling and work experience of migrants have a smaller effect on U.S. earnings than comparable skills acquired by the native-born (Chiswick 1980). Chiswick's data indicated, nevertheless, that earnings parity would be achieved fairly quickly as a result of the motivation and abilities of most immigrants. Fourteen years after arrival, immigrants would be earning as much as native-born Americans; thirty years after entry, immigrants' income would be 10 percent higher than that of comparable American males (Chiswick, 1978).

Other studies have confirmed that after substantial initial loss of occupational status, immigrants tend to be upwardly mobile. For example, Gurak's 1981 survey of 904 Colombian and Dominican first-generation immigrants living in non–Puerto Rican areas in Manhattan and Queens, found significant upward mobility for respondents from the first jobs they held in this country to those they held just before or during the survey. Immigrants' first jobs were often as unskilled industrial labor. Approximately 63 percent had their first jobs in the manufacturing sector (about 36 percent in garment manufacturing), but mobility out of this sector was relatively rapid (Gurak and Kritz 1988a: 43). With each succeeding job, migrants moved further away from manufacturing, into clerical or sales work and, to a lesser extent, professional or management positions. Both Colombian and Dominican men experienced substantial mobility, and once they took their first jobs here, Colombian men had almost no downward mobility. About 12 percent of Dominican men and women were downwardly mobile after their first job, while 9 percent of Colombian women and only 3 percent of Colombian men were (ibid.: 19).

Other researchers have been less optimistic. Borjas's studies of immigration (1990, 1989) indicate that at time of entry (at age twenty) men who migrated between 1975 and 1979 earned 21 percent less than native-born Americans. He projected that in twenty years' time the gap would narrow to 13 percent, but even after forty years the predicted wage differential would be, on average, 12 percent. While immigrants arriving in the United States in the late 1960s did better at matching native-born Americans' wage levels, those arriving in the 1970s did much worse, and decades later the earnings of both cohorts were likely to remain below the earnings of the native-born. Borjas concludes that "new waves of immigrants are unlikely to assimilate fully into the U.S. labor market during their lifetimes" (1990: 107). Most analysts take this more pessimistic view that immigrants' occupational position declines upon arrival, and their earnings may never equal those of workers born in the United States.[1]

Portes and Bach's study (1985) goes beyond an analysis of immigrant earnings to examine the decline in occupational status and diminished expectations experienced by male immigrants. They conducted three surveys of the same group of Mexican and Cuban immigrants from 1973 to 1979, tracking occupational mobility and attitudinal changes over time. Their results indicate that both groups suffered significant initial downward mobility. While Mexicans at the lower end of the occupational scale were somewhat upwardly mobile, there were steep declines in the proportion of those who were employed as white-collar and intermediate service workers (clerks, tailors, barbers, and so forth). Cuban immigrants, who were more middle-class than their Mexican counterparts (25 percent had been in white-collar occupations before leaving Cuba), experienced even greater downward mobility. After three years in the United States only 10 percent held white-

[1] Historically only a small fraction of immigrants to the U.S. were able to progress to a better occupation during their lifetimes (Bodnar, 1985: 169–75). On this issue Bodnar concludes: "Although most immigrants had no other direction to go but upward if they remained in the United States, the overall impression from historical mobility studies is that such movement was an unrealistic expectation in their lifetimes . . . significant occupational mobility was not normally part of the immigrant experience in industrial America" (ibid.: 170–71). Cited in Borjas 1990. See also Barry Eichengreen and Henry A. Gemery, "The Earnings of Skilled and Unskilled Immigrants at the End of the Nineteenth Century," *Journal of Economic History* 46 (June 1986): 441–54; and Chiswick 1978. Related studies include: Francine Blau, "Immigration and Earnings in Early Twentieth Century America," *Research in Population Economics* 2 (1980): 21–41; Gregory deFreitas, "The Earnings of Immigrants in the American Labor Market," Ph.D. diss., Columbia University, 1980; and Long 1980.

collar jobs. Former white-collar workers swelled the proportion of Cuban immigrants who held positions as semiskilled industrial workers (a category of jobs held by 8 percent in Cuba, but by 29 percent in this country), unskilled laborers (which rose from 5 percent to 10 percent), and skilled laborers (from 7 percent in Cuba to 13 percent in the United States). These figures are, Portes and Bach note, "a reflection of the downward shift in the entire group's occupational status" (1985: 191).

There is no doubt that the initial downward mobility shared by most male immigrants is traumatic. In interviews in Queens, informants often related vivid stories of their first job experiences. For many middle-class immigrants from Latin America arrival in the U.S. meant having to do manual labor for the first time in their lives. A Colombian man told me that at home he had worked in the Central Bank, but had been laid off: "I came here to work . . . Here there is work, if and when you look for it. . . The first place I worked was [in a factory] putting the legs onto ladders. I had never done manual work in my life. I had always worked in an office."[2] This downward mobility can be a discouraging experience. "Take the case of professionals," said the president of the Ateneo Ecuatoriano, himself a doctor. "They become completely disillusioned . . . they have to survive however they can, doing whatever they can."[3] There are a lot of professionals who end up driving cabs, and washing dishes in restaurants, said the director of a Latin American social agency.[4] This strikes hard, noted a Colombian, "in the general case of the professional . . . the educated person . . . a former bank employee for instance, who finds himself here with an ignorant person from Guatemala, cleaning floors together."[5]

Perhaps as important as their initial downward mobility is the gap between the jobs immigrants aspired to and those they ended up holding. For example, in Portes and Bach's study, in 1973 four out of every five Mexican immigrant men aspired to skilled employment; only one in five had achieved it by 1979. In addition, 11 percent were employed as unskilled laborers in 1979, though only 5 percent had initially expected such jobs. The gap between Cuban migrants' occupational expectations and their subsequent attainments was even greater. Nearly 32 percent had aspired to intermediate service work; only 5.9 percent held positions in this sector by 1979. Few of those who had wanted to become professionals (13.8 percent in 1973) had

[2] Interview (in Spanish), September 10, 1991.

[3] Interview (in Spanish), May 10, 1991.

[4] Interview (in Spanish), July 23, 1991.

[5] Interview (in Spanish), July 16, 1991. Aside from betraying the upper-middle class prejudice of the speaker, with its emphasis on "being cultured" and having an education, the remark also reflects the perceived hierarchy among Latin American countries.

reached their goal (6.4 percent) by 1979. Although by 1979 they had partially recovered their lost status, Mexican and Cuban migrants still had not reached the level of their original occupations or achieved their expectations for life in the United States (Portes and Bach, 1985: 196).

Maintaining Status

The loss of occupational status may not be crucial, however, to immigrants' sense of identity and definitions of success. As we saw in Chapter 5, most Latin Americans who emigrate to the United States for economic reasons are often uncertain how long they will stay in this country. Many come as sojourners, with thoughts of going back after a few years.[6] Asked why they came to this country, many male immigrants say they want to improve their economic situation.[7] But the fruits of their efforts are not meant to be enjoyed here. As one Dominican man put it, "I just want to make enough [to live well in the Dominican Republic], and then go back."[8] In their home countries many of these migrants are perched precariously on the edge of the middle class.[9] As migrants, they succeed by accumulating as much as possible as quickly as possible and then returning. The income they earn here may be enough to bolster and secure their class status at home (Pessar 1987: 104; Bray 1984). To accomplish their goal, immigrants take on work they would not normally consider in their home countries—as factory laborers, for instance. A Colombian woman pointed out that "a lot of people are satisfied, say, with looking for a job and earning good money; they say 'This is sufficient, because I'm not going to stay here long—I'm going back to Colombia.'"[10] Thus finding a job—any job—is more important than job security or benefits.[11]

If short-term accumulation is the goal that immigrants, particularly sojourners, seek, then immediate short-term downward mobility may not mat-

[6] It is important to maintain the distinction between the *ideology* of return and what immigrants actually do. Many migrants remain in the U.S. far beyond the time they intended, and many end up staying permanently (see Chapter 5).
[7] See note 2, Chapter 5.
[8] Conversation (in Spanish), March 15, 1991.
[9] See note 9, Chapter 5.
[10] Interview (in Spanish), August 28, 1991.
[11] According to Hoskin (1989) those who anticipate only a temporary stay will most likely limit their expectations to economic betterment (see also Castles and Kosack 1973; Rist 1978; Piore 1979; Portes and Bach 1985). Pessar notes that it may seem odd that women garment workers are overwhelmingly satisfied with their work, in spite of the fact that many Americans would see them as working in dead-end working class jobs. But these jobs allow them to invest in consumer products which give them increased social standing in their home country (Pessar 1987).

ter so much to them if they are earning enough to save for their return. Nonetheless, they may act to minimize their status inconsistency—the difference between education and abilities achieved and recognized in their countries of origin, and the occuational positions they hold in this country—in two ways. First, they may decide to remain within an ethnic enclave, or in the absence of a full enclave, at least to stay within the labor market networks established by co-nationals or other Latinos. In these ethnic enclaves migrants are sheltered from some of the ruptures brought about by immigration—the loss of localized kin and social networks, the inability to transfer skills and education, and the like. As long as they do not leave the enclave, they may be able to apply their knowledge and contribute their skills in much the same way they did in their country of origin. Portes and Wilson argue that the "payoff of education, occupational status, and objective information appears as great among those employed in enclave enterprises as for those working in the mainstream center economy" (1980: 314; see also Portes and Bach 1975). Though the income and occupational effects of the enclave economy have been challenged or qualified by other researchers (Gilbertson and Gurak 1993; Zhou and Logan 1989; Sanders and Nee, 1987), it is clear that ethnic enclaves provide social benefits as well, among the most important of which is sustaining male immigrants' self-image by bringing them together with others in the same situation.

The second way in which male immigrants can assuage their feelings of status inconsistency is through participation in immigrant organizations.[12] Migrant sojourners join organizations to reconstruct the social networks and perpetuate socialization patterns of the home country. The president of the Comité Cívico Ecuatoriano said that "when I came to this country, I sat inside my apartment, and went from home to work and back again. I didn't know the other Ecuadorians I came into contact with. Eventually I started going to social clubs. I ran into people I didn't even know were here, people I knew from back home."[13] Ethnic organizations offer immigrants an alternative to adaptation to the receiving country by providing an environment which, like the ethnic enclave, recognizes their social standing in spite of whatever downward economic mobility they may have suffered in

[12] Association members are disproportionately male (Georges 1984: 17). Immigrants participate in these organizations even though the costs in time and energy are high. As one Colombian activist put it: "If I had two jobs, one in a factory, and one in something else—sweeping and cleaning somewhere—I wouldn't be able to sit down like we do, for a meeting of two or three hours. Because I would rather rest." Interview, August 14, 1991. Many people attend immigrant community events that have low costs and some entertainment value; dances are very popular, as are the yearly festivals and parades. But active membership generally comes after some time in the United States, especially after achieving economic stability.

[13] Interview (in Spanish), July 12, 1991.

the United States.[14] The president of the Organization of Colombian Professionals noted:

> There are many professionals who feel completely isolated because of the fact of their having been professionals, and then coming to this country and finding a completely different situation; it produces chaos. So we have to extract the professional [from his life here] even if he's working in a factory, and we invite him to our meetings, and we make him participate. There's nothing in our by-laws that asks whether a person is [still] a professional; as long as they have graduated from a university . . . we don't even worry if they are illegal or citizens. . . . Many find a satisfaction in meeting professionals again, and talking of things that a person often doesn't have the opportunity to talk about. Often a person arrives to this country completely alone, without—from the social perspective—any contact at all other than with a class of persons with no education, and in poor working conditions.[15]

In this manner the problem of status inconsistency is, to a degree, set aside —again, as long as immigrant men remain in the social environs of immigrant organizations.[16]

In the social networks of the ethnic economic enclave and those of the immigrant organization, a Latin American male's status depends, initially at least, on what he was *before*, not what he is now. Based on his status in his home country, he will be welcomed into organizations in this country where members hold similar status, regardless of his current occupation.[17] His status in an immigrant organization, however, depends on whether he would

[14] This situation resembles Wirth's description of immigrants nearly seventy years ago: "As the colony grows, the immigrant finds in it a social world. In the colony he meets with sympathy, understanding and encouragement. There he finds his fellow countrymen who understand his habits and standards and share his life experience and viewpoint. In the colony he has status, plays a role in the group. In the life of the colony's streets and cafes, in its church and benevolent societies, he finds response and security. In the colony he finds that he can live, be somebody, satisfy his wishes—all of which is impossible in the strange world outside" (1929: 141).

[15] Interview (in Spanish), July 16, 1991.

[16] This clannishness can be frustrating when viewed from the perspective of the political activist. A Puerto Rican activist in Queens asked "What are we doing in Queens? . . . Everyone in their little group. . . . Power is concentrated in their families and their communities. They really don't want to talk to Americans. . . . I don't understand it, I try to understand it; believe me, I try. I try to comprehend people who become doctors, they become lawyers, they own their own businesses and then they stay within the immediate safe environment of that community." Interview, June 10, 1991.

[17] Organizations are implicitly organized along Latin American class lines. Professional organizations cater to upper-middle-class professionals, social and cultural organizations to a broader middle class, and sports organizations to the middle and lower middle class. See Sassen-Koob 1979; Altamirano 1990.

hold his original status again if he returned. His status here is provisional, and dependent on his status in his home country. Thus a man may find it in his interest to emphasize his ties to his country of origin, and the possibility of his return, however hypothetical. This emphasis, of course, has effects on the political and organizational life of the immigrant community.

With the loss of status in the receiving country, men tend to form and lead ethnic organizations whose focus is the country of origin. There are dozens of such Latin American immigrant organizations in Queens. They all raise money for charitable concerns such as orphanages and hospitals in the home country. For example, the Dominican club Hermanos Unidos, in Corona, collects money for gifts and medical supplies to take down to poor neighborhoods in the Dominican Republic each year. They give out sports equipment, clothing, wheelchairs, and crutches, among other things, to children, the elderly, and the infirm of their hometowns.[18]

Because of the role ethnic institutions play in validating social status achieved in the home country, men are generally not interested in seeing ethnic institutions shift their orientation toward the receiving country. Such a shift would undermine their provisional status, particularly if they were newly arrived, and particularly if they are leaders in the organizations. Leadership positions are almost entirely filled by men,[19] and leaders especially depend on the homeward orientation of the immigrant organizations for their status in the immigrant community.[20] Thus in the short run the organizations in the immigrant community will be unlikely to serve as instruments of resocialization by redirecting immigrants' focus to social and political issues in the United States.

Hoskin writes "almost by definition, ethnic organizations value continuity of identification over change to the norms of the host society" (1989: 354). While she may be correct, she does not offer an explanation of *why* organizations might retard immigrant orientation to the receiving country.

[18] Author's fieldnotes, Club Hermanos Unidos, December 6, 1992.

[19] For men's views about women's lack of capacity for leadership, see Chapter 9. Women hold office in immigrant women's organizations, but in settings with both sexes present they are rarely elected to the presidency or vice-presidency. More often they hold the position of "secretary"—a position with a great deal of responsibility but very little power to lead or command. Women's position in these organizations is changing, but very slowly.

[20] The editor of the *Noticiero Colombiano* noted that there is an immigrant upper middle class that has assimilated into American society and lost contact with what they would call the "ghetto," but they come back every now and then to eat at a restaurant, or go dancing. Ethnic leadership does not come from this stratum, he said, but from bourgeois professionals whose clientele live in areas of ethnic concentration (a kind of Gramscian "organic" leadership). But for these professionals from outside, leadership is purely instrumental, not a matter of ethnic loyalty: "If they were practicing law in a Chinese neighborhood, they would suddenly become interested in the problems of the Chinese." Interview (in Spanish), February 24, 1992.

I argue that gendered social roles and expectations explain a great deal about the continuation of patterns of socialization and organization from the home country. As the years pass, however, things may change. First, if and when a different status is obtained as the result of upward mobility in the new society, then it may be less painful for men to change the direction of immigrant organizations. Of course if immigrants are not successful in rebuilding their status, they may redouble efforts to maintain a social sphere separate from the society they live in, enforcing ethnic boundaries and maintaining an ideology of return to the home country. The second possibility is that a younger leadership, primarily born or raised in the United States, will eventually challenge the first-generation immigrant leaders and attempt to reorient the focus of these organizations. As of now this potential for change in orientation is only slowly being realized. However, there is one final possibility for change—through the adoption of dual citizenship.

Resolving the Dilemma through Dual Citizenship

Some of the leadership of Latin American immigrant organizations have made an attempt to resolve, or at least attenuate, the dilemma of choosing between two mutually exclusive political identities by pushing for dual citizenship in their countries of birth. In theory, dual citizenship allows immigrants to become American citizens without losing all their rights as nationals in their country of origin. Though the United States does not formally recognize dual citizenship, in practice an immigrant can retain his or her nationality in two (or more) countries at once. An American citizen cannot claim a formal attachment to another country, but a citizen from another country may, upon taking on American citizenship, passively retain citizenship rights in their country of origin if it does not recognize, or is indifferent to, the new attachment formed in the United States.[21] At the time of this writing, eight Latin American countries—Argentina, Uruguay, Panama, El Salvador, Brazil, and most recently Colombia, Ecuador, and the Dominican Republic—have recognized the continuation of nationality despite the acquisition of citizenship in another country. Several other countries, including Mexico, are seeking to follow their example.

[21] See section 349 (a) of the Immigration and Nationality Act [8 U.S.C. 148]. In order for loss of U.S. citizenship to occur, it must be established that citizenship in another country was obtained voluntarily by a person 18 years or older with the intention of relinquishing United States citizenship. Even if a person acquires another nationality, and goes as far as to serve in another country's government or military, if they do not have the express intention of giving up their American citizenship it is difficult to lose it.

Argentina, Uruguay, and Panama have formally recognized dual citizenship of their nationals in other countries for decades.[22] Argentina and Uruguay have followed the Italian model: citizenship is acquired at birth, and cannot be abrogated by other subsequent changes in allegiance or status. Citizens abroad retain rights even if they naturalize in another country, and can retain the use of both passports. If they wish, they can participate in the elections of the home country upon their return. In this model, dual citizenship allows immigrants to take on other political allegiances without jeopardizing their standing with their countries of origin. It may not allow them full and equal political rights while residing abroad, but it usually allows for the recuperation of those rights if and when immigrants return to the home country. Brazil and El Salvador are more recent examples of this top-down approach, orchestrated from within the legislature as a kind of afterthought, with little concerted pressure from the immigrant community abroad.[23]

In the Colombian, Ecuadorian, and Dominican cases the impetus for dual citizenship came from these countries' populations in the United States, particularly New York City, and not from within these nations themselves. Immigrants repatriate hundreds of millions of dollars a year to their kin in Latin America, having a significant impact on local economies (Gurak and Kritz 1984; Portes and Grosfoguel 1994). Settlements of immigrants from all three countries have become important campaign stops for politicians seeking to raise funds for political races in these countries. Immigrants have been able to translate this economic muscle into political leverage, winning concessions from political parties and legislatures in their countries of origin regularizing their status as citizens and allowing dual citizenship, ownership of land, and easy access when returning, among other things. The successes of some nationalities have inspired other immigrant groups in New York City to petition and lobby for similar benefits.

Colombian organizations in New York began lobbying in Colombia for dual citizenship after meeting with a group of visiting Colombian senators

[22] Uruguay at least since the establishment of its 1967 constitution, and Panama at least since its 1972 constitution. Caribbean countries with large percentages of their populations abroad have also allowed dual citizenship from very early on. St. Vincent and Grenada, for instance, have offered full citizenship to their subjects abroad regardless of other allegiances they may take (Basch, Schiller, and Szanton-Blanc 1994: 127).

[23] See Marc Margolis, "South America: Constitutional Reform Flickers out in Brazil," *Los Angeles Times*, April 23, 1994, p. A2. In seven months of attempting constitutional reform, Brazil's congress was largely ineffectual, passing only four minor changes. One of these was allowing Brazilians with foreign passports the right to dual citizenship. El Salvador passed its dual nationality law in 1980, just as the country embarked on a ten-year civil war. By its end, a tenth of the Salvadoran population were refugees abroad.

in 1987. The timing was propitious. About a year later, with the process of constitutional reform underway in Colombia, they received notice that some legislators would work to see that changes would be introduced favoring Colombian nationals abroad. A group of Colombians in New York immediately set up a committee—the Comité Colombiano Pro-Reforma Institutional: Doble Nacionalidad y Circunscripción Electoral en el Exterior—which, among other things, collected 5,000 signatures at the Colombian Festival held in Flushings Meadow Park that year in support of a petition in favor of dual citizenship.[24] The amended constitution was approved in Colombia on July 4, 1991, incorporating guarantees for Colombians overseas.[25] Included were provisions that allowed Colombians overseas to become citizens of another country without losing their rights as Colombians, to elect a senator to represent them from abroad, and to vote directly in Colombia's presidential elections.[26] The Colombian success demonstrated to other Latin American immigrant groups in New York City that lobbying the home country for dual citizenship provisions could in fact be effective.

Ecuadorians' effort first began in 1967, when a group of immigrants in New York petitioned for the right of citizens abroad to vote in Ecuador's elections; there was, however, no response from the Ecuadorian government (a military regime at the time). In 1979 a group of Ecuadorian expatriates in Queens put together an organization to lobby for dual citizenship (Ecuatorianos por la Consecución y Conservación de la Doble Nacionalidad), and submitted a formal proposal; again there was no response from the government.[27] In 1983 an Ecuadorian congressional committee proposed that citizens abroad should participate in national elections from overseas consulates (following the Colombian model), but the proposal was shelved. After 1990, with concomitant proposals being discussed in Colombia, the pace picked up: letters were sent from the immigrant community in

[24] Conversation, president, Colombian Charities, May 13, 1992.

[25] It's curious to note how minuscule a role dual citizenship played in the debates on constitutional reform in the Asamblea Constitucional. In Colombia itself people were much more interested, for example, in whether divorce would be allowed for Catholics, departmental governors would be elected directly, or abortion legalized. "Poll by El Tiempo, Radio Caracol, and CNC: Opinions Divided on Recall Elections," *El Tiempo* (Bogotá, Colombia), May 27, 1991, p. A1, reported in FBIS *Latin American Report*, July 8, 1991, pp. 54–58.

[26] Flyer, FEDOCOL, Segundo Foro Cívico, June 9, 1991; also "A Partir de Hoy Entra en Vigencia Nueva Constitución de Colombia," *Noticias del Mundo*, July 5, 1991, and "La Colombia de Jackson Heights," *El Diario/La Prensa*, July 18, 1991.

[27] Carlos Garcia, "Piden al Congreso y Gobierno Ley Doble Nacionalidad," *Noticias del Mundo*, September 18, 1991.

New York and elsewhere to the legislature in Quito; dual ditizenship was endorsed by the Sixth Congress of the Federation of Ecuadorian Organizations in 1991, and a delegation representing Ecuadorians in New York was sent to argue their case in March 1992.[28] With Colombia close to approving dual citizenship that year, Ecuadorians seemed ready to follow their example. The Extraordinary Congress convoked to amend the constitution became stalemated, however, and was dissolved, throwing the future of the project in doubt.[29] After some fits and starts, the Ecuadorian legislature finally approved dual nationality in May 1995.

The debate over dual citizenship for Dominicans abroad also accelerated after 1990. A constitutional amendment had been debated in the Dominican Republic for at least ten years (Georges 1984: 36). Both of the major political parties supported some kind of dual citizenship provision in theory, but legislation was never approved. The possibility of dual citizenship seemed a convenient symbolic gesture made to the large immigrant community in the United States. In 1992, for instance, then-president Joaquín Balaguer released a statement indicating he favored the idea, but there was no effort to actually see it through into law.[30] The Dominican legislature began reforms in 1994 to establish the principle of dual citizenship, but it was the presidential elections of 1996 that signaled a real shift. Both candidates who made it to the final round said they favored legislation legalizing dual citizenship and permitting Dominicans living abroad to vote wherever they live—perhaps at the closest consulate. (If implemented, this change would make the New York metropolitan area the second largest concentration of potential voters in Dominican presidential elections, exceeded only by Santo Domingo, the capital.) During the campaign the newly elected president, Leonel Fernandez Reyna, had said he planned to establish a "Ministry of the Diaspora," and José Francisco Peña-Gomez, the defeated candidate, had promised to allow the election of congressional deputies to represent Dominicans living abroad.[31] Legislation allowing dual citizenship was passed by the Dominican House of Deputies in 1996.

[28] Eudoro Hinojosa, "La Doble Nacionalidad Ecuatoriana: Cronolgía y Progreso," *Noticias del Mundo,* July 1, 1992.

[29] Carlos Garcia, "Irrenunciabilidad Nacionalidad Ecuatoriana es Grata Realidad," *Noticias del Mundo,* January 14, 1994; "En Grave Peligro Aprobación de Irrenunciabilidad de la Ciudadanía Ecuatoriana," *Noticias del Mundo,* March 2, 1994.

[30] "Balaguer Favorece Doble Nacionalidad Dominicanos," *Noticias del Mundo,* May 29, 1992; Reginaldo Atanay, "Para Los Dominicanos: Es Bueno Ser Ciudadanos de EEUU?" *El Diario/La Prensa,* March 12, 1992.

[31] Larry Rohter, "New York's Dominicans Taking Big Role in Island Elections," *New York Times,* June 29, 1996, pp. A1, A24.

The Success of Immigrant Lobbying

The Colombian, Ecuadorian, and Dominican successes raise at least two questions: Why, if immigrants were seeking to lower costs of participation in the American system, did they turn to lobbying their countries of origin? And why should their home countries have paid them any attention? The answers are interrelated. It is significant, but not surprising, that the appeals are being directed toward their home country, and not worked out through the political system here in the United States. Migrants provide remittances to their families,[32] which are a major source of small investment funds and foreign currency exchange for many countries in Latin America and the Caribbean (Basch, Schiller, and Szamton-Blanc 1994: 259).[33] Political candidates routinely come to the United States to raise money for their campaigns in the home countries and to build ties with the community abroad. As a consequence, immigrants have leverage with these politicians, in both opposition and governing parties, in a way they do not (yet) with candidates and elected officials in American politics.

Dominicans residing in New York, for example, have long been an important source of contributions for political campaigns in the Dominican Republic. Dominican politicians routinely make trips to the city to hold fund-raisers for their political campaigns back home, emphasizing the ties between the two communities. While running for president in 1996, for instance, Leonel Fernandez capitalized on his New York upbringing: "I am a product of New York City" he proclaimed.[34] Incomes which, in absolute terms, are several times the norm for their compatriots in their country of origin make Dominicans in New York significant potential campaign donors, and the importance of these funds has increased as the community has grown larger, more established, and more prosperous. Dominicans in New York probably raise hundreds of thousands of dollars for Dominican politicians in Dominican election cycles, much of it at $150-a-head dinners in Washington Heights, Corona, or the Bronx.[35] Peña-Gomez, the runner-

[32] No reliable data exists on the total value of these remittances, since most of the money is sent through private or unofficial channels. However, remittances to Mexico have been estimated at $3.6 billion, and those to El Salvador at more than $150 million, every year. See Donna Mungen, "Los Angeles Times Interview: José Angel Pescador," *Los Angeles Times*, April 7, 1996, p. M3, and Montes Mozo and Garcia Vasquez 1988.

[33] Basch, Schiller, and Szanton-Blanc note, too, that Filipinos abroad are now requesting the right to vote in Phillipine elections; the right to own land in the Phillipines while a foreign citizen without special regulation; dual citizenship; and the right to run for office while a dual citizen (1994: 259).

[34] Rohter, "Island Elections."

[35] Ibid.

up in the 1996 presidential race, said the role that Dominicans in New York play "is absolutely decisive." As a major source of political donations, Dominicans in New York are worth placating. So when they asked for changes that would regularize their membership status in their country of origin, Dominican politicians were receptive. However, it should be noted that the laws were relatively easy to pass—they are largely symbolic and hence relatively costless. Allowing Dominicans to vote in national elections from abroad and giving them representation in the national assembly are much more controversial and costly, and hence less likely to be implemented.[36]

The Mexican case is slightly different, being driven not only by the growing presence and economic potential of Mexican immigrants in the United States, but also by Mexican party politics. By the time of the 1988 presidential elections in Mexico, California and Texas were well-established campaign stops for Mexican politicians in the opposition parties of the Partido Autonomo Nacional (PAN) and Partido Revolucionario Democrático (PRD), and, increasingly, for the governing Partido Revolucionario Institucional (PRI) as well. Governors of Mexican states met regularly with residents abroad for consultations, support, and contributions.[37] For the first time, Mexican opposition parties directly appealed to the emigrant vote by promising dual citizenship rights and the ability to vote from Mexican consulates in the United States. The PRD, in fact, launched a petition drive to collect signatures from Mexican nationals in California supporting the voting rights of Mexicans in the United States.[38] The 1988 elections were a warning signal to the ruling PRI party that the Mexican expatriate electorate was up for grabs, but it was only with the broader opening in Mexican politics in the summer of 1996 that the PRI, along with the opposition parties, agreed in principle to a series of political reforms including a commitment to a constitutional amendment that would give Mexican nationals residing abroad the right to cast absentee ballots for president in the year 2000 (like Colombians in the United States).[39] In spite of the large numbers of potential vot-

[36] Currently to vote in a national election, Dominicans abroad must return to vote in their home country. Proposals to allow voting from abroad were, as of 1997, still under discussion.

[37] During 1990 and 1991, the governors of the states of Zacatecas, Chihuahua, Jalisco, Nayarit, Sinaloa, and Baja California visited Los Angeles (most of them more than once) to meet with their respective *colonias*. Immigrant communities of people from Oaxaca, Durango, Michoacán, and Colima are also working to establish relationships with the governments of their home states (Gonzalez Guttierez 1993: 229).

[38] Dresser 1993: 100. See also "A Mexican Right to Vote from Abroad: A Key Strategy for Expanding Mexican Democracy" proposal presented to the statewide meeting of the PRD, Riverside, California, July 1, 1991.

[39] Sam Dillon, "Major Party Deal in Mexico to Bring Political Reforms," *New York Times*, July 27, 1996, pp. A1–A2; Sam Dillon, "Mexico Is Near to Granting Expatriates Voting Rights," *New York*

ers in the United States (somewhere between 500,000 and five million[40]), it is unlikely, if the experience of other countries is any indication, that anywhere near a majority of those eligible will vote. But campaigning by Mexican candidates in major emigrant settlements such as Los Angeles, Houston, and Chicago will no doubt increase. In 1995 the Mexican government began considering the adoption of a constitutional amendment that would allow Mexicans abroad to retain a nonvoting Mexican cultural "nationality" while taking foreign citizenship, as well as exemption from certain restrictions on property rights.[41]

Immigrant lobbying of their home countries works best when the goal of the lobbying is relatively costless to politicians or is perceived to be of ultimate benefit to the country of origin. Having some form of economic leverage—whether in terms of campaign contributions, remittances, or possible future reinvestment in the home country—strengthens immigrants' bargaining position. Acquiring allies among opposition or governing parties (ready to harvest the support of emigrants for their own ends) can be key to getting proposals through the legislative mazes of the home countries.

What Will Dual Citizenship Mean?

There is no single, uniform logic behind Latin American immigrants' push for dual citizenship other than that of easing the tension of irreconcilable citizenships. The Ecuadorian effort, for instance, was couched in economic terms understandable and acceptable to those holding to the idea of return: "Dual citizenship . . . would permit the entry of valuable capital, like the money saved over many years, and the retirement pensions of many compatriots. . . . [In addition] the international experience acquired would propel economic development and the creation of jobs for thousands of Ecuadorians."[42]

Colombians emphasize participation in both the home country and the United States; thus dual citizenship appeals to those who will stay and those who wish to return. The president of Colombia's Liberal Party in New York City stated: "The Colombian community [in New York] should have a presence in Colombian politics as well as American politics. . . . Now that the law

---

Times, June 16, 1996, p. A4. Voting by citizens of other countries living in the U.S. is not so unusual as it might seem: in 1996, 20,000 Poles cast ballots at consulates in four cities in the United States. Dillon, "Voting Rights."

[40] Ibid.

[41] Seth Mydans, "The Latest Big Boom Is Citizenship," *New York Times*, August 11, 1995, p. A12.

[42] Carlos Garcia, "Otra Voz de Apoyo a la Doble Nacionalidad de Ecuatorianos," *Noticias del Mundo*, August 21, 1991.

has been passed so that no Colombian . . . will lose their nationality, this will open a large political arena . . . the Colombian community will organize, and should organize in the United States."[43]

There are factions among Colombians pulling in both directions. The following exchange occurred at a meeting of some of the leaders of Colombian organizations:

J: The important thing is to first solve our problems here.

S: Dual citizenship opens the doors to enter into politics here. . . .

F: If we live here, and have children, and pay taxes, then we should have a say . . . but we should also have the right to participate in Colombia, to vote in the presidential elections there. Many Colombians come here to save a little money, and then return to buy a house for their retirement.

J: That's how we come here. But . . . people have children, they stay here for twenty-five years.

R: Many people go back to Colombia. Unfortunately, we haven't done it ourselves.

J: It makes more sense to work in this country than over there. . . . We have to have priorities. I suggest we establish our priorities in the community here. To see how we can get involved in the political process here.

R: I think we should be involved in politics in Colombia.[44]

The differences in strategy can be traced, for the most part, to differences of leadership: in the Colombian community it is passing to a younger generation (born in the home country, but politicized here), while Ecuadorian organizations are led, primarily, by older first-generation immigrants.

While some immigrant leaders want dual citizenship because they believe it will lower the costs of eventual return to their countries of origin, others who have worked for years toward this goal believe it will lower the costs of naturalizing in the United States. The motives for lowering the costs of U.S. naturalization may differ, but they all have the same end—to facili-

[43] Interview, president, Partido Liberal Colombiano, August 9, 1991.

[44] FEDOCOL meeting (in Spanish), July 11, 1991 (J, S, and R are male; F is female). This same division gets played out in other organizational settings as well. Tim Golden, a reporter for the *New York Times*, told me of the tensions at a Lions Club meeting between the old guard who wanted to keep a focus on the home country, and a younger generation of activists more interested in the immigrant situation in New York City (interview, April 1, 1991). And while some of the leadership of the Partido Liberal Colombiano favor active involvement in American electoral politics, the Conservative Party is moribund, and representatives of the Alianza Democratica, a party on the left of the political spectrum in Colombia, have been more interested in getting people to vote in Colombia's elections (Author's fieldnotes, "Colombia, Una Patria Que Nos Espera," forum held by the Alianza Democratica, in Jackson Heights, June 11, 1992).

tate membership in two political communities. But whatever the motives for dual citizenship, it paradoxically allows Latin American immigrants in New York the freedom to become participating members of the polity in which they reside. Immigrants from countries that have allowed dual citizenship over a period of time—Argentina and Panama, for instance—have naturalization rates significantly higher than those of other Latin American immigrant groups in New York City. The naturalization rate for Argentines in New York City, for example, is 40.9 percent, and for Panamanians, 54.4 percent. These compare with an average rate of 27 percent for the top ten Latino groups in the city, and an average rate of 23 percent for those groups without the option of dual citizenship.[45] In the long run, then, dual citizenship is likely to facilitate the insertion of Latin American immigrants into membership and participation in American politics.

[45] Calculated from Rodriguez et al. 1995: 15, table 3. See the 1990 INS *Statistical Yearbook* (Immigration and Naturalization Service 1991: 101) as well. For contrary data see Yang 1994: 473–74. Yang found that dual citizenship did *not* encourage naturalization, calculating that the odds of naturalization of immigrants from countries which recognize dual citizenship were about 20 percent smaller than those of citizens without dual citizenship. He speculates that this may be due to immigrants' confusion, or perceptions that dual citizenship adds more responsibilities. I think the data set in this case may not be sufficiently well-defined.

9

Wanting In: Latin American Immigrant Women and the Turn to Electoral Politics

In their attempts to resolve the dilemma of having to choose between two irreconcilable polities, mainstream immigrant organizations, dominated by men, appeal to their countries of origin to allow dual citizenship. Women and others on the margins of immigrant organizational structures choose instead to appeal directly to arbiters in their present political environment. The choice of strategy, I argue, is gendered.

Not only are women in general more likely than men to shift their cultural orientation toward the United States, but female activists are more inclined to participate in American politics. This chapter explores both phenomena. In particular, Latina immigrant activists' identity as women, together with their political socialization here and in their country of origin, leads them to become more involved than men in American politics, and inclines them to be more likely to look here, rather than to their countries of origin, for solutions to ease the costs of participation within the American political system.

Women and Immigration

In the last fifteen years there has been some change in the study and evaluation of immigration patterns. Previously it was assumed that men migrated first, and women and children followed; men were assumed to have made most of the decisions about immigration—when and where it would take place. In the 1970s there was a new recognition in the academic literature that decisions took place within households, and that therefore one had to

Table 18. Sex ratios among legal immigrants in New York City, 1982–1989

Country of origin	Number of women: 100 men
Top twenty countries	106
Colombia	115
Honduras	111
El Salvador	106
Dominican Republic	105
Ecuador	104
Peru	103
All immigrants	102

Source: Salvo and Ortiz 1992: 74, figure 4.3.

look at each person's strategy within the context of families. With this revised perspective there is increasing recognition of the extent to which legal immigration to the United States is, by a small but significant margin, female. In the last few decades, the United States has received more immigrant women than men from almost every sending country.[1] This is true for New York City as well (see Table 18). Immigrants from the Dominican Republic and Colombia make up the first and second largest non–Puerto Rican Latino migrant populations in New York. From 1982 to 1989 women made up, respectively, 51 percent and 54 percent of the migrant stream from these countries to the city (Salvo and Ortiz 1992: 74); from 1976 to 1978 the percentages were as high as 57 percent and 66 percent respectively (Gurak and Kritz 1982: 16).

Arriving to the United States as members of households, Latin American women often share with men the idea of returning to their home country. The goal of rapidly accumulating savings in order to return requires women to play a much greater role in contributing to the household's income, and they are much more likely to work in New York City than they are in the home country. For example, Pessar found that while 31 percent of Dominican women were employed at some time before migration, 91.5 percent worked for pay at some time in the United States and 51 percent were in the work force at the time of the study (1987: 105–6). Similarly, Gurak and

[1] Prior to 1930, the annual sex ratios of new immigrants to the United States was usually over 120 males for every 100 females. This was primarily determined by immigration law: until 1952, women could not sponsor their spouses. Changes in immigration law allowed women to become "pioneer" immigrants (Salvo and Ortiz 1992: 73–74). For an overview of sex ratios and female immigration to the United States see Houston, Kramer, and Barrett 1984; for an overview of some of the recent literature on women and immigration see Pedraza 1991.

Kritz found that 57 percent of Colombian women worked prior to immigrating, 92.7 percent had worked in the United States, and 66 percent were then in the work force (1982:18; 1984). Women's employment goes counter to middle-class expectations in the home country, but is rationalized—perhaps more by their husbands than by the women themselves—by saying that it will only be for a short while.[2] Women's work is justified as long as it is for the good of the family.[3] It is not meant to be not an end itself.[4]

Immigrant women's entrance into the work force does not entail economic or social parity with immigrant men. More women work after coming to the United States, but the jobs they take are more likely than men's to be low-skill work in manufacturing or the garment industry. Women stay at such jobs longer than men and are less upwardly mobile. Women generally work fewer hours and less regularly (and get paid less for the work they do than do men[5]), in part because work does not relieve them of their traditional family responsibilities (Pesquera 1993; Marx Ferree 1979).[6] Still,

[2] It is still a point of pride for a husband to say that his wife has "never had to work" [*Mi mujer nunca ha tenido que trabajar*], as a Peruvian told me over beers. "My father worked on the docks near Callao, in Peru. He worked there his whole life. Now look where I am." Part of making it into the middle class is seeing to it that the women in the household don't work (author's fieldnotes, Club Hermanos Unidos, March 18, 1991). Grasmuck and Pessar note that women themselves may also feel ambivalent about their work: "The bourgeois standard of living the female immigrant and her family hope to emulate is a standard informed by Dominican values. These hold that the women shall remain in the home and the man shall be the sole breadwinner. . . . Thus most of our female informants spoke of their tenure of work outside the house as temporary . . . to 'help her husband out'" (1991: 154–55).

[3] Marx Ferree (1979) interprets women's traditional role as protecting the respectability of the family. Work is only justified when employment is an effort to restore the status and respectability of the family, as in the United States. Women can then take jobs without guilt or ambivalence.

[4] But in many cases having women enter the workplace is necessary. Immigration disrupts the familiar support networks of kin and friends and causes a turning inward to the nuclear family. Occasional support through these dispersed networks is still important, however. The majority of immigrants have received some assistance in the form of housing, food and clothing, employment, money, and emotional support from kin and friends. For example, 70 percent of both Colombians and Dominicans learned of their current job through family or friends (Gurak and Kritz 1984).

[5] García Castro on Colombian immigrant women (1982a: 27) and Gurak on Dominican and Colombian women (1987); see also Urrea Giraldo 1982. Data in these papers is based on the survey of Dominican and Colombian migrants directed by Douglas Gurak at Fordham University in 1981. On gendered differences in the occupational mobility of Cuban and Mexican immigrants, see Sullivan 1984:1057–59. For a more general discussion of the downward mobility of women immigrants see Long 1980.

[6] In her study of Cuban immigrant women in Florida, Marx Ferree (1979) notes that "although virtually all the women said that a woman has the obligation to work when the family is financially pressed, less than half (42%) felt the husband had a similar obligation to help with the housework when his wife is employed."

married women and married women with children both show greater labor force participation than female heads of households (Gurak and Kritz 1992: 7; Chaney 1980a: 289; also see MacPherson and Stewart 1989: 66). However, these women's role in the family does affect their choice of jobs. Women are more likely than men to take jobs in smaller businesses in the immediate neighborhood, or in Queens (although many still work in Manhattan), presumably so they can stay closer to their families, and to take more flexible jobs at lower pay (Garcia Castro 1982a: 27). Women are still expected to play certain traditional roles in the family, particularly with respect to children, while engaging in work.

Despite the difficulties, employment gives immigrant women economic resources they did not have in their home country. Employment may even be easier in this country for women than for men, and although they often work fewer hours, they make a significant contribution to the household's total income. As women take pay home, this may lead to a renegotiation of decision-making in households where couples are married. Whereas prior to immigration the senior male usually controlled all household expenditures or allocated an allowance to his spouse, in the United States the most common practice becomes the "pooled household" where all income earners put earnings in a common pot and jointly decide how the money will be spent (Pessar 1987: 121; Grasmuck and Pessar 1991: 148).[7] Women may keep part of their paychecks for their own expenses and remittances (Gonzalez 1976: 37–38; Pessar 1987: 122).[8]

As women experience the benefits of working and controlling their earnings, their long-term strategies can begin to diverge from men's (Hondagneau-Sotelo 1994: 100; Hondagneau-Sotelo 1992; Grasmuck and Pessar 1991: 156, 158). While men hold to the maxim that "five dollars spent here means five more years before returning home," women may begin spending savings in this country. This progressively postpones return to

[7] In a survey of 55 households before migration from the Dominican Republic, men exercised control over the budget in 69% of households. Where men controlled the budget, 26% of the time they oversaw all expenses, and 74% of the time they gave their spouses a household allowance. Thirty-one % of the pre-migration households pooled their income, but these were almost all female-headed households. Once in the United States, 69% of households pool income (58% of these were nuclear families, and 42% were female-headed) (Pessar 1987: 121).

[8] In the 1981 Gurak and Kritz survey 60% of the male immigrants and 53.6% of the Colombian women sent remittances to their home countries. Dominican women are less likely to send money. The amount sent averaged $100 per month for Colombian males, $94 for Dominican males, $70 for Colombian women, and $60 for Dominican women (Gurak and Kritz 1984). My Dominican neighbor said she usually sent between $100 and $200 a month when she was employed, but hadn't sent anything in a while. Her mother would know something was wrong because she hadn't sent anything (author's fieldnotes, January 22, 1991).

their country of origin, where opportunities for work are limited and social controls are stricter (Grasmuck and Pessar 1991: 156; Pessar 1987: 123; Garcia Castro 1982a: 30–31). Women are aware that return will mean, in most cases, going back to the male head-of-household pattern, and they may not be eager to relinquish their newfound decision-making authority (Hondagneau-Sotelo 1994: 146; Grasmuck and Pessar 1991: 155). A group of my neighbors, all women, raised such issues in talking about their relationships with men. Elizabeth and Anna said they don't want men to support them; they have no intention of being obligated to men. My next-door neighbor, on the other hand, said that when she married her first husband at age eighteen her husband supported her and she didn't have to work (she is now separated from her husband and lives with her daughter). Elizabeth and Anna both said they left home to get away from that feeling of obligation.[9] Having their own means of income allows women to enter into relationships with men on their own terms. Such independence extends as well to their relationships with family authority in general. A woman who had left her husband in Colombia and come with her daughter to New York told me about her strict upbringing: "My father used to lock the telephone in his closet so that I couldn't talk with any boys. . . . My brothers were given the keys to the house when they were older, but I have never had a key to the house, not even now, when I go to visit. When I want to stay out late I have to ask for a key to the house."[10] She thinks this experience may be why she came to the United States. In short, women have economic and personal incentives for abandoning the original strategy of accumulation and return. They may reevaluate the idea that success entails a return to the home country and staying means failure. Staying, for women, may be a significant improvement in their situation.

Immigrant women's desire to change the terms of their relationships can lead to conflict. Married women, for example, might find that their husbands are not willing to renegotiate household decision-making. A neigh-

[9] Author's fieldnotes, April 1, 1991.

[10] Conversation (in Spanish), August 14, 1991. Note the similar cases discussed by Nancie Gonzalez (1976). She cites, for example, the situation of a widow who by staying in New York avoided pressures to conform to social expectations of how she should manage her money and children if she returned to the Dominican Republic. Garcia Castro (1982a: 31) also notes that immigration may serve as an escape from social pressures and obligations. She quotes a Colombian woman in New York City: "Here I am freer. There everyone in my family used to pressure me. . . . 'Where are you going? Why are you coming back so late?'" (see also Cruz 1980b, and Cruz 1980c). Garcia Castro notes that younger women are more likely to view immigration as a way of escaping restrictions and constraints, while older women see it in terms of the economic benefits (1982a: 25).

Table 19. Marital status of first-generation immigrants in Queens, 1990

	% Married	% Widowed	% Divorced	% Separated	% Never married
Men	51.2	1.0	5.7	3.8	38.3
Women	46.7	6.5	9.7	6.7	30.4

Source: 1990 Census, Public Use Microdata Sample.

bor told me she was having trouble because she was out of work, and her husband wouldn't help support her son. She was working in a temporary job from 10 to 4 answering the phones. Her boss, a woman, gave her seventy dollars a day. "That's good work," she said. "I almost feel like skipping the apartment, leaving everything, and going into hiding." She said she had told her husband that she was tired of having her hands in the dishwater; she felt he was threatened by her trying to better herself (*tratando de subir*). "A lot of Dominican men are like that," said another woman who was listening.[11] This conflict over gender roles can lead to additional strains on marriages already taxed by the migration process, and by the dilemma over whether or not to stay in the United States (Grasmuck and Pessar 1991: 156). Separation and divorce are common—many women become heads of households after immigration to the United States (Gilbertson and Gurak 1994; Landale and Ogena 1995). Data from the 1990 Public Use Microdata Sample indicate that 22 percent of women were either widowed, separated, or divorced (see Table 19). Gurak and Kritz estimate that about 44 percent of Dominican women and 25 percent of Colombian women in New York City have experienced some kind of marital disruption.[12]

[11] Author's fieldnotes, March 30, 1991. Another illustration of male chauvinism from an English class I was teaching: two Dominican men, a Dominican woman and two Colombian women were present, and Miriam, another Colombian woman, is late for class. I call her home and her husband tells me she's out. After I hang up, Miguel suggests Sonia call, so that Miriam's husband won't be concerned about the strange man calling for his wife. Sonia asks him if he would worry if a man called his wife on the phone. Miguel says that his wife shouldn't be getting phone calls from men. "So you're a *machista*," Sonia responds. "Won't you trust your wife?" "No," says Miguel (author's fieldnotes, April 1, 1991).

[12] In Pessar's interviews with 55 households, 18 had experienced separation or divorce once in the U.S. "and in most instances the man's reluctance to temper his patriarchal attitudes and behavior was a crucial factor in the breakup. Nonetheless, in most cases the senior male adapted relatively easily to a more egalitarian form of domestic organization" (1987: 123). More broadly, Gurak and Kritz's survey found that marital disruptions occurred for about 25% of Colombian women and both Colombian and Dominican males, but for 43.8% of Dominican women. Thirty-two % of Dominican women were divorced, as opposed to 17.5% of Colombian women (Gurak and Kritz 1982: 21).

Women and Settlement

Women on their own have to develop alternative economic strategies,[13] since working full-time at low wages and simultaneously bringing up children is next to impossible.[14] Women who find themselves in this situation are likely to receive assistance from the state. In general immigrant women are more aware than immigrant men of social welfare programs; their co-workers and friends, most of whom are women, keep them apprised of what programs are available.[15] In times of sustained need women are much more likely to turn to government programs than men.[16] A large number of immigrant women receive welfare or aid for their dependent children (AFDC)—56 percent of Dominican women, for example, and 25 percent of Colombians (Gurak and Kritz, 1982; 1984). Note that this is closely correlated with the percentage of women in each group who are single heads of household with children: 63 percent of Colombian and 88 percent of Dominican female heads of household receive welfare benefits, and 45.7 percent of Colombians and 69 percent of Dominicans receive AFDC (Gurak and Kritz 1992: table 1). Child care is prohibitively expensive, and networks for child care (through friends or relatives) which existed in the home country are missing or unreliable. A Colombian woman described how she would get

[13] Among these strategies is supplementing income with work in the informal economy. My next-door Dominican neighbor M. undertook several small entrepreneurial ventures to earn enough to pay her rent. She would get merchandise from a friend in Manhattan and then resell it in Queens. She sold perfumes and clothing, and raffled a ring and Bulova watch (author's fieldnotes, February 8, 1991; February 23, 1991; July 21, 1991).

[14] Norma, a Dominican woman, is somewhat of an exception, but her experience shows some of the costs of being a single working mother. She has been working as a garment worker, ironing finished pieces, for seventeen years at the same factory. She says she does one thousand pieces a day. She could make $400 a week when times were good, but now times were bad and she was only making $65 a week. She has been alone with her daughter for seven years, since her husband left her. She says she has no vices or trouble with men. She takes care of her apartment and pays her rent. The only things she allows herself are cigarettes and to "tomarme mi romo cada dia" (drink a small airplane-sized bottle of rum a day) (author's fieldnotes, February 22, 1991).

[15] Abused wives, for instance, often get advice from other immigrant women in their neighborhoods, telling them where to go and what services are available. M., my next-door neighbor, found out about assistance for women and infant children (WIC) from her cousin in Brooklyn and, in turn, gives people advice on how to get public assistance (author's fieldnotes, February 20, 1991; March 17, 1991).

[16] Gurak and Kritz found that significant percentages of female immigrants were aware that they could obtain assistance from governmental agencies; 24% of Dominicans, and 19% of Colombians said they would turn first to these agencies in a financial crisis (Gurak and Krtiz 1984).

home from work at eleven at night, and her daughter would be ravenous so she would cook her a meal. She hired a baby-sitter, but the baby-sitter was expensive, and she was trying to work and study at the same time. "Really," she said, "I didn't know anyone here—not my parents, my family, no one."[17] Without the social networks that existed in their home countries women turn for help to city and state agency programs; being alone with children means that women are more likely than men to have contact with the institutions and programs of the federal and local government.

The existing sociological literature is lax in looking at women's experience with their children or child care except as it affects the mother's ability to work. Even working women continue to be the primary caretakers of their children and, as such, come into contact with a range of public institutions through their children—the health care and educational systems, in particular. One of my neighbors in Queens, for instance, used to work in a garment factory, but she quit when she was seven months pregnant with her second child. Now she has her first two children in child care, and she has to drop them off there at 6:30 every morning, and be at work by 7:30. At the time, she was pregnant with her third child, and she would go periodically with a friend who was also expecting to the hospital in Elmhurst for prenatal care.[18] In addition to health care providers, schools also play a key role in the lives of immigrant mothers. Education is seen by immigrants as the primary path for social improvement (*la manera de subir, de mejorarse*)—not always for themselves, but certainly for their children (García Castro 1982: 24; Pessar 1987: 124)—and mothers will go out of their way to take jobs that are flexible enough to allow them to see their children to and from school. Again, this gives immigrant women much more contact with public institutions than immigrant men.

It is easy to see how men's and women's economic strategies begin to diverge with their experiences in this country. If they stay married or attached, women acquire greater independence and power with their income, which gives them an increased incentive to stay in this country. If they separate, even if they wish to go back, their strategy will likely change perforce; accumulating savings becomes almost impossible with the strain of raising children and working. In either case, if they have children they will come into contact with a wide range of public institutions, giving them a broader experience of governmental structures than immigrant men have. In general, then, immigrant women have both negative and positive incentives to orient their strategies toward this country, and away from their country of origin.

17 Interview (in Spanish), July 17, 1991.

18 Conversation (in Spanish), September 19, 1991.

Table 20. Sex ratios of persons naturalized in New York City, 1982–1989

Country of origin	Number of women: 100 men	
	Naturalization	Legal immigration
Dominican Republic	149	105
Colombia	145	115
Ecuador	116	104
Cuba	110	Not applicable
Honduras	161	111
El Salvador	161	106
Peru	109	103
All Immigrants	118	102

Source: Salvo and Ortiz 1992: 147. For other evidence of the correlation between gender and naturalization see Yang 1994: 472. If we take into account that illegal immigration probably includes more men than women, the ratio of women to men naturalizing is likely to be even higher. Naturalization rates for Latin American immigrants in general tend to be low. By contrast immigrants from Asian countries have naturalization rates in excess of 50% during this time period (Warren 1988, cited in Grasmuck and Pessar 1991: 207).

These incentives generally lead to an increased desire to stay in the United States,[19] a desire which, among other things, translates into eventual naturalization. A survey of immigrants from seven Latin American countries suggests that women tend to become citizens much more often than men (see table 20), even taking into account their greater proportion among legal immigrants to the city.[20] This is particularly true for Dominicans and Colombians, who are the second and third largest Latino populations in the city after the Puerto Ricans, and for Hondurans and Salvadorans.

These differences, however, are not sufficient to explain why women are disproportionately represented as the mediators between governmental institutions and other immigrants. After all, while the majority of women may

[19] Without presenting data from his 1981 survey, Gurak states: "Women appear more likely to settle in New York than do males. Those interviewed definitely have longer term settlement intentions than do males" (Gurak 1988a: 37). Chaney (1980a) also states that women, particularly married women, are often the most eager to stay.

[20] In general, being widowed or divorced is correlated with citizenship for both men and women. Based on the 1990 census Public Use Microdata Sample for Queens, immigrant men and women with these marital statuses are more likely to become citizens than those who are separated or have never married, with married individuals falling somewhere in between. Forty-one % of divorced women, and 31% of married women are citizens, for example, but only 18% of those who have never married. The respective figures for men are 36%, 31%, and 17%. However, since more than twice as many women as men experience a disruption of their marriages, it follows that more women than men become citizens.

shift their orientations somewhat to further their interests and those of their families, this doesn't mean that they will necessarily choose a life of political activism. Though immigrant women are more likely to become citizens than men, and perhaps more likely to vote once they are citizens,[21] few will devote their full energies to political involvement. Many women view politics with suspicion,[22] and the number of women so involved is actually quite small. For this select group of women, activism is reinforced by other factors in their lives.

Women and Politics

Like men, women participate actively in immigrant organizations, but the organizations are usually founded and run by men. Male domination of organizations is especially evident in the Dominican community in Queens, which revolves around social clubs. The Hermanos Unidos club in Corona, for example, has about 350 male members and twenty-five female members.[23] South American organizations have a more even sex ratio in their membership, but men monopolize leadership posts in almost all of these groups too (except those which are specifically women's groups, or *ramas femininas*—women's branches—of more general [male] groups). Men are presidents and vice-presidents; women are minor functionaries. "A lot of men," said one female Colombian activist, "think that power is something they hold privately and personally for themselves. It's accepted that women will organize. But if a woman pushes for leadership, this creates certain worries, a certain discomfort. They feel a woman can be secretary or serve in public relations but that none really has the ability for leadership."[24] Women are allowed to run the concessions stands and prepare events, while

[21] ABC exit polls taken in New York City during the 1988 presidential elections found that Latino voters were 43% male and 57% female in the primaries, and 47% male and 53% female in the general elections. In assembly district 30, in Queens, Latino registered voters are 46% male and 54% female; in council district 25, they are 45% male and 55% female (Baca, 1991).
[22] Pessar quotes one woman who commented, "It isn't a good thing getting involved in politics" (*no esta bien meterse en la política*). Another said "A person comes to no good in politics" (*La persona se va abajo con la política*) (Pessar, 1987: 114). Views such as these are commonplace.
[23] Author's fieldnotes, Club Hermanos Unidos, December 6, 1992.
[24] Interview (in Spanish), November 4, 1991. A Puerto Rican activist took the path of less resistance: "I had no problems because I wasn't aspiring to any position. I am a person who has volunteered her time. I wasn't looking for any position, or any job in any community, or anything like that. So I had no resistance whatsoever. . . . I had my job and wasn't looking for what they had to offer. . . . I wasn't competition for anyone, so I had no resistance whatsoever. . . . Like I say, you're a volunteer and no one will resent you." Interview, August 29, 1991.

men do the public speaking and posturing.[25] At a citywide public forum, a Colombian organizer sat and took names by the door. I asked her how she had gotten stuck with that job. "This is women's work" she said sarcastically. "You'll never see a man doing this."[26] The handful of organizations specifically organized by and for Latin American women provide some outlet for their initiative and leadership, but these organizations, like those dominated by men, are also generally oriented toward the home country rather than toward American politics. The difference is that the women in these organizations often play a dual role: they are also involved as activists and organizers for Latin American immigrant interests in New York.

Women, like men, draw on their pre-migratory experiences for the knowledge and expertise needed to run organizations. Activist women's initial experiences with politics are usually in their country of origin. Their first mentors are members of their own families who initiate them into political and organizational life—their parents, siblings, aunts, and others, both men and women. One Ecuadorian woman, for instance, told me she had been influenced by her mother: "Well, my mother was always very active. My mother was a teacher, and for her education was fundamental, and she always encouraged my education. She was very active, as well; she was a member of the Press Club, for example, and a member of *la Sociedad de Quiteños*."[27] A Colombian woman said that her father and sister had been very involved in politics. Her father was most involved, although only in campaign work. She got interested, and now "it's stuck in my blood."[28] Another Colombian said her father had taken her to meetings of the Conservative Party in Cali. Later she joined the Conservative Youth organization. "I learned how to be a leader at home," she said. "It's like a virus. It doesn't leave you later."[29] Activist women often comment on how their political interests are something inherited, almost genetic.[30] This inheritance becomes a model for their political work in the United States.

Latina activists' political socialization, however, is also partly the result of sharing many of the same experiences of other Latin American immigrant

[25] For an especially insightful treatment of this phenomenon see Hardy-Fanta 1993; also Naples 1991 and Pardo 1990.

[26] Author's fieldnotes, Latino Voting Rights Committee, public forum, November 12, 1991.

[27] Interview (in Spanish), February 24, 1992.

[28] Conversation (in Spanish), October 21, 1991.

[29] Interview (in Spanish), November 4, 1991.

[30] The metaphor of politics passed on biologically, carried in the blood somehow, is a common one. Another Colombian woman notes that "my aunt was very involved in community activities. She was the wife of a newspaper publisher. She was interested in women's issues at a time when it wasn't popular to do so. Maybe it's carried in the genes somehow." Interview, November 8, 1991.

women—work, marriage, motherhood. Like many other immigrant women, their initial years in this country are taken up with work and family. "There was a time," one woman said, "when I was only a housewife [*una madre de familia*], until my children were a little older."[31] As women have more time for themselves, husbands have difficulties accepting their new roles and commitments, and often oppose the idea of their wives getting involved in organizing and going off alone to meetings. A Latina block leader told me ruefully: "I saw myself as a politician. [She laughs]. I like it a lot. . . . But here my husband has clipped my wings. Because he doesn't think that women should go out and scream and yell. I do my things, but only up to a point, so he doesn't have a problem with it. After all, this is my house, and I have to take care of the house as well. And little by little I get him used to it, I get him used to it. So, if I, if my husband had backed me, I would be doing politics, yes. Because I like politics."[32]

Activists' full devotion to organizational life often does not begin until such concerns are taken care of in one way or another. Their children grow older, or they are divorced, both situations giving them greater independence. Like other immigrant women, activists' experiences with families and work often lead them to reevaluate their commitments.

It is true that many of these activists are less vulnerable than other immigrant women. Many of them have college educations and are fluent in English, whereas most immigrants must try hard to know enough of the language to defend themselves (*para defenderse*), and women generally know less English than men (Garcia Castro 1982a). Finally, their employment, often initially in the social service bureaucracy, gives them both financial security and an entrée into American political life. These advantages are crucial and provide activists with many of the necessary skills to work as intermediaries between immigrants and the local and state governments. As women talk about their work they recognize the special role they play. An Ecuadorian activist describes her work in Queens family court:

> I had a certain political interest there too, if you want to call it that, because I realized that the Hispanic woman who went to the court to ask for help with her family problems (and I say Hispanic *woman* because it was mostly the His-

[31] Interview (in Spanish), February 24, 1992.

[32] Interview (in Spanish), May 1, 1991. An Ecuadorian woman I spoke with in the waiting room of a school for English said she didn't belong to any Ecuadorian clubs because her husband didn't like it (author's fieldnotes, January 31, 1991). Rose Rothschild, manager of Community Board 4, said her opinion was that "Hispanics don't participate. From what I understand, the husbands do not want their wives to go out. At night and things like that." Interview, April 22, 1991.

panic woman who sought help) had a lot of difficulties—she didn't know the system, she didn't understand, she was poorly informed. . . . The courts had interpreters and we were the bridge that helped a person make herself understood in the institution, but we also helped a little to orient her in this country, right?[33]

If Latina activists become mediators between immigrants and the governmental bureaucracies, they are also acknowledging and building on their experiences as immigrants and as women.

While men are likely to keep a sojourner mentality, and organizations dominated by men will focus on the home country, activist immigrant women are more likely to turn to the problems of the immigrant community in this country. An Ecuadorian woman noted:

> It was natural that people who came over in large numbers would want to get together, so they formed civic organizations. And men were always the leaders, because in Latin America men were always the leaders. Women in politics were seen as strange. When I was growing up as a girl in Ecuador, it was not the thing for women to do. Men here are more interested in politics there. They do good things, raise money, but they are not interested in what goes on here. They have status in the community; they are *caciques* [leaders]. But they aren't interested in starting over—to begin with, to have to learn English. If they got involved in politics here they wouldn't be *caciques* anymore. They would only play a small part. So women and Puerto Ricans tend to dominate local politics in Queens. Puerto Ricans because of their experience in politics. Women because they are willing to work with others.[34]

Activist women have both the motive and the opportunity to play the role of political intermediaries.[35] As immigrants, Latinas' primary loyalties remain with their home countries, but as women they find themselves facing new problems in New York. Despite their skills, they are marginalized within immigrant organizations and so turn to alternative forms of participation.

[33] Interview (in Spanish), February 24, 1992. The Queens family court in particular served as a socializing experience for many of the Queens Latina leadership. Many of them initially worked there, and the friendships they established became the foundation for much of the Latina activists' social network in Queens.

[34] Interview, April 17, 1991. Men's concern with protecting their established status is echoed in another interview: "[Women] are more ready to participate. Men only participate if you give them a position on the leadership. You have to give men a position. Women are prepared to be only members." Interview (in Spanish), November 4, 1991. See also Hardy-Fanta 1993.

[35] This seems to be true of immigrant women across ethnic groups. See Hardy-Fanta 1993; Ui 1991.

For city and state government agencies looking for people to serve as intermediaries between government and the fast-growing population of immigrants, these activist women are ideal. For the women themselves, these positions offer the chance for leadership unavailable in immigrant organizations. These mediating roles may be frustrating—women remain beholden to their political patrons within New York's political establishment—but the activity also gives women a great deal of visibility among Latin American immigrants in Queens and makes them likely contenders for political office, should any choose to run.

Electoral Redistricting in Queens

Latina activists occupy a peculiar niche in New York City politics. As intermediaries with the broader American political establishment, they have some influence both within and outside the immigrant community, but they remain on the margins of both the American and the immigrant institutional establishments. Their role and their resources (along with their allies, who are often equally as marginalized in the immigrant community)[36] are perforce limited, particularly within the parameters of New York City politics. The role they generally play is to gently prod the immigrant community in the direction of increased participation in American politics. They organize registration and naturalization tables on street corners and fairs, endorse local politicians and work for their campaigns, hold fund-raisers for candidates they like, and try to get out the vote. In short, they act much as other emerging interest groups do in American politics, the one difference being that they still identify themselves as members of the Latin American immigrant community. Along with the maturing second generation, they represent the rise of a new ethnic politics in the city.

Unable to appeal for aid from the larger first-generation immigrant community, and confronted by steep costs of entering New York City's hegemonic electoral political arena, Latina activists and their allies must look elsewhere for support. Coalition partners within the city are either unlikely or problematic; immigrant activists in Queens have little to offer in return for inclusion in any coalition except their presence. Unlike their male coun-

[36] Latino gays and lesbians, for example, who are disproportionately concentrated in the Jackson Heights area, are more likely to remain in the United States rather than plan on return to their countries of origin. For this reason they, like women, are more likely to naturalize and participate politically than immigrant men. Unfortunately, there are no hard data on the numbers involved. For a fictional account of Latino gay life in Queens see Jaime Manrique, *Latin Moon in Manhattan* (New York: St. Martin's Press, 1993).

terparts in the mainstream organizations, they have little leverage. However, by stepping outside the local political realm, and turning to an outside arbiter, these activists were able in the crucial instance of electoral redistricting in the city and state in 1991 to play a role in shaping a Latino district in Queens. By appealing for federal government intervention they were able to trump resistance at the city level.

Redistricting in 1991 was different from any political reapportionment in New York City within recent memory because it actually *was* a redistricting—the drawing of entirely new districts—and not simply incremental fiddling with district boundaries, as is usually the case.[37] The actual task of redistricting was assigned to a commission appointed by the mayor to expand the number of City Council districts from 35 to 51. The possibilities for significantly expanding minority representation on the council prompted Latino organizations—in particular the Puerto Rican / Latino Coalition for Voting Rights, the Puerto Rican Legal Defense and Educational Fund, and the Puerto Rican / Latino Voting Rights Network—to enter the process and present a number of proposals to the commission for an increase in the number of Latino districts.

The expansion of minority districts was actively resisted in Queens. On the one hand, incumbent politicians were nervous because redistricting meant changes that were not fully under their control; on the other, the possibility of minority districts in Queens was perceived by white ethnics as a threat to their sense of community as neighborhood. They argued that *ethnic* redistricting was a break with tradition. Neighborhood boundaries were being violated by newly drawn district lines, with neighborhoods partitioned among various political districts in order to group minorities together. The two arguments paralleled and reinforced one another.

At public hearings held by the state's task force for reapportionment, the refrain of native-born blacks and whites (there were few immigrants present) was: "They're dividing the community."[38] Jackson Heights and Corona, with their mixed populations of new immigrants and long-term residents, were at the center of the controversy in Queens. White ethnic residents in Jackson Heights mobilized so that "traditional" borders wouldn't be broken and the "community" split. They used the language of the civil rights move-

[37] Redistricting was largely a result of the 1989 Supreme Court decision which upheld the dismantling of the old Board of Estimates and shifted power to an expanded City Council. See Chapter 4.

[38] Author's fieldnotes, public hearing, New York State Legislative Task Force on Demographic Research and Reapportionment, Queens Borough Hall, February 13, 1992. At another occasion, state senator Leonard Stavinsky said the redistricting plan "partitioned and destroyed" neighborhoods.

ment to defend themselves against implicit charges of discrimination and to undercut the arguments for creating separate minority districts, charging that minority districts would lead, in fact, to resegregation along racial lines. For example, Rudy Greco, president of the Jackson Heights Beautification Group, testified: "Jackson Heights shouldn't be penalized for having desegregated [in the '60s and '70s]. We worked hard to integrate and now Jackson Heights is being resegregated. . . . The people of the community are up in arms. . . . You have created a black district, a white, and an Hispanic district where blacks, whites, and Hispanics used to live together.[39]

Helen Sears, one of two Democratic district leaders for the area, read a similar statement:

> It takes decades and decades to build a community. It doesn't happen overnight. It takes effort and thought to keep a community intact. We worked during the civil rights era to integrate our schools. Jackson Heights has children from [many] countries, speaking [many] languages. The area is one of the most diverse in New York City. Now we see a reversal—you are going to split the area into a white district, an Hispanic district, and an area of blacks. . . . This doesn't recognize that people live side by side. It ignores communities. . . . Keep Jackson Heights intact. This is the most un-American thing, gerrymandering the district lines.[40]

In their public rhetoric, white ethnics defended Jackson Heights as a *place*, protesting the elevation of ethnicity above locality as the deciding principle of political community.

The city commission, in drawing the lines for new council districts, did not entirely agree with the "neighborhood as community" argument. Many of their lines crossed "traditional" boundary lines. But they did use census figures to make the argument that Latinos in certain areas of the city—primarily in Queens, where no one of Latin American origin had ever been elected to political office—were not sufficiently concentrated residentially to be able to draw majority-Hispanic districts. The commission presented

[39] Author's fieldnotes, president of the Jackson Heights Beautification Group, speaking at a redistricting meeting, February 13, 1992. Desegregation in Jackson Heights meant participating in New York City's plan for "paired schools." P.S. 148 was paired with P.S. 127 in East Elmhurst. The plan was highly unpopular. It "made it difficult for people to buy homes, you know, with families. They didn't want to do it. You could stand on my doorstep and look up the street, see the school, and my children can't go there . . . it was a flop. Most of the parents sent their kids to parochial school or private school, or they didn't buy homes in the community." The school pairing plan was dropped in the late 1980s. Interview, president of the Jackson Heights Neighborhood Association, April 29, 1991.

[40] Author's fieldnotes, February 13, 1992.

its final maps on June 3, 1991.[41] The redistricting plans still had to be approved by the U.S. Justice Department, however, since three out of five of New York's boroughs are covered by the 1965 Voting Rights Act and its amendments—Manhattan, Brooklyn, and the Bronx (but not Queens).[42] It was at this juncture that the mostly female activists from the Queens Hispanic Coalition and the Queens Hispanic Political Action Committee joined other Latino interest groups to circumvent the city's political establishment by appealing directly to the Justice Department.

The Justice Department's Civil Rights Division was sympathetic to the appeal. Despite its lackluster record under a Republican administration, John Dunne, the assistant attorney general in charge of the division, indicated that he was concerned about the maps drawn up by the city, particularly in parts of Brooklyn and the Bronx, and, unofficially, in Queens. On July 19, 1991, after hearing the protests and testimony of various Latino groups involved, the Justice Department turned down the city's proposed redistricting plan, saying it "consistently disfavored" Hispanic voters in violation of the law.[43] It took another two weeks of negotiations before the Justice Department approved a final version of the districts on July 26th. The new maps included alterations favoring Latino representation in the city, including the formation of a majority-Latino district in the Jackson Heights–Corona area of Queens.[44] In the new maps Latinos made up 55 percent of the population of the 21st council district in Queens (from 49.6 percent previously). Ironically the creation of these new boundaries actually *reduced* the number of registered minority voters: the district changed from having 44 percent black registered voters and 33.5 percent Hispanic registered voters, to 22.3 percent black voters, and 24.5 percent Hispanic voters.[45]

In the end, when the electoral districts were drawn and the plan was approved by the city, white ethnic voices were drowned out. Although they had the ear of the local political machinery, they couldn't convince the Justice Department that their vision of neighborhoods as the basis of political com-

[41] Jerry Gray, "Council District 21 Creates an Angry Hispanic Majority," *New York Times*, July 19, 1991, p. B1; Sam Roberts, "As Population Grows, Hispanic Power Lags," *New York Times*, July 18, 1993, p. B4. For an insiders' view of the redistricting process see Macchiarola and Diaz 1993.

[42] These three boroughs fell under the Act because historically 50% or less of their minority populations were registered to vote, which placed them in the same category as most counties in the South.

[43] Frank Lynn, "Districting Is His Case," *New York Times*, July 26, 1991, p. B2; Robert Pear, "U.S. Rejects New York Plan for City Council Districts; Finds Hispanics Hurt," *New York Times*, July 20, 1993, p. A1.

[44] Robert Pear, "New York's Plan Wins Backing: U.S. Justice Department Approves City Council District Map," *New York Times*, July 27, 1991.

[45] Felicia Lee, "Panel Approves Revised Plan for New York's Council Seats," *New York Times*, July 26, 1991.

munity was adequate, that it included everyone equally, without discrimination. They couldn't argue against the fact that while Latinos are 20 percent of the borough's population, no Latino had yet held elected office. Though the vast majority of Latin American immigrants had little interest in the apportionment dispute, it was relatively easy for a small group of Latino activists (most of them women involved in U.S. electoral politics in the Jackson Heights–Corona area) to go to Washington and lobby the lawyers at the Department of Justice. Once there, they persuaded the Justice Department counsels that the city's redistricting lines were discriminatory and that the relevant definition of "community" should not be the municipally defined neighborhood but the ethnic origin of the population. Only in this way, they argued, could a Latino be elected to political office in Queens.

The activists' task was successful, first of all, because the federal government's definition of who counts as Hispanic corresponded with and reinforced some facets of Latino immigrant activists' self-identification.[46] Of course, it also helped that the Justice Department's political motivations—the desire for a Republican administration to show up the failings of Democratic machine politics in New York City, and build political support among the growing Latino population—momentarily coincided with the activists' own.[47] But the 1991 City Council redistricting indicated both the strengths and weaknesses of the activists' approach. A relatively small group of men and women were able to appeal for intervention from the federal government for a "Hispanic" district in Queens, but were unable to run a candidate of their own for the district. Helen Marshall, an African American of Caribbean descent, and a former New York State assemblywoman, ran with backing from the Democratic Party in Queens, and won the seat in November, 1991.

The Turn to Electoral Politics

It's clear the situation for Latin American immigrants in Queens and in New York City is changing rapidly, particularly following the reapportionment of electoral districts. Immigrants and immigrant groups—particularly those

[46] See Chapter 6. On the role of the state in bolstering or creating ethnic identities, see Anderson 1983: 168. Also also Richard Handler, *Nationalism and the Politics of Culture in Quebec* (Madison: University of Wisconsin Press, 1988), and Michael Herzfeld, *Anthropology through the Looking Glass: Critical Anthropology on the Margins of Europe* (New York: Cambridge University Press, 1987).

[47] Sam Roberts, "The Legal Mosaic and Political Art of Council Maps," *New York Times*, July 22, 1991, p. B10; "Problems Seen in Council Map by Justice Department," *New York Times*, July 18, 1991, p. B4.

already on the margins of the immigrant communities—are beginning to redirect their efforts toward their communities in the United States, rather than anticipating return to their countries of origin. The change in women's long-term strategies, especially, is reflected in their higher naturalization and participation rates in American politics. It is reflected as well in the willingness of Latina activists to do more than simply mirror the ambivalence of mainstream immigrant organizations.

It is uncertain, though, how this initiative will translate in electoral politics. Until now Latin American women have been likely to play the role of ethnic intermediaries, serving as facilitators or negotiators between immigrants and the American political and bureaucratic systems, and Latin American men have taken charge of the mainstream immigrant organizations. It's still an open question as to which leadership cluster will be better positioned to enter the electoral sphere. On the one hand, immigrant women have more experience in dealing with American institutions, and so might seem to be the natural choices to step into electoral politics, as elected positions are to some degree an extension of that mediating role. On the other hand, activist women have been able to succeed in constructing the mediating role because this role has been undervalued by the rest of the immigrant population; men are still seen by many immigrant men *and* women as providing the more appropriate leadership for the community. Until now male leadership has focused its energies in first-generation organizations, where men can maintain their social status even if their economic status declines. However, over time, as participation in the American sphere becomes more valued, men may begin to supplant women as the most visible intermediaries between immigrants and the broader society.

In one scenario, then, men will run for electoral office, crowding women to the background. Some women activists are convinced that men will want those leadership positions regardless of whether they are qualified, and are concerned that women might cede them these positions, if that is the price for men's participation: "Women participate more because they have a more responsible vision of what is going on. They are more ready to participate. Men only participate if they have a position of leadership. You have to give men a position [with a title]. Women are readier to just be members."[48] One woman activist noted cynically that if a seat opened up, men would want to run for it, and more qualified women would be shunted aside. Even if there are women who would be more qualified candidates, the expectations are that men will likely step forward to take any open positions. Four Latino men did run in City Council district 25 after the new redistricting in 1991.

[48] Interview (in Spanish), November 4, 1991.

None had any political experience, and all lost. No women ran. As one Puerto Rican activist said, "it's a very interesting thing, which drives me crazy: that's women's work. The guys run for office, and the women help them get there."[49]

But events may turn out otherwise. Nydia Velasquez and Elizabeth Colon, the two leading candidates against Stephen Solarz in the 1992 primary elections for congressional district 12 (which includes parts of Elmhurst, Jackson Heights and Corona in Queens, and also stretches into Brooklyn and Manhattan) were both Puerto Rican women who had come into politics through community organizations and mediating institutions between government and Puerto Rican migrants. In an upset victory, Nydia Velasquez won the primary, and went on to be elected the first Puerto Rican congresswoman. Though both women are Puerto Rican and not immigrants per se, they indicate the potential women may have of using the intermediary positions they occupy to launch electoral political careers, and the support they may be able to garner from Latino voters willing to accommodate themselves to the idea of female leadership. So things may be changing. A Colombian respondent captured the mood: "It's time," she stated, "that we stop letting ourselves be used. If [men] aren't going to give us what they promised, then we aren't going to help them or support them either."[50]

Regardless of whether future Latino electoral candidates in Queens are women or men, their efforts will have been greatly facilitated by the groundwork laid by a group of first-generation immigrant activists, for the most part women. These activists have worked to lower the costs of participation for new Hispanic voters by encouraging voter registration and participation, building ties with elected officials within the Democratic and Republican Parties, laying the foundations for independent Latino political organizations, and working for majority-Hipanic districts in the area.

[49] Interview, April 17, 1991.
[50] Interview (in Spanish), August 28, 1991.

V

CONCLUSION: THE NEW AMERICANS

10

Liminality and Democratic Citizenship

Immigration is often described as if it were a liminal experience, in which immigrants have to go through a kind of rite of passage to get to a goal on the other side.[1] This liminality is usually seen from two very different perspectives. From that of the host country, immigration is a liminal condition leading eventually, but inevitably, to becoming American. From the point of view of the sojourner, immigration may be imagined as a rite of passage leading to a return to the home country with status and economic position secured. Both involve successful passage through the middle ground of the immigrant experience—taking on a nebulous identity, and occupying a marginal position in society. But the immigration experience may in fact be neither of these. What if there is no other side to the liminal? Delayed or delaying, first-generation immigrants may find themselves trapped betwixt and between. Victor Turner, who developed the idea of liminality, foresaw this possibility; he called it a "marginal state," in which there is no assurance of resolving its inherent ambiguity.

Being In-between

This book argues that the lives of first-generation Latin American immigrants are characterized by this sense of marginality: they have ties to two nations, and are unwilling or unable to cut ties fully to either. A Colombian

[1] See Victor Turner (1974), particularly the essays "Social Dramas and Ritual Metaphors" and "Pilgrimages as Social Progress." See also Turner 1969 and Norton 1988.

in Queens, for example, noted that "a person can spend ten or twenty years [in the United States], and have the exact same problem [of fitting in]. . . . There is something innate in this culture . . . which sets us apart. An *Hispano*, a complete *Hispano* in the first generation, will never enter 100 percent into the culture."[2] Yet immigrants who return to their countries of origin experience feelings of disconnectedness as well. A Uruguayan immigrant told me about a group that had been formed in Uruguay called "Ex-residents of the United States," whose members have all lived in New York City. They meet regularly, like a support group. At the meeting he went to, he said, "there were twenty people in the room . . . all with one thing in common: nobody knew what to do. Whether to stay in Uruguay, or to come back here. That is to say, they missed many things from here, but they knew that there they were doing things they couldn't do here. So then it's the life of the Eternal Immigrant."[3]

Immigrants' marginality is particularly evident in the sphere of formal politics. Latin American immigrants may *like* the United States, but even though surveys indicate they desire to stay, the great majority have not yet become citizens, and have not become involved in formal political institutions. How do we reconcile these two things—the desire to become a member of a polity, but the reluctance to actually do so? This study suggests that the answer lies in the formal and institutional irreconcilability of the two polities between which they are caught.

I argued in the first part of this book that Latin American immigrants find Queens to be a somewhat inhospitable political environment. Political parties are not eager to spend the resources of their debilitated machines on mobilizing new entrants, so they wait instead for those on the margins to mobilize first, before accepting them as full-fledged political actors. To become such a political actor is to become a voting citizen. But for many Latin American immigrants, becoming a U.S. citizen means breaking definitively with the myth of return and cutting formal ties with their countries of origin. Faced with political options that require them to choose one country or the other, Latin American immigrants choose neither. Instead they operate on the margins of both.

To escape the mutually exclusive choices demanded by formal politics, Latin American immigrants turn to a politics of in-between. As I indicated in the second part of this book, such a strategy allows them to express their ties to both polities (though maintaining distance from formal political commitments) through the manipulation of multiple identities. These identi-

[2] Interview (in Spanish), July 16, 1991.
[3] Interview (in Spanish), January 9, 1992.

ties draw on continuities from immigrants' countries of birth, but respond to conditions in this country. The politics of identity plays out through breaks and continuities both in the forms of organization and repertoires of actions of Latin American immigrants in Queens, and in individual immigrants' own search for an equilibrium between the two polities.

Immigrants have had to struggle to find this balance between the two polities on their own. Neither their countries of origin nor the United States have been particularly receptive to, or even aware of, the dilemma Latin American immigrants face. In the United States, for instance, the fact that many Latin American immigrants do not participate in formal politics has gone almost unnoticed. Despite the increasing attention being paid to the "immigrant problem," Latin American immigrants remain in this sense invisible.

First-generation immigrants search to find ways out of this liminal space between two nations, and in the third section of this book I outlined the gendered strategies they have pursued to achieve this end. On the one hand, mainstream immigrant organizations have petitioned their countries of origin for the right to dual citizenship, for avoiding the loss of their original citizenship when naturalizing as Americans reduces the costs immigrants confront as they try to decide where to direct their political resources. On the other hand, activist women and others on the margin of the immigrant community focus on politics in this country, appealing to the federal government, for example, to intervene in local politics, a strategy that in Queens resulted in the literal re-drawing of the political playing field.

Lowering the Costs for Noncitizens

These strategies have successfully reduced some of the costs of political membership and participation in the United States. Achieving dual citizenship on the one hand and the creation of minority voting districts on the other has alleviated immigrants' political marginality. Neither approach, however, is sufficient in itself.

Achieving dual citizenship seems to come close to resolving the dilemma of liminality, especially in reducing costs of naturalization in the United States. There are, of course, practical difficulties with dual citizenship. How will the states involved deal with such mundane matters as taxation, divorce, and military service? In practice, though, the United States, like every other nation, already deals with these problems. It tolerates dual citizenship in a variety of circumstances: if a child is born outside the United States in a country which grants its own citizenship at birth, for instance, or if one of a child's parents is a citizen of another country, which then may make citizenship claims as well (Tiao 1993: 210).[4] All democratic polities have to deal, at some level, with multiple loyalties. The problems are not resolved by arguing for exclusive citizenship. Given the increasing complexities of the real world, dual citizenship may actually simplify rather than complicate the picture. But there is a more fundamental problem.

Dual citizenship may seem to slice through immigrants' Gordian knot and thereby reduce the costs they face. Theoretically at least it allows immigrants to make the choice of membership and participation as they wish. However, this view implicitly assumes that political incorporation is largely the responsibility of each individual, and that immigrants will participate as they learn enough of the civic language of the United States to be participants. This view doesn't recognize the *other* costs which immigrants may face as they try to enter the formal political sphere.

Although Latin American immigrants, once naturalized, tend to have high registration rates,[5] these don't necessarily translate into actual participation in formal politics. The NALEO National Latino Immigrant Survey, for example, indicates that voting rates are significantly lower than rates of registration.[6] Even Asian immigrants to the United States, who have much higher naturalization rates than Latin American immigrants (Barkan 1983), naturalized citizens still have much lower registration and participation rates in electoral politics than whites do, even accounting for socioeconomic differences (Lien 1995; Lien 1994). It appears that immigrants may be encountering additional barriers to full participation, reflected in low rates of registration and low rates of turnout (DeSipio 1996; Schmidt 1992). Full citizenship requires not only formal membership, but participatory inclusion as well.

The second strategy that immigrants in Queens have chosen to pursue—appealing to the federal government to step in at key moments in the redistricting process, and lobbying for changes that would increase Hispanic

[4] In *Kawakita v. U.S.* (343 U.S. 717), the Supreme Court stated that dual nationality is a "status long recognized in the law" and that "a person may have and exercise rights of nationality in two countries and be subject to the responsibilities of both. The mere fact that he asserts the rights of one citizenship does not . . . mean that he renounces the other."

[5] Celia Dugger, "Immigrant Voters Reshape Politics," *New York Times*, March 10, 1996, p. 1, 28. More than two-thirds of new citizens in New York City register immediately after the naturalization ceremony, according to the New York Immigrant Coalition. The NALEO National Immigrant Survey found registration rates of 80% or more for most groups of naturalized Latin American immigrants; Mexicans are the exception with registration rates of "only" 70% (Pachón and DeSipio 1994: 87).

[6] In Pachón and DeSipio's sample the turnout for Dominicans, South Americans and Central Americans in the 1984 presidential elections was around 50%; Mexican participation was lowest at 38%, and Cuban participation highest at 71% (Pachón and DeSipio 1994: 88).

representation—does circumvent some of the opposition to immigrant political incorporation on the part of political parties, which are far from eager to expend resources on the recruitment of marginal political players and actively resistant to sharing political spoils with newcomers. But this strategy will not work on its own. The new City Council district drawn in Corona in 1991 as a "Latino district" did not elect a Latino to office; despite the preponderant Hispanic population, too few Latinos are citizens and voters. In effect, Latinos remain a minority. There is the danger that such districts will remain "rotten boroughs"—electing representatives who are chosen by only a few, without recognizing the needs of the many. So formal inclusion is not sufficient.

Dual citizenship and federal intervention in the redistricting process may be significant first steps toward political participation, but they are not panaceas. The two strategies are complementary—one ameliorating the costs of membership, the other, of representation—but neither fully addresses the question of *participation*. Both solutions are driven by elites within the immigrant community, appealing to either their country of origin or to the authorities in their country of residence, for end runs around the formal costs imposed on citizenship and representation. But they do not result in the automatic incorporation and participation of immigrants in politics, nor indicate in what shape or form this incorporation will take place. The work of naturalizing, registering, and mobilizing immigrants in this country still lies ahead.

Alternative Proposals and Their Problems

The dilemma of being caught between two nations is by no means unique to Latin American immigrants in Queens. Political incorporation of immigrants is a global problem. There are larger population movements in the world today than at any other time in history. The UN reports that in 1992 there were one hundred million people living in countries other than their country of origin last year, twice the number of 1989. Two percent of the world's population is residing in a country other than that of their birth, and this can only be expected to increase (United Nations Population Fund, 1993: 7). The numbers of people immigrating, migrating, or simply dislocated from one country to another underscores the urgency of addressing their insertion and participation in political life.

The scope of the problem has drawn the attention of an increasing number of scholars and policymakers, who have raised some hard questions about the definition of citizenship, the place of participation, and the role of the state. Their suggestions about resolving or mitigating the dilemma of liminality fall into two clusters. The first proposal argues that increasing global internationalization makes the notion of national citizenship increasingly archaic and obsolete, and recommends a notion of transnational citizenship instead. The second view sets out a case for localized political rights for long-term residents in host countries. In this perspective, local citizenship should make up for the deficiencies of national citizenship. There are problems with both of these solutions.

The first proposal draws on the notion of transnationalism for a reconception of our very ideas of citizenship (Rouse 1995; Bamyeh 1993; Sutton 1992; Appadurai 1990; Benmayor 1988). Theorists of transnationalism focus on "the manner in which migrants, through their life ways and daily practices, reconfigure space so that their lives are lived simultaneously within two or more nation-states" (Basch, Schiller, and Szanton-Blanc 1994: 28; see also Duany 1994; Portes and Grosfoguel 1994; Glick-Schiller et al. 1992; Rouse 1991; Sutton 1987). "Over time and with extensive movement back and forth, communities of origin and destination increasingly comprise transnational circuits—social and geographic spaces that arise through the circulation of people, money, goods and information . . . . Over time, migrant communities become culturally "transnationalized," incorporating ideologies, practices, expectations, and political claims from both societies to create a 'culture of migration' that is distinct from the culture of both the sending and receiving nation" (Massey and Durand 1992: 8).

This new migrant political space is not simply the manifestation of a "deterritorialized state," in which the migrants' home state extends its claims across the boundaries of other states to include its citizens who may live physically dispersed, but who "remain socially, politically, culturally, and often economically part of the nation-state of their ancestors" (Basch, Schiller, and Szantos-Blanc 1994: 8).[7] Instead, proponents of the transnational perspective stress that there is the emergence of a new formulation for citizenship: a *postnational*, or *transnational*, citizenship, with its basis in an international human rights regime (Jacobson 1996; Soysal 1994: 1, 165–66). With individual rights disassociated from the state, the importance of

[7] Many nations—Korea, Mexico, Turkey, Algeria among them—maintain a claim on their nationals abroad. One example of this was the "tenth department" popularized by President Aristide of Haiti when he was in exile in the United States in the early 1990s: in addition to the nine administrative divisions on the island, he included Haitians living in the United States (Basch, Schiller, and Szanton-Blanc 1994: 146–47). But this claim is rarely more than rhetorical, stopping far short of equal political and civic rights. In spite of the language of the "citizens abroad," for instance, the Haitian legislature turned down any inclusion of Haitians as dual citizens (ibid.: 212). Participatory citizenship is not encouraged.

national citizenship is fading away. Territorial boundaries are increasingly less relevant as an organizing principle of social interaction (Basch, Schiller, and Szanton-Blanc 1994: 52; Duany 1994: 2–3; Sutton 1992: 237). Individuals' identities are increasingly characterized by fluid, multiple attachments that stretch across frontiers in a "single field of social relations" (Basch, Schiller, and Szanton-Blanc 1994: 5).

The problem with this perspective is that it doesn't take politics seriously. The proposal for transnational citizenship is, perhaps, the logical extension of T. H. Marshall's influential argument including social and economic rights in addition to political rights under the conception of citizenship (1950), but it turns Marshall's argument around and focuses on civil and social rights at the *expense* of political rights. Citizenship is more than a formal status of basic equality in a community, entitling one to a set of rights—it is also an expression of one's membership in a *political* community (Kymlicka and Norman 1995: 301), which entails deliberation and decision-making. The transnational proposal sees citizenship as the holding of a set of rights, but not as participation in deliberation. The descriptions of mechanisms and institutions of participation by authors pursuing this line of thought tend to be thin, or more likely, nonexistent.[8] The fact is, it is hard to think of having functioning democratic institutions without, in some form, the presence of the state.[9]

The second set of proposals acknowledges the importance of political life, and the need to incorporate immigrants at the margins. Limiting participation in political life to citizens, critics argue, is a significant limitation on representative democracy (Hammar 1990b: 2). The solution is to allow participation in local politics to all long-term permanent residents (Rodriguez et al. 1995; Schmidt 1992, Hammar 1990a, 1990b and 1989). Local citizenship would not only give immigrants a voice in the decision-making process, but also serve as a political apprenticeship, allowing those on the margins to educate themselves as citizens (Bauböck 1994: 102).[10] Participa-

[8] Soysal might disagree with this characterization of her argument; she calls for a "post-national citizenship confer[ring] upon every person the right and duty of participation in the authority structures and public life of a polity, regardless of their historical or cultural ties to that community" (Soysal 1994: 1). Nonetheless, this strand of her thought remains underdeveloped and rather vague.

[9] It may very well be true that national, territorial notions of citizenship are inadequate, as some have argued (Connolly 1993), so that we need a new theory of universalistic citizenship to fit an increasingly global economy (Soysal 1994; Bauböck 1994; Turner 1986). But until an institutional framework is in place to guarantee democratic practices at the international level, it would not do to ignore the importance of political citizenship in the nation-state.

[10] This view draws on the standard arguments of democratic participatory theorists. See Barber 1984; Pateman 1970. It is concerned less with policy outcomes than with politics as a tool for human moral development.

tion in the local community is seen as the wellspring of citizenship (Lowndes 1995: 162; de Tocqueville [1835] 1946: 66).

The objection to the local citizenship approach is certainly not that it's impracticable. Some version of local political rights have been granted to noncitizens in a half-dozen European countries since the 1970s (Miller 1989: 129–32).[11] This solution has even been tried before in the United States: noncitizen suffrage was allowed in this country from 1789 to 1924. Immigrants had the right to vote in local and sometimes national elections by signing "first papers"—a declaration of the intent to become a citizen (Raskin 1993; Tiao 1993; Rosberg 1977). A total of eighteen states, mostly in the midwest and western United States, experimented with noncitizen suffrage until increasing hostility to immigrants led to a backlash and repeal of voting rights. In the nineteenth century, Raskin observes that voting by aliens in local elections was explicitly seen as a kind of "civic education and training for the fuller rights of national citizenship" (1993: 1454). Although today every state in the union requires that voters in statewide and federal elections be citizens (Tiao 1993: 177), there is no constitutional prohibition stopping states from allowing immigrants to vote. In fact, there are still places in the United States where noncitizens can vote in elections—New York school board elections, as I've noted (and those in Chicago). Takoma Park, Maryland, gave noncitizens the right to vote in municipal elections in 1992.[12]

The main drawback of local enfranchisement for citizens is not its feasibility, but that, as the earlier experimentation with immigrant suffrage in the United States illustrates, it is reversible. Where they are not guaranteed by the Constitution, noncitizen suffrage and political participation are always precarious.[13] Local citizenship shares many of the same problems as the notion of postnational citizenship. It allows multiple memberships in various polities, but not equal membership. The modern notion of citizenship secures equal membership for all members of a society. Local citizenship takes the idea of politics—particularly through local participation—seriously, but in the end, is also an argument for a kind of secondary membership status in the polity.[14]

[11] The right to vote in local-level elections has been granted in Sweden, Norway, Denmark, Finland, the Netherlands, Ireland, and the Swiss cantons of Neuchâtel and Jura.

[12] In 1992 the New York State Assembly's Task Force on New Americans also recommended a bill that would extend the vote to noncitizen residents. As of this writing, nothing has come of this proposal. See Deborah Sontag, "Advocates for Immigrants Explore Voting Rights for Noncitizens," *New York Times*, July 31, 1992, p. B1.

[13] For the courts' position on this issue see the discussion in Tiao 1993: 176–80.

[14] In more ways than one. As the Fainsteins point out, involvement in local politics by itself is often frustratingly ineffectual. Even though participatory mechanisms may exist, these may not allow people to affect the larger context which affects them—decisions made at the state or na-

Both "transnational citizenship" and local citizenship are partial, insubstantial, and insecure. Both of them, by themselves, are simulacra of full citizenship. Even if the gap between the rights held by resident aliens and those held by citizens has been shrinking to the point of meaninglessness, as some authors have charged (Schuck 1989; Schuck and Smith 1985), these rights are still less secure and more easily modified than the rights of citizens (Carens 1989: 36). Full citizenship must be basic—constitutional—to a democratic polity. It cannot exist at the whim or discretion of the state.

Raising the Costs for Noncitizens

In any case, it seems the current of American politics, rather than moving toward lowering costs for noncitizens to enter the polity, is headed in the opposite direction. In response to the perceived crisis of illegal immigration, local, state and federal governments have begun trying a number of strategies since the late 1980s to raise the costs of noncitizenship. It is now more difficult for noncitizens to receive social welfare benefits,[15] to receive an education,[16] or to speak a language other than English.[17] These laws and proposals may be intended primarily as symbolic gestures, but their general effect is to reduce the access of both legal and undocumented immigrants to government services, and to political participation more generally.

---

tional level. Particularly in an increasingly global, internationalized economy, the effect of local politics, while not insignificant, is restricted (Fainstein and Fainstein 1993; Peterson 1981). It is, in the end, a very limited kind of participation.

[15] Benefits have been denied to undocumented residents, both at the state level and increasingly at the national level. Proposition 187 in California, passed in November 1994, authorized a cutoff of a range of benefits for undocumented aliens living in the state. In August 1996 the U.S. Congress followed suit, cutting welfare, medicaid, and social security benefits not only to undocumented residents but to legal permanent residents as well. See Robert Pear, "Clinton Says He'll Sign Bill Overhauling Welfare System," *New York Times*, August 1, 1996. See also "Immigration Bill Seeks to Cut Welfare Abuse," *Christian Science Monitor*, April 20, 1996.

[16] Following California's lead, Congress has also considered proposals to allow states to deny education benefits to the children of undocumented immigrants. See Eric Schmitt, "Immigration Overhaul Moves toward Vote," *New York Times*, August 2, 1996.

[17] Since 1986 at least 23 states, 41 counties, and 15 cities have passed measures making English the official language of that jurisdiction (see "Suffolk Vote Backs Making English Official Language," *New York Times*, August 14, 1996, p. B5). In 1996 a similar measure was approved by the U.S. House of Representatives, making it likely that the matter will continue to be addressed at the federal level as well (see "House Votes English Official Language," Reuters, August 1, 1996; Carl Schmitt, "A Law to Learn 'Em a Thing or Two about the English Language," *New York Times*, July 28, 1996). This in spite of the fact that research on language acquisition has generally indicated that contemporary immigrants are learning English as fast, or faster, than earlier generations of arrivals. See Portes and Schauffler 1994.

The new policies may have had the perverse effect of actually increasing the number of people applying for naturalization. While there were 384,000 new citizens in 1992, more than one million people became citizens in 1994, and again in 1995.[18] Some views, Proposition 187 in California, or Congress' cutting back on benefits for legal and illegal immigrants, or the push for making English the "official language" of the United States may be all for the good, because they encourage people to become citizens (Glazer 1996). If naturalization by intimidation works, perhaps there won't be a marginalized population of nonimmigrants to worry about in the United States.

There is the possibility that the dramatic increase in naturalization figures may be a one-time occurrence. The numbers reflect the bulge of undocumented aliens who became permanent residents under the 1986 Immigration Reform and Control Act: slightly more than three million people became legal residents of the United States under the one-time amnesty offered by that legislation. These new legal residents became eligible for citizenship in 1993, so that one would expect a short-term bulge of citizenship applications as this group joins the normal numbers of immigrants seeking naturalization. However, as the numbers of naturalizations continues onward, this explanation seems increasingly unsatisfactory.

A second possibility raises more troubling questions. Even if people are becoming citizens as a result of the latest anti-immigrant backlash, do we really want people to choose citizenship under duress? T. S. Eliot's Thomas Becket notes: "The last temptation is the greatest treason / To do the right thing, for the wrong reason." Is revoking or removing benefits really the way we want to go about encouraging people to become citizens? Having chosen naturalization purely instrumentally, what kind of citizens will they be? What will citizenship mean to them, except a choice of status as a safe haven? Do we want citizens by intimidation? The answer to this last question, it is fairly clear, should be "no." Commitment to a democratic citizenship depends on a noncoercive choice of membership and participation.

The Worth of Citizenship

The situation in the United States is far from bleak; the choice of American citizenship, unlike that of many countries, remains relatively open and transparent. The situation here is unlike that of some nations in Europe, for instance, where there can be a formidable set of administrative barriers

[18] Naturalization rates for New York City almost doubled from 1994 to 1995, to 141,235. The number of new citizens in the city in 1992 was only 43,447. See Celia Dugger, "Immigrant Voters Reshape Politics," *New York Times*, March 10, 1996, pp. 1, 28.

that keep immigrants from becoming naturalized citizens (de Rham 1990; Layton-Henry 1990). Aside from residency and language requirements, what is basically required of new citizens here is an affirmation of shared principle. Naturalization, like political participation more broadly, is largely up to the individual. It is largely because citizenship has been assumed to be unproblematic that the issue has been absent from the public discourse.

The United States, however, now has a large and growing population of first-generation immigrants, many of whom find themselves on the margins of political life. For many of them, taking on American citizenship is problematic. They perceive costs to naturalizing as American citizens, both from the unfriendly structure of party politics in the United States and from within their own immigrant communities. As a result, large numbers of people find themselves in between, living on the margins of formal politics.

Some observers justify this marginalization by saying the problem is only temporary, since of course immigrants' children are automatically citizens.[19] From this point of view the problem, if there is any, lasts only a generation. Of course, this means that a generation of new immigrants is left largely outside the polity, many of them for decades. If 50 percent of Latin American immigrants in Queens still do not naturalize after twenty years, what does this mean for democratic politics in New York City? If two-thirds or so of all first-generation immigrants remain outside formal electoral politics, what implications does this have for the practice of democracy in the United States? Nor is it likely that the effects of this political marginalization will stop at the first generation. If political behavior is learned, particularly from one's parents, what are the prospects for political participation in the second generation? If their parents are outside the polity, what opportunity will these new Americans have for civic education and participation in political life? Participation creates democratic citizens by fostering political learning, a sense of investment in the political system, and tolerance for the views of others. People learn to become citizens not by watching and waiting, but by *doing*.

There are two courses of action. First, we must reemphasize the importance of formal political participation in this country. The absence of a good

[19] At least for now. There is the possibility that, as Governor Wilson of California has suggested, the proposal to do away with the Fourteenth Amendment to the Constitution will be taken seriously. There are some indications that in the 1996 election year, the Republican Party was beginning to consider this alternative, at least at the symbolic level, introducing a bill to the House to this effect and writing into their party platform support for a constitutional amendment denying citizenship to children born to illegal immigrants. See Neil Lewis, "Bill Seeks to End Automatic Citizenship for All Born in the United States," *New York Times*, December 14, 1995, p. A26; David Rosenbaum, "Platform Unit Acts on Illegal Immigrants' Children," *New York Times*, August 6, 1996, p. A12. For a cautionary discussion, see "Birthright Citizenship Amendment: A Threat to Equality," *Harvard Law Review* 107 (1994): 1026–43.

many first-generation immigrants from this arena diminishes the meaningfulness of democracy not only for them, but also for the larger polity. Certainly efforts to extend participation in local politics should be encouraged. However, particularly in light of the immigrant experience in Queens, it is clear that participatory outreach cannot rely solely on the exertions of political parties. If new immigrants are to become full participants in the political process, their mobilization by other local institutions and organizations must be supported and extended. At the national level the situation requires valuing citizenship once again and making a concerted effort to extend citizenship to permanent residents in the United States. We surely wish to avoid returning to the chauvinism and blind patriotism of the turn of the century, exemplified by President Theodore Roosevelt, who stated with conviction that "we can have no 'fifty-fifty' allegiance in this country. Either a man is an American and nothing else, or he is not an American at all."[20]

Second therefore, we should reconsider the exclusivity of American citizenship and acknowledge the existence of dual nationalities. This will almost certainly raise the ire of those who wish to protect outmoded ideas of sovereignty, or insist that dual loyalties will undermine notions of national security. But the demand that politics be exclusive does not recognize the realities of an increasingly mobile and interdependent world. What is crucial is not to deny the mobility of people, but to try and build systems of political representation that can accommodate this new reality. We should therefore consider recognizing dual citizenship for first-generation immigrants, thereby facilitating their transition into the U.S. polity.

The United States seems to have abdicated any responsibility for the incorporation of new members into the practice of democratic politics. The costs of entering the polity have been left entirely up to new citizens to carry. In the short run, the displacement of these costs ensures that new members entering the polity take an inordinately long time to become active participants in the decisions which concern us all. In the long run, these costs undermine democratic institutions and practices. Democracies benefit from having active citizens, not apathetic residents. Good citizens do not come from nowhere, and good citizenship is not automatic; both must be nurtured. If we value our democratic institutions, then the responsibility for ensuring active citizenship is at least in part collectively our own.

[20] Address in New York, September 19, 1917, published in Roosevelt's *Works* (New York: G. P. Putnam's Sons, 1900), chap. 21, p. 38; cited in Schlesinger 1992: 35.

Appendix
Methodology and Interview Sample

This book is based primarily on qualitative survey methods, that is, open-ended interviews in conjunction with participant observation fieldwork. Qualitative methodology is not as useful a predictive tool as a standardized survey can be, but it can facilitate the construction of explanatory theory. More important, qualitative methods allow us to build theory through respondents' own self-interpretations and the observation of their everyday practices. In this book this theoretical approach means looking at the meaning of political participation through the views and experiences of first-generation Latin American immigrants themselves.

What can qualitative fieldwork do that cannot be achieved through survey work? Hochschild in *What's Fair?* sets out four claims for qualitative analysis. First, qualitative work may not provide conclusive "proof," but may resonate with the reader's own experience, so as to be persuasive or at least suggestive. Second, this kind of approach may discover theoretical questions which later may be formalized into hypotheses to be tested by quantitative social science methods. Third, instead of inferring the link between variables as quantitative research does, qualitative research can draw responses from actors showing how they link these variables in their own minds. "The conclusions from both types of research may be equally valid, even identical, but they emerge from different types of data, which are collected in different ways to yield different types of explanations for the same phenomenon." Fourth, Hochschild argues that qualitative research can generate findings that survey research cannot—implying that survey data may be "limited by either a failure of imagination or the exigencies of statistical techniques." In addition, qualitative work, being unconstrained by methodological considerations that require the inflexible continuity of research design and questions, can generate new theory and findings by taking change into account and breaking out of inherited categories. In these cases, qualitative analysis "may find results where surveys find only noise" (Hochschild 1981: 24–25).

Qualitative fieldwork is similar to photography. One photographer has noted that "A portrait is a likeness. The moment an emotion or fact is transformed into a photograph it is no longer a fact but an opinion. There is no such thing as inaccuracy in a photograph. All photographs are accurate. None of them is the truth."[1] Like photographic portraits, ethnographic studies in the social sciences do not claim to capture truth—only an accurate likeness. For the social scientist, the problem with qualitative work is that it is often difficult to generalize findings among a delimited group of people to a larger population. I work with this potential problem in two ways. First, by interweaving the interviews together with participant observation and fieldwork, and second, by setting the interviews and fieldwork in the context of survey and census data (Becerra and Zambrana 1985; Massey 1987). The combination of overlapping materials drawing on distinct methodologies allows me to make broader inferences and draw bolder conclusions from the interviews than would be possible using any single method on its own.

My fieldwork consists of notes taken as a participant observer at immigrant events and meetings, as well as records of day-to-day activities in the neighborhoods of north-central Queens. The fieldwork took eighteen months, from January 1991 to September 1992. In addition to this informal data-gathering, more formal open-ended interviews were carried out among contacts made during the fieldwork period. One hundred and twelve structured open-ended interviews were completed during a twelve-month period, from March 1991 to February 1992, all with adult respondents eighteen and older. Each of these interviews lasted between forty-five minutes and two hours.[2] Subjects for the interviews were drawn initially from public notices put out by community agencies and organizations active in the area, as well as lists of names drawn up by community groups or local government officials. Additional contacts were generated from initial

[1] Richard Avedon, quoted in Vicki Goldberg, "In the Game of Portraiture, the Photographer Almost Always Wins," *New York Times*, March 14, 1994, sec. 2, p. 37.

[2] Almost all the interviews were taped. Some respondents preferred not to have their interviews recorded. In these cases, I took extensive notes, and used these and my own recollection of the conversation to reconstruct the interview. In the body of the book, I make a distinction between formal taped interviews and more informal unrecorded interviews and conversations. In my footnotes I refer to the former as "Interview" and the latter as "Conversation."

interviews, in "snowball" fashion, and some were established directly while residing in the area. Through participant observation I was able to interact with people over a period of time and in a number of different contexts, which made the process of approaching them for interviews substantially easier. The refusal rate from potential interviewees was less than 3 percent.

The interviews and participant observation generated information about immigrants' experiences with immigration and with their work, their families, and their involvement in organizational life. I asked respondents about their views of community, leadership, politics, and politicians, as well as about their feelings toward other nationalities and ethnic groups. The questions were not strictly structured; their purpose was to give the interviewees the opportunity to present their views in their own language.

All methodologies have their biases. My own work reflects certain sampling biases inherent in snowball sampling. The interview sample was not randomly chosen—the group of interviewees was put together through press clippings, lists kept by the Hispanic Liaison in the office of the Queens borough president, and the suggestions of interviewees themselves. These were not "typical" immigrants. Of the ninety-five taped interviews of first-generation immigrants, eighty were with individuals who were members of political, professional, cultural, or sports organizations. Another seventeen interviews were completed with native-born Puerto Ricans and Anglo-Americans who were also involved in political or associational life, for a total of 112 interviews. The sample is heavily skewed toward those who are already active in some form of organizational life (though not in what they would consider to be "political" life); that is to say, toward people who are both visible and accessible. There were both pragmatic and methodological reasons for choosing this strategy. On the pragmatic side, approaching people already accustomed to visibility simplified problems of establishing trust, probably the single largest difficulty in a study of immigrants (Massey 1987; Cornelius 1982; Hendricks 1980). Organizational activists are also more self-conscious about their position in this country as immigrants. Methodologically, this choice of sample allowed me to test hypotheses about socioeconomic status and political participation with the very people one would expect to be most *likely* to participate in formal politics, but who did not (Verba et al. 1993). The reasons they indicated for why they did not, and the alternatives they constructed for themselves instead, are at the heart of this study.

The sample is somewhat skewed in other ways as well. First of all, the interviews represent some national groups better than others. Of the seven largest national groups in the first-generation Latino immigrant population

Table A.1. Taped interviews by national origin, first-generation immigrants, Queens

	Number of interviews	% of interview sample	% of Latino immigrant population, Queens
Colombian	35	40	26.2
Ecuadorian	19	22	14.0
Dominican	8	9	16.6
Argentine	5	6	2.8
Honduran	5	6	1.4
Cuban	4	5	6.6
Uruguayan	3	3	.9
Peruvian	2	2	6.9
Mexican	2	2	4.8
Nicaraguan	2	2	.9
Chilean	2	2	1.2
Panamanian	1	1	1.4
Salvadoran	1	1	4.9
Total	89		

in Queens, two are relatively overrepresented; the rest, consequently, are underrepresented (see Table A.1). Colombians and Ecuadorians account for 62 percent of the taped interviews, but only 40 percent of first-generation immigrants in Queens. Dominicans and Peruvians, the third and fourth largest population groups, are relatively underrepresented. The deficiency in the number of Dominican interviews was made up, in large part, by informal participant observation as a member of the Dominican social club Hermanos Unidos in Corona, the neighborhood where I lived while conducting my fieldwork. The underrepresentation of Cubans, Salvadorans, and Mexicans is not problematic for the purposes of this project. Cubans had unique circumstances of arrival into the United States, which led to relative ease of entry into formal political participation here. Salvadorans and Mexicans, for their part, are still relative newcomers into the northeastern United States, and New York in particular. The great majority of immigrants from these two countries have arrived in the last ten years. As obtaining citizenship and initiating formal political participation seems to hinge on the length of stay in the United States, these populations are still too recent to be fully relevant to the concerns of this study.

Second, the interviews overrepresent the views of male immigrants relative to those of women (see Table A.2). Most of my informants were active in immigrant organizations; as organizational leadership is preponderantly male, this tended to skew the sample toward men. Still, there are enough

Table A.2. Taped interviews by gender, first-generation immigrants, Queens

	Number of interviews	% of sample	% of Latino immigrant population, Queens
Men	60	63	48.1
Women	35	37	51.9
Total	95		

Table A.3. Taped interviews by occupation, first-generation immigrants, Queens

Occupation	Number of interviews	% of interviews	% of Latino immigrant population, Queens
Professional	49	51.6	9.5
Business owner	12	12.6	1.3
Technical			3.5
Sales/clerical	3	3.2	13.7
Personal services			2.2
Skilled labor			5.0
Building maintenance	1	1.1	6.6
Textile work	1	1.1	5.2
Food preparation			6.4
Transportation			4.6
Construction			6.6
Factory work	4	4.2	6.2
Household staff			2.3
Not in the labor market	9	9.5	26.0
Unknown	16	16.8	
Total	95		

formal interviews with women (supplemented by participant observation and informal conversations) to give a good sense of gender differences in immigrants' approaches to and opinions about politics.

Third, the formal interviews concentrate on a relatively small sector of the Latin American immigrant population in Queens. This is clear when we look at the class makeup of the interview sample through respondents' occupations—despite limitations, still the best indicator I have for putting the taped interviews in the context of class (see Table A.3). Categories in the table are broad. First, "professional" includes those employed in everything from engineering to teaching, and ranges from clergy to college students. Second, the category "not in the labor market" lumps together women and men from various class backgrounds who are not holding or seeking jobs. The interviews are drawn overwhelmingly from the middle- and upper middle-class among these first-generation immigrants. But the class bias of the formal interviews only reinforces the thrust of the question I wish to explain. Why is it that even Latin American immigrants with relatively high socioeconomic status take so long to become formally involved in U.S. politics?

References

Abramson, Paul. 1983. *Political Attitudes in America: Formation and Change*. New York: W. H. Freeman.

Ackelsberg, Martha. 1984. "Women's Collaborative Activities and City Life: Politics and Policy." In *Political Women: Current Roles in State and Local Government*, ed. Janet Flammang, pp. 242–59. Beverly Hills: Sage.

Acuña, Rodolfo. [1972] 1981. *Occupied America: The Chicano's Struggle toward Liberation*. San Francisco: Canfield Press.

Adler, Norman, and Blanche Doris Blank. 1975. *Political Clubs in New York*. New York: Praeger.

Agger, Robert E., Daniel Goldrich, and Bert E. Swanson. 1964. *The Rulers and the Ruled: Political Power and Impotence in American Communities*. New York: Wiley.

Alba, Richard, 1990. *Ethnic Identity: The Transformation of White America*. New Haven: Yale University Press.

Alba, Richard, Nancy Denton, Shu-Yin Leung, and John R. Logan. 1995. "Neighborhood Change under Conditions of Mass Immigration: The New York City Region, 1970–1990." *International Migration Review* 29(3):625–56.

Alford, Robert, and Harry Scobie. 1968. "Sources of Local Political Involvement." *American Political Science Review* 62(4):1192–206.

Almond, Gabriel, and Sidney Verba. 1963. *The Civic Culture*. Princeton, N.J.: Princeton University Press.

Altamirano, Teófilo. 1992. *Exodo: Peruanos en el Exterior*. Lima, Peru: Fondo Editorial, Pontifica Universidad Católica del Peru.

———. 1990. *Los Que Se Fueron: Peruanos en los Estados Unidos*. Lima, Peru: Fondo Editorial, Pontifica Universidad Católica del Peru.

Alvarez, Robert. 1987. "A Profile of the Citizenship Process among Hispanics in the United States." *International Migration Review* 21(2):327–51.

Anderson, Benedict R. [1983] 1992. *Imagined Communities: Reflections on the Origin and Spread of Nationalism.* New York: Verso.

Andrade, Sally. 1982. "Family Roles of Hispanic Women: Stereotypes, Empirical Findings, and Implications for Research." In *Work, Family, Women: Latina Women in Transition,* ed. Ruth E. Zambrana, pp. 95–106. New York: Hispanic Research Center, Fordham University.

Aponte, Richard. 1991. "Urban Hispanic Poverty: Disaggregations and Explanations." *Social Problems* 38(4):516–28.

Appadurai, Arjun. 1990. "Disjuncture and Difference in the Global Cultural Economy." *Public Culture* 2(2):1–24.

Arian, Asher, Arthur S. Goldberg, John Mollenkopf, and Edward Rogowsky. 1991. *Changing New York City Politics.* New York: Routledge.

Astudillo, Jaime, and Claudio Cordero. 1990. *Huayrapamushcas en USA: Flujos Migratorios de la Region Centro-Sur del Ecuador a los EEUU.* Quito, Ecuador: Editorial El Conejo.

Atunes, George, and Charles M. Gaitz. 1975. "Ethnicity and Participation: A Study of Mexican-Americans, Blacks and Whites." *American Journal of Sociology* 80(5):1192–211.

Auster, Lawrence. 1991. *The Path to National Suicide: An Essay on Immigration and Multiculturalism.* Monterey, Va.: American Immigration Control Foundation.

Austin, D. Mark, and Yoko Baba. 1990. "Social Determinants of Neighborhood Attachment." *Sociological Spectrum* 10(1):59–78.

Avey, Michael. 1989. *The Demobilization of American Voters: A Comprehensive Theory of Voter Turnout.* New York: Greenwood.

Baca, Eddie. 1991. *A 1991 Status Report on the New York Puerto Rican/Latino Voter and Population.* New York: Management Consultants.

Bailey, Thomas, and Roger Waldinger. 1991. "The Changing Ethnic/Racial Division of Labor." In *Dual City: Restructuring New York,* ed. John Hull Mollenkopf and Manuel Castells, pp. 43–78. New York: Russell Sage Foundation.

Bamyeh, Mohammed A. 1993. "Transnationalism." *Current Sociology* 41(3):1–95.

Barber, Benjamin. 1984. *Strong Democracy: Participatory Politics for a New Age.* Berkeley: University of California Press.

Barber, James. 1969. *Citizen Politics.* Chicago: Markham.

Barkan, Elliot. 1983. "Whom Shall We Integrate? A Comparative Analysis of the Immigration and Naturalization Trends of Asians before and after the 1965 Immigration Act, 1951–1978." *Journal of American Ethnic History* 3 (Fall):29–57.

Barrera, Mario. 1979. *Race and Class in the Southwest.* Notre Dame, Ind.: University of Notre Dame Press.

Barrera, Mario, Charles Ornelas, and Carlos Muñoz. 1972. "The Barrio as Internal Colony." In *People and Politics in Urban Society,* ed. Harlan Hahn, pp. 465–98. Beverly Hills: Sage.

Barth, Frederik. 1969. "Introduction." In *Ethnic Groups and Boundaries: The Social Organization of Culture Difference,* ed. Frederik Barth, pp. 9–38. Boston: Little, Brown.

Basch, Linda. 1987. "The Politics of Caribbeanization: Vincentians and Grenadians in New York." In *Caribbean Life in New York: Sociocultural Dimensions*, ed. Constance R. Sutton and Elsa Chaney, pp. 160–81. New York: Center for Migration Studies.

Basch, Linda, Nina Glick Schiller, and Cristina Szanton-Blanc. 1994. *Nations Unbound: Transnational Projects, Postcolonial Predicaments, and Deterritorialized Nation-States.* Basel, Switzerland: Gordon and Breach.

Bauböck, Rainer. 1994. *Transnational Citizenship: Membership and Rights in International Migration.* Brookfield, Vt.: Edward Elgar.

Becerra, Rosina, and Ruth E. Zambrana. 1985. "Methodological Approaches to Research on Hispanics." *Social Work Research and Abstracts* 21(2):42–49.

Beck, Roy. 1994. "The Ordeal of Immigration in Wausau." *The Atlantic Monthly* 273(4):84–97.

Bell, Daniel. 1975. "Ethnicity and Social Change." In *Ethnicity: Theory and Practice*, ed. Nathan Glazer and Daniel P. Moynihan, pp. 141–74. Cambridge: Harvard University Press.

Bendixen and Associates. 1991. "WXTV Public Opinion Poll." October.

Benmajor, Rina. 1988. "Crossing Borders: The Politics of Multiple Identity." *Centro de Estudios Puertorriqueños Bulletin* 2(3):72–77.

Bennet, Stephen Earl, and David Resnick. 1990. "The Implications of Nonvoting for Democracy in the United States." *American Journal of Political Science* 34(3):771–802.

Berelson, Bernard. 1952. "Democratic Theory and Public Opinion." *Public Opinion Quarterly* 16(3):313–30.

Berelson, Bernard, Paul Lazarsfeld, and William McPhee. 1954. *Voting: A Study of Opinion Formation in a Presidential Campaign.* Chicago: University of Chicago Press.

Black, Jerome H. 1982. "Immigrant Political Adaptation in Canada: Some Tentative Findings." *Canadian Journal of Political Science* 15(1):3–27.

Blauner, Bob. 1972. *Racial Oppression in America.* New York: Harper and Row.

Blumenthal, S. 1970. "The Private Organization in the Naturalization and Citizenship Process." *International Migration Review* 5(4):448–63.

Bodnar, John. 1985. *The Transplanted: A History of Immigrants in Urban America.* Bloomington: Indiana University Press.

Bogen, Elizabeth. 1987a. "Recent Statistics on New York City Immigration." In *Immigration in New York*, ed. Elizabeth Bogen, pp. 33–49. New York: Praeger.

———, ed. 1987b. *Immigration in New York.* New York: Praeger.

Bonacich, Edna. 1980. "Class Approaches to Ethnicity and Race." *The Insurgent Sociologist* 10(2):9–23.

———. 1972. "A Theory of Ethnic Antagonism: The Split Labor Market." *American Sociological Review* 37(5):547–59.

Borjas, George. 1990. *Friends or Strangers: The Impact of Immigrants on the U.S. Economy.* New York: Basic Books.

———. 1989. "Immigrant and Emigrant Earnings: A Longitudinal Study." *Economic Inquiry* 27 (January):21–37.

Bouvier, Leon, and Lindsey Grant. 1994. *How Many Americans? Population, Immigration, and the Environment.* San Francisco: Sierra Club Books.

Brady, Henry E., Sidney Verba, and Kay Lehman Schlozman. 1995. "Beyond SES: A Resource Model of Political Participation." *American Political Science Review* 89(2):271–94.

Brauen, Marsha, and Kathryn Newcomer. 1977. "Political Socialization: A Topical Bibliography." *Youth and Society* 8(3):299–320.

Bray, David. 1984. "Economic Development: The Middle Class and International Migration in the Dominican Republic." *International Migration Review* 18(2): 217–36.

Brea Franco, Julio. 1986. "Reforma Electoral y Representación Política en el Sistema Electoral Dominicano." In *Sistemas Electorales y Representación Política en Latinoamerica,* ed. Fundación Friedrich Ebert, pp. 227–64. Madrid, España: Graficos Geranios S.A.

Brecher, Charles, and Raymond D. Horton with Robert A. Cropf and Dean Michael Mead. 1993. *Power Failure: New York City Politics and Policy since 1960.* New York: Oxford University Press.

Brimelow, Peter. 1995. *Alien Nation: Common Sense about America's Immigration Disaster.* New York: Random House.

———. 1992. "Time to Rethink Immigration?" *National Review* 44(12):30–46.

Brodkin Sacks, Karen. 1988. "Gender and Grassroots Leadership." In *Women and the Politics of Enlightenment,* ed. Ann Bookman and Sandra Morgen, pp. 77–96. Philadelphia: Temple University Press.

Caldeira, Gregory, Aage R. Clausen, and Samuel C. Patterson. 1990. "Partisan Mobilization and Electoral Participation." *Electoral Studies* 9(3):191–204.

Calderon, Jose. 1992. "'Hispanic' and 'Latino': The Viability of Categories for Panethnic Unity." *Latin American Perspectives* 19(4):37–44.

Calvo, Manuel A., and Steven Rosenstone. 1989. *Hispanic Political Participation.* San Antonio, Tex.: Southwest Voter Research Institute.

Camacho, David E. 1987. "Chicano Urban Politics: The Role of the Political Entrepreneur." Mexican American Studies and Research Center, University of Arizona, Working Paper Series. June.

Campbell, Angus, Philip E. Converse, Warren E. Miller, and Donald Stokes. 1960. *The American Voter.* New York: Wiley.

Campbell, Angus, Gerald Gurin, and Warren E. Miller. 1954. *The Voter Decides.* Evanston, Ill.: Row, Peterson.

Cardona Gutierrez, Ramiro, Carmen Ines Cruz, and Juanita Castaño. 1980. "El Proceso migratorio en Colombia: el flujo a los Estados Unidos." In *El Exodo de colombianos: un estudio de la corriente migratoria a los Estados Unidos y un intento para proporcionar el retorno,* ed. Ramiro Cardona Gutierrez and Sara Rubiano de Velasquez, pp. 55–141. Bogotá, Colombia: Ediciones Tercer Mundo.

Carens, Joseph. 1989. "Membership and Morality: Admission to Citizenship in Liberal Democratic States." In *Immigration and the Politics of Citizenship in Europe and North America,* ed. William Rogers Brubaker, pp. 31–50. Lanham, Md.: University Press of America.

Castles, Stephen, and Godula Kosack. 1973. *Immigrant Workers and Class Structure in Western Europe.* New York: Oxford University Press.

Castro Caycedo, German. 1989. *El Hueco: La Entrada Ilegal de Colombianos a Estados Unidos Por Mexico.* Bogotá, Colombia: Planeta.

Cattan, Peter. 1993. "The Diversity of Hispanics in the U.S. Work Force." *Monthly Labor Review* 116(8):3–16.

Chambers, Iain. 1994. *Migrancy, Culture, Identity.* London: Routledge.

Chaney, Elsa. 1980a. "Colombians in New York City: Theoretical and Policy Issues." In *Sourcebook on the New Immigration,* ed. Roy Simon Bryce-Laporte, pp. 285–94. New Brunswick, N.J.: Transaction Books.

———. 1980b. "América Latina en los Estados Unidos: colombianos en Nueva York." In *El Exodo de colombianos: un estudio de la corriente migratoria a los Estados Unidos y un intento para proporcionar el retorno,* ed. Ramiro Cardona Gutierrez and Sara Rubiano de Velasquez, pp. 191–236. Bogotá, Colombia: Ediciones Tercer Mundo.

Chiswick, Barry. 1980. "Immigrant Earnings Patterns by Sex, Race, and Ethnic Groupings." *Monthly Labor Review* 103(10):22–25.

———. 1978. "The Effect of Americanization on the Earnings of Foreign-born Men." *Journal of Political Economy* 86 (October):897–921.

———. 1976. "An Analysis of the Economic Progress and Impact of Immigrants." Final Report to the U.S. Department of Labor, Employment, and Training Administration. University of Illinois, Chicago.

Cohen, Abner. 1985. *The Symbolic Construction of Community.* London: Tavistock.

Cohen, Jean. 1985. "Strategy or Identity: New Theoretical Paradigms and Contemporary Social Movements." *Social Research* 52(4):663–716.

Cohen, Steven Martin, and Robert E. Kapsis. 1978. "Participation of Blacks, Puerto Ricans, and Whites in Voluntary Associations: A Test of Current Theories." *Social Forces* 56(4):1052–71.

Commons, John R. 1907. *Races and Immigrants in America.* New York: Macmillan.

Connolly, William. 1993. "Democracy and Territoriality." In *Rhetorical Republic: Governing Representations in American Politics,* ed. Frederick M. Dolan and Thomas L. Dunn, pp. 249–74. Amherst: University of Massachusetts Press.

———. [1974] 1983. *The Terms of Political Discourse.* Princeton, N.J.: Princeton University Press.

Conway, M. Margaret. 1991. *Political Participation in the United States.* Washington, D.C.: CQ Press.

Cornelius, Wayne. 1982. "Interviewing Undocumented Immigrants: Methodological Reflections Based on Fieldwork in Mexico and the U.S." *International Migration Review* 16(2):378–411.

Cornwell, Elmer E. 1964. "Bosses, Machines, and Ethnic Groups." *Annals of the American Academy of Political and Social Science* 353 (May):27–39.

Crotty, William. 1971. "Party Effort and Its Impact on the Vote." *American Political Science Review* 65(2):439–450.

Cruz, Carmen Inés. 1980a. "The Migration Process in Colombia: Some Considerations about Its Causes and Consequence." In *Sourcebook of the New Immigration*, ed. Roy Simon Bryce Laporte, pp. 85–97. New Brunswick, N.J.: Transaction Books.

———. 1980b. "Experiencia de un matrimonio inmigrante en Nueva York." In *El Exodo de colombianos: un estudio de la corriente migratoria a los Estados Unidos y un intento para proporcionar el retorno*, ed. Ramiro Cardona Gutierrez and Sara Rubiano de Velasquez, pp. 165–70. Bogotá, Colombia: Ediciones Tercer Mundo.

———. 1980c. "De Secretaria a empleada domestica." In *El Exodo de colombianos: un estudio de la corriente migratoria a los Estados Unidos y un intento para proporcionar el retorno*, ed. Ramiro Cardona Gutierrez and Sara Rubiano de Velasquez, pp. 171–79. Bogotá, Colombia: Ediciones Tercer Mundo.

Cutright, Phillips. 1963. "Measuring the Impact of Local Party Activity on the General Election Vote." *Public Opinion Quarterly* 27(3):372–86.

Dahl, Robert. 1993. "Finding Competent Citizens: Improving Democracy." *Current* 351 (March-April):23–29.

———. 1977. "On Removing Certain Impediments to Democracy in the United States." *Political Science Quarterly* 92(1):1–20.

———. 1961. *Who Governs?* New Haven, Ct.: Yale University Press.

———. 1956. *Preface to Democratic Theory*. Chicago: University of Chicago Press.

Danielson, Michael N., and Jameson W. Doig. 1982. *New York: The Politics of Urban Regional Development*. Berkeley: University of California Press.

De Giovanni, Frank F., and Lorraine C. Minnite. 1991. "Patterns of Neighborhood Change." In *Dual City: Restructuring New York*, ed. John Hull Mollenkopf and Manuel Castells, pp. 267–311. New York: Russell Sage Foundation.

de la Garza, Rodolfo O., ed. 1987. *Ignored Voices: Public Opinion Polls and the Latino Community*. Austin, Tex.: Center for Mexican American Studies, University of Texas.

de la Garza, Rodolfo O., and Angelo Falcón. 1992. "Identity, Policy Preferences, and Political Behavior: Preliminary Results from the Latino National Political Survey." New York: Institute for Puerto Rican Policy.

de la Garza, Rodolfo O., Louis DeSipio, F. Chris Garcia, John Garcia, and Angelo Falcón. 1992. *Latino Voices: Mexican, Puerto Rican, and Cuban Perspectives on American Politics*. Boulder, Colo.: Westview Press.

del Pinal, Jorge, and Carmen de Naves. 1990. *The Hispanic Population of the United States, March 1989: Current Population Report*. Washington, D.C.: U.S. Department of Commerce.

DeMartini, Joseph R. 1983. "Social Movement Participation: Political Socialization, Generational Consequences, and Lasting Effects." *Youth and Society* 15(2):195–233.

Dennis, Jack. 1991. "Theories of Turnout: An Empirical Comparison of Alienationist and Rationalist Perspectives." In *Political Participation and American Democracy*, ed. William Crotty, pp. 23–65. Westport, Ct.: Greenwood.

Denton, Nancy, and Douglas Massey. 1989. "Racial Identity among Caribbean

Hispanics: The Effect of Double Minority Status on Residential Segregation." *American Sociological Review* 54 (October): 790–808.

de Rham, Gérard. 1990. "Naturalization: The Politics of Citizenship Acquisition." In *The Political Rights of Migrant Workers in Western Europe*, ed. Zig Layton-Henry, pp. 158–86. London: Sage Publications.

DeSipio, Louis. 1996. "Making Citizens or Good Citizens? Naturalization as a Predictor of Organizational and Electoral Behavior among Latino Immigrants." *Hispanic Journal of Behavioral Sciences* 18(2): 194–213.

———. 1994. "Immigrants to Voters: Electoral Empowerment Strategies Based on Latino Non-citizens." Paper presented at the Midwest Political Science Association, Chicago, April 14–16.

———. 1993. "Counting on the Latino Vote: Mobilizing U.S. Citizen Non-voters as a Tool for Latino Electoral Empowerment." Paper presented at the meeting of the American Political Science Association, Washington, D.C., September 2–5.

———. 1987. "Social Science Literature and the Naturalization Process." *International Migration Review* 21(2): 390–405.

DeSipio, Louis, and Rodolfo de la Garza. 1992. "Making Them Us: The Political Incorporation of Immigrant and Non-immigrant Minorities in the United States." In *Nations of Immigrants: Australia, the United States, and International Migration*, ed. Gary P. Freeman and James Jupp, pp. 202–16. Melbourne: Cambridge University Press.

DeSipio, Louis, and Harry Pachón. 1992. "Making Americans: Administrative Discretion and Americanization." *Chicano-Latino Law Review* 12 (Spring): 52–66.

DeSipio, Louis, Harry Pachón, Sonia Ospina, and Eric Popkin. 1994. "The Political Incorporation of 'New' Latino Immigrant Populations: The Dominicans, Colombians, Salvadorans, and Guatemalans." Paper presented at the meeting of thc American Political Science Association, New York City, September 1–4.

Diaz-Briquets, Sergio, and Melinda Frederick. 1984. "Colombian Emigration: A Research Note on Its Probable Quantitative Extent." *International Migration Review* 18(1): 99–110.

Didion, Joan. [1979] 1990. *The White Album.* New York: Farrar, Straus and Giroux.

Downs, Anthony. 1957. *An Economic Theory of Democracy*. New York: Harper and Row.

Drennan, Matthew P. 1991. "The Decline and Rise of the New York Economy." In *Dual City: Restructuring New York*, ed. John Hull Mollenkopf and Manuel Castells, pp. 25–42. New York: Russell Sage Foundation.

Dresser, Denise. 1993. "Exporting Conflict: Transboundary Consequences of Mexican Politics." In *The California-Mexico Connection*, ed. Abraham Lowenthal and Katrina Burgess, pp. 82–112. Stanford, Calif.: Stanford University Press.

Duany, Jorge. 1994. "Quisqueya on the Hudson: The Transnational Identity of Dominicans in Washington Heights." Dominican Research Monographs, CUNY Dominican Studies Institute.

Dwyer, Christopher. 1991. *The Dominican Americans.* New York: Chelsea House.

Eckstein, Harry H. 1966. *Division and Coherence in Democracy*. Princeton, N.J.: Princeton University Press.

Enelow, James, and Melvin J. Hinich. 1984. *The Spatial Theory of Voting: An Introduction*. New York: Cambridge University Press.

Enloe, Cynthia. 1981. "The Growth of the State and Ethnic Mobilization: The American Experience." *Ethnic and Racial Studies* 4(2):123–36.

Erie, Stephen. 1988. *Rainbow's End: Irish-Americans and the Dilemmas of Urban Machine Politics, 1840–1984*. Berkeley: University of California Press.

Espenshade, Thomas, and Katherine Hempstead. 1996. "Contemporary American Attitudes toward U.S. Immigration." *International Migration Review* 30(2): 535–70.

Fainstein, Norman I., and Susan S. Fainstein. 1993. "Participation in New York and London: Community and Market under Capitalism." In *Mobilizing the Community: Local Politics in the Era of the Global City*, ed. Robert Fisher and Joseph Kling, pp. 52–74. Newbury Park, Calif.: Sage.

———. 1988. "Governing Regimes and the Political Economy of Development in New York City, 1946–1984." In *Power, Culture and Place: Essays on New York City*, ed. John Hull Mollenkopf, pp. 161–99. New York: Russell Sage Foundation.

Fainstein, Susan, and Norman I. Fainstein. 1991. "The Changing Character of Community Politics in New York City: 1968–1988." In *Dual City: Restructuring New York*, ed. John Hull Mollenkopf and Manuel Castells, pp. 315–32. New York: Russell Sage Foundation.

Fendrich, James M. 1977. "Keeping the Faith or Pursuing the Good Life: A Study of the Consequences of Participation in the American Civil Rights Movement." *American Sociological Review*, 42(1):144–57.

Fernandez, Celestino, Maria Luisa Frias, and Juan L. Gonzales. 1984. "Factors Affecting the Rate of Naturalization among Mexican Immigrants: Research Findings and Field Observations." In *Proceedings of the First National Conference on Naturalization and Citizenship*, ed. Harry Pachón. Washington, D.C.: NALEO.

Finifter, Ada, and B. Finifter. 1983. "Political Socialization of International Migrants: American Immigrants in Australia." Paper presented at the American Political Science Association meeting, Washington, D.C., September 1–4.

Fischer, Claude. 1977. "Perspectives on Community and Personal Relations." In *Networks and Places: Social Relations in an Urban Setting*, ed. Claude Fischer, pp. 1–16. New York: Free Press.

Fitch, Robert. 1993. *The Assassination of New York*. New York: Verso.

Forbes, Jack. 1992. "The Hispanic Spin: Party Politics and Governmental Manipulation of Ethnic Identity." *Latin American Perspectives* 19(4):59–78.

Fowlkes, Diane. 1984. "Conceptions of the 'Political': White Activists in Atlanta." In *Political Women: Current Roles in State and Local Government*, ed. Janet Flammang, pp. 66–86. Beverly Hills: Sage.

Freeman, Gary P. 1979. *Immigrant Labor and Racial Conflicts in Industrial Societies: The British and French Experience, 1945–1975*. Princeton, N.J.: Princeton University Press.

Fuentes, Annette. 1992. "New York: Elusive Unity in La Gran Manzana." *NACLA: Report on the Americas* 26(2):27–34.
Fukuyama, Francis. 1993. "Immigrants and Family Values." *Commentary* 95(5): 26–33.
Gans, Herbert. 1962. *The Urban Villagers: Group and Class in the Life of Italian Americans*. New York: Free Press.
Gant, Michael M., and William Lyons. 1993. "Democratic Theory, Non-voting, and Public Policy: The 1972–1988 Presidential Elections." *American Politics Quarterly* 21(2):185–204.
Garcia, Jesus M., and Patricia Montgomery. 1992. *The Hispanic Population in the United States: March 1991*. Washington, D.C.: U.S. Department of Commerce.
Garcia, John A. 1986. "Caribbean Migration to the Mainland: A Review of Adaptive Experiences." *Annals of the American Academy of Political and Social Science* 487 (September):114–25.
———. 1984. "Hispanic Naturalization: Socio-economic Considerations." In *Proceedings of the First National Conference on Naturalization and Citizenship*, pp. 22–23. Washington, D.C.: NALEO.
———. 1981. "Political Integration of Mexican Immigrants: Explorations into the Naturalization Process." *International Migration Review* 15(4):608–25.
Garcia Belaunde, Domingo. 1986. "Sistema Electoral y Representación Política en el Perú Actual." In *Sistemas Electorales y Representación Política en Latinoamérica*, ed. Fundación Friedrich Ebert, pp. 43–74. Madrid, España: Graficos Geranios S.A.
Garcia Castro, Mary. 1982a. "Women in Migration: Colombian Voices in the Big Apple." *Migration Today* 10(3–4):23–32.
———. 1982b. "'Mary' and 'Eve's' Social Reproduction in the 'Big Apple'—Colombian Voices." Center for Latin American and Caribbean Studies. New York University, Faculty of Arts and Science.
Geertz, Clifford. 1963. "The Integrative Revolution: Primordial Sentiments and Civil Politics in New States." In *Old Societies and New States*, ed. Clifford Geertz, pp. 105–57. New York: Free Press.
Georges, Eugenia. 1990. *The Making of a Transnational Community: Migration, Development, and Cultural Change in the Dominican Republic*. New York: Columbia University Press.
———. 1989. "Participación política de una población hispana: los dominicanos en la ciudad de Nueva York." In *Dominicanos Ausentes*, ed. Eugenia Georges, pp. 183–211. Santo Domingo: Fundación Friedrich Ebert.
———. 1984. "New Immigrants and the Political Process: Dominicans in New York." New York Research Program in Inter-American Affairs, New York University.
Gerson, Kathleen, C. Ann Steuve, and Claude S. Fischer. 1979. "Attachment to Place." In *Networks and Places: Social Relations in an Urban Setting*, ed. Claude Fischer, pp. 139–61. New York: Free Press.
Gilbertson, Greta, Joseph Fitzpatrick, and Lijun Yang. 1996. "Hispanic Intermar-

riage in New York City: New Evidence from 1991." *International Migration Review* 30(2):445–59.

Gilbertson, Greta, and Douglas Gurak. 1994. "Household Transitions in the Migrations of Dominicans and Colombians to New York." *International Migration Review* 28(1):22–45.

———. 1993. "Broadening the Enclave Debate: The Labor Market Experiences of Dominican and Colombian Men in New York City." *Sociological Forum* 8(2): 205–20.

Gimenez, Martha E. 1992. "U.S. Ethnic Politics: Implications for Latin Americans." *Latin American Perspectives* 19(4):7–16.

———. 1989a. "Latino/Hispanic—Who Needs a Name? The Case against a Standard Terminology." *International Journal of Health Services* 19(3):557–71.

———. 1989b. "The Political Construction of the Hispanic." In *Estudios Chicanos and the Politics of Community, Selected Proceedings*, ed. Mary Romero and Cordelia Candelaria, pp. 66–85. Colorado Springs, Colo.: National Association for Chicano Studies.

Giordano, Jaime, and Daniel Torres, eds. 1986. *La Identidad cultural de hispanoamérica: discusión actuál.* Santiago de Chile: Instituto Profesional del Pacifico.

Gitelman, Zvi. 1982. *Becoming Israelis: Political Resocialization of Soviet and American Immigrants.* Westport, Ct.: Greenwood.

Glazer, Nathan. 1996. "Reflections on Citizenship and Diversity." In *Diversity and Citizenship: Rediscovering American Nationhood*, ed. Gary Jeffrey Jacobson and Susan Dunn, pp. 85–100. Lanham, Md.: Rowman and Littlefield.

———. 1983. "The Politics of a Multiethnic Society." In *Ethnic Dilemmas: 1964–1982*, ed. Nathan Glazer, pp. 315–36. Cambridge: Harvard University Press.

Glazer, Nathan, and Daniel Patrick Moynihan. 1970. *Beyond the Melting Pot: The Negroes, Puerto Ricans, Jews, Italians, and Irish of New York City.* Cambridge: MIT Press.

Glick-Schiller, Nina, Linda Basch, and Cristina Blanc-Szanton, eds. 1992. *Towards a Transnational Perspective on Migration: Race, Class, Ethnicity, and Nationalism Reconsidered.* New York: Annals of the New York Academy of Sciences.

Gonzalez, Nancie. 1976. "Multiple Migratory Experiences of Dominican Women." *Anthropological Quarterly* 49(1):36–44.

González Gutiérrez, Carlos. 1993. "The Mexican Diaspora in California: Limits and Possibilities for the Mexican Government." In *The California-Mexico Connection*, ed. Abraham Lowenthal and Katrina Burgess, pp. 221–38. Stanford, Calif.: Stanford University Press.

Goode, Judith. 1990. "A Wary Welcome to the Neighborhood: Community Responses to Immigrants." *Urban Anthropology* 19(1–2):125–53.

———. 1989. "Negotiating Hispanic Identity in a Multi-Ethnic Community: The Philadelphia Case." Paper delivered at the Latin American Studies Association meeting, Miami, December.

Gordon, Milton. 1964. *Assimilation in American Life: The Role of Race, Religion, and National Origins.* New York: Oxford University Press.

Grant, Madison, and Charles Stewart Davidson. 1930. *The Alien in Our Midst, or 'Selling Our Birthright for a Mess of Pottage.'* New York: Galton Publishing.

Grasmuck, Sherri, and Patricia Pessar. 1991. *Between Two Islands: Dominican International Migration.* Berkeley: University of California Press.

———. 1989. "International Migration, the State, and Households: The Case of the Dominican Republic." Paper presented to the meeting of the Latin American Studies Association, San Juan, Puerto Rico, September.

———. 1984. "Immigration, Ethnic Stratification, and Native Working Class Discipline: Comparison of Documented and Undocumented Dominicans." *International Migration Review* 18(3):692–713.

Grebler, Leo. 1966. "The Naturalization of Mexican Immigrants in the United States." *International Migration Review* 1 (Fall):17–31.

Greely, Andrew. 1985. *Why Can't They Be Like Us? America's White Ethnic Groups.* New York: Dutton.

Green, Charles, and Basil Wilson. 1990. *The Struggle for Empowerment in New York City.* New York: McGraw Hill.

Greenstein, Fred. 1965. *Children and Politics.* New Haven, Ct.: Yale University Press.

———. 1964. "The Changing Pattern of Urban Party Politics." *Annals of the American Academy of Political and Social Science* 353 (May):2–13.

Guest, Avery M., and Barrett A. Lee. 1983. "Consensus on Locality Names within the Metropolis." *Sociology and Social Research* 67(4):374–91.

Gurak, Douglas. 1987. "Family Formation and Marital Selectivity among Colombian and Dominican Immigrants in New York City." *International Migration Review* 21(2):275–298.

Gurak, Douglas, and Joseph P. Fitzpatrick. 1982. "Intermarriage among Hispanic Ethnic Groups in New York City." *American Journal of Sociology* 87(4):921–34.

Gurak, Douglas, and Mary M. Kritz. 1996. "Social Context, Household Composition, and Employment among Migrants and Nonmigrant Dominican Women." *International Migration Review* 30(2):399–422.

———. 1992. "Social Context, Household Composition, and Employment among Dominican and Colombian Women in New York." Revision of paper published in the *Proceedings of the Peopling of the Americas Conference,* May 1992.

———. 1988a. "Labor Force Status and Transitions of Dominican and Colombian Immigrants." Report to the Division of Immigration Policy and Research, Bureau of International Labor Affairs.

———. 1988b. "New York Hispanics: A Demographic Overview." In *The Hispanic Experience in the United States: Contemporary Issues and Perspectives,* ed. Edna Acosta-Belén and Barbara Sjostrom, pp. 37–76. New York: Praeger.

———. 1987. "Family Formation and Marital Selectivity among Colombian and Dominican Immigrants in New York City." *International Migration Review* 21(2):275–97.

———. 1984. "Kinship Networks and the Settlement Process: Dominican and

Colombian Immigrants in New York City." *Research Bulletin* (Hispanic Research Center, Fordham University) 7(3–4):7–11.

———. 1982. "Women in New York City: Household Structure and Employment Patterns." *Migration Today* 10(3–4):15–21.

Hagan, Jacqueline Maria. 1994. *Deciding to Be Legal: A Maya Community in Chicago.* Philadelphia: Temple University Press.

Hammar, Tomas. 1990a. "The Civil Rights of Aliens." In *The Political Rights of Migrant Workers in Western Europe,* ed. Zig Layton-Henry, pp. 74–93. London: Sage.

———. 1990b. *Democracy and the Nation State: Aliens, Denizens, and Citizens in a World of International Migration.* Aldershot, England: Avebury Press.

———. 1989. "State, Nation, and Dual Citizenship." In *Immigration and the Politics of Citizenship in Europe and North America,* ed. William Rogers Brubaker, pp. 81–96. Lanham, Md.: University Press of America.

Handlin, Oscar. 1959. *Immigration as a Factor in American History.* Englewood Cliffs, N.J.: Prentice-Hall.

———. [1951] 1973. *The Uprooted: The Epic Story of the Great Migrations that Made the American People.* Boston: Little, Brown.

———. 1941. *Boston's Immigrants: A Study of Acculturation.* Cambridge: Harvard University Press.

Hardy-Fanta, Carol. 1993. *Latina Politics, Latino Politics: Gender, Culture, and Political Participation in Boston.* Philadelphia: Temple University Press.

Hartsock, Nancy. [1974] 1981. "Political Change: Two Perspectives on Power." In *Building Feminist Theory: Essays from Quest, a Feminist Quarterly.* New York: Longman.

Hayes-Bautista, David. 1980. "Identifying 'Hispanic Populations: The Influence of Research Methodology on Public Policy." *American Journal of Public Health* 70(4):353–56.

Hechter, Michael. 1971. "Towards a Theory of Ethnic Change." *Politics and Society* 2 (Fall):21–45.

Henderson, Thomas. 1976. *Tammany Hall and the New Immigrants: The Progressive Years.* New York: Arno Press.

Hendricks, Glenn. 1980. "The Illegal Migrant: Some Research Strategies." In *Sourcebook on the New Immigration,* ed. Simon Royce-Laporte, pp. 373–78. New Brunswick, N.J.: Transaction Books.

———. 1974. *The Dominican Diaspora From the Dominican Republic to New York City: Villagers in Transition.* New York: Teacher's College Press, Columbia University.

Hernández, Ramona, and Silvio Torres-Saillant. 1994. "Dominicans in New York: Men, Women, and Prospects." Unpublished ms., City University of New York.

Hernández Becerra, Augusto. 1986. "Elecciones, Representación y Participación en Colombia." In *Sistemas Electorales y Representación Política en Latinoamérica,* ed. Fundación Friedrich Ebert, pp. 120–39. Madrid, España: Graficos Geranios S.A.

Hero, Rodney. 1992. *Latinos and the U.S. Political System: Two-tiered Pluralism.* Philadelphia: Temple University Press.

Higham, John. 1955. *Strangers in the Land: Patterns of American Nativism 1896–1925*. New Brunswick, N.J.: Rutgers University Press.

Hillery, George A. 1955. "Definitions of Community: Areas of Agreement." *Rural Sociology* 20 (June): 11–123.

Himmelweit, Hilde. 1983. "Political Socialization." *International Social Science Journal* 35(2): 237–56.

Hinojosa Cardona, Eudoro. 1992. *Doble Nacionalidad*. New York: Federación de Entidades Ecuatorianas en el Exterior.

Hirschman, Charles. 1986. "The Making of Race in Colonial Malaya: Political Economy and Racial Ideology." *Sociological Forum* 1(2): 330–61.

Hobsbawm, Eric. 1985. "Introduction: Inventing Traditions." In *The Invention of Tradition*, ed. Eric Hobsbawm and Terence Ranger, pp. 1–14. New York: Cambridge University Press.

———. [1969] 1981. *Bandits*. New York: Pantheon.

Hochschild, Jennifer. 1981. *What's Fair? American Beliefs about Distributive Justice*. Cambridge: Harvard University Press.

Hondagneau-Sotelo, Pierrette. 1994. *Gendered Transitions: Mexican Experiences of Immigration*. Berkeley: University of California Press.

———. 1992. "Overcoming Patriarchal Constraints: The Reconstruction of Gender Relations among Mexican Immigrant Women and Men." *Gender and Society* 6(3): 393–415.

Horowitz, Donald. 1977. "Cultural Movements and Ethnic Change." *Annals of the American Academy of Political and Social Science* 433 (September): 6–18.

———. 1975. "Ethnic Identity." In *Ethnicity: Theory and Experience*, ed. Nathan Glazer and Daniel Patrick Moynihan, pp. 111–140. Cambridge: Harvard University Press.

Hoskin, Marilyn. 1990. *New Immigrants and Democratic Society: Minority Integration in Western Democracies*. New York: Praeger.

———. 1989. "Socialization and Anti-socialization: The Case of Immigrants." In *Political Learning in Adulthood: A Sourcebook of Theory and Research*, ed. Roberta Sigel, pp. 340–77. Chicago: University of Chicago Press.

Houston, Marion, Roger Kramer, and Joan Mackin Barrett. 1984. "Female Predominance in Immigration to the United States since 1930: A First Look." *International Migration Review* 18(4): 908–59.

Howard, Dick. 1989. *Defining the Political*. London: Macmillan.

Hunter, Albert. 1974. *Symbolic Communities: The Persistence and Change of Chicago's Local Communities*. Chicago: University of Chicago Press.

Hunter, Albert, and Suzanne Staggenborg. 1986. "Communities Do Act: Neighborhood Characteristics, Resource Mobilization, and Political Action by Local Community Organizations." *Social Science Journal* 23(2): 169–80.

Hyman, Herbert. 1959. *Political Socialization: A Study in the Psychology of Political Behavior*. Glencoe, Ill.: Free Press.

Immigration and Naturalization Service. 1991. *1990 Statistical Yearbook of the Immigration and Naturalization Service*. Washington, D.C.: U.S. Department of Justice.

Institute for Puerto Rican Studies. 1992. "The Distribution of Puerto Rican and Other Selected Latinos in the U.S.: 1990." *Datanote* 11 (June).

Inter-Racial Council. 1920. *Proceedings of the National Conference on Immigration.* New York: Inter-Racial Council.

Isaacs, Harold. 1975. *The Idols of the Tribe.* New York: Harper and Row.

Jackson, Kenneth, ed. 1995. *The Encyclopedia of New York.* New Haven, Ct.: Yale University Press.

Jacobson, David. 1996. *Rights across Borders: Immigration and the Decline of Citizenship.* Baltimore: Johns Hopkins University Press.

Jaret, Charles. 1991. "Recent Structural Changes and U.S. Urban Ethnic Minorities." *Journal of Urban Affairs* 13(3):307–36.

Jarvenpa, Robert. 1985. "The Political Economy and Political Ethnicity of American Indian Adaptations and Identities." In *Ethnicity and Race in the U.S.A.*, ed. Richard Alba, pp. 29–48. New York: Routledge and Kegan Paul.

Jenkins, J. Craig. 1983. "Resource Mobilization Theory and the Study of Social Movements." *Annual Review of Sociology* 9:527–53.

Jennings, James. 1988. "The Puerto Rican Community: Its Political Background." In *Latinos in the Political System,* ed. F. Chris Garcia, pp. 65–80. Notre Dame, Ind.: University of Notre Dame Press.

Jennings, James, and Monte Rivera, eds. 1984. *Puerto Rican Politics in America.* Westport, Ct.: Greenwood.

Jennings, Jerry T. 1993. *Voting and Registration in the Election of November 1992.* Washington, D.C.: U.S. Department of Commerce.

———. 1991. *Voting and Registration in the Election of November 1990.* Washington, D.C.: U.S. Department of Commerce.

———. 1989. *Voting and Registration in the Election of November 1988.* Washington, D.C.: U.S. Department of Commerce.

Johnson, Haynes. 1994. *Divided We Fall: Gambling with History in the Nineties.* New York: W. W. Norton.

Jones, Delmos. 1987. "The 'Community' and Organizations in the Community." In *Cities of the United States: Studies in Urban Anthropology,* ed. Leith Mullings, pp. 99–121. New York: Columbia University Press.

Jones-Correa, Michael, and David Leal. 1996. "Becoming 'Hispanic': Secondary Panethnic Identification among Latin American Origin Populations in the United States." *Hispanic Journal of Behavioral Sciences* 18(2):214–54.

Kasarda, John. 1985. "Urban Change and Minority Opportunities." In *The New Urban Reality,* ed. Paul Peterson, pp. 33–68. Washington, D.C.: Brookings Institution.

Kasinitz, Philip, 1992. *Caribbean New York: Black Immigrants and the Politics of Race.* Ithaca, N.Y.: Cornell University Press.

———. 1987. "Conflicts and Constituencies: The City's 'New Immigrants.'" *Dissent* 34 (Fall):496–506.

Kasinitz, Philip, and Judith Freidenberg-Herbstein. [1987] 1994. "The Puerto Rican Parade and West Indian Carnival: Public Celebrations in New York City."

In *Caribbean Life in New York City: Sociocultural Dimensions*, ed. Constance Sutton and Elsa M. Chaney, pp. 305–26. New York: Center for Migration Studies.

Katznelson, Ira. 1981. *City Trenches: Urban Politics and the Patterning of Class in the United States*. Chicago: University of Chicago Press.

Keller, Suzanne. 1968. *The Urban Neighborhood*. New York: Random House.

Kelly, Rita Mae, and Jayne Burgess. 1989. "Gender and the Meaning of Power and Politics." *Women and Politics* 9(1):47–82.

Kibria, Nazli. 1993. *Family Tightrope: The Changing Lives of Vietnamese Americans*. Princeton, N.J.: Princeton University Press.

———. 1990. "Power, Patriarchy, and Gender Conflict in the Vietnamese Immigrant Community." *Gender and Society* 4(1):9–24.

Kitschelt, Herbert. 1985. "New Social Movements in West Germany and the United States." *Political Power and Social Theory* 5:273–324.

Kline, Harvey. 1985. "Colombia: Modified Two-party and Elitist Politics." In *Latin American Politics and Development*, ed. Howard J. Wiarda and Harvey Kline, pp. 249–70. Boulder, Colo.: Westview.

Kornblum, William, and James Beshers. 1988. "White Ethnicity: Ecological Dimensions." In *Power, Culture and Place: Essays on New York City*, ed. John Hull Mollenkopf, pp. 201–22. New York: Russell Sage Foundation.

Kritz, Mary, Charles Keely, and Silvano Tomasi, eds. 1981. *Global Trends in Migration: Theory and Research on International Population Movements*. New York: Center for Migration Studies.

Kymlicka, Will, and Wayne Norman. 1995. "Return of the Citizen: A Survey of Recent Work on Citizenship Theory." In *Theorizing Citizenship*, ed. Ronald Beiner, pp. 283–322. Albany: SUNY Press.

Landale, Nancy, and Nimfa Ogena. 1995. "Migration and Union Dissolution among Puerto Rican Women." *International Migration Review* 29(3):671–92.

Lane, Robert. 1959. *Political Life: Why People Get Involved in Politics*. Glencoe, Ill.: Free Press.

Layton-Henry, Zig. 1991. "Citizenship and Migrant Workers in Western Europe." In *The Frontiers of Citizenship*, ed. Ursula Vogel and Michael Moran, pp. 107–24. London: Macmillan.

———, ed. 1990. *The Political Rights of Migrant Workers in Western Europe*. London: Sage.

Lazarfeld, Paul, Bernard Berelson, and Hazel Gaudet. 1948. *The People's Choice*. New York: Columbia University Press.

Leavitt, Roy, and Mary E. Lutz. 1988. "Three New Immigrant Groups in New York City: Dominicans, Haitians, and Cambodians." New York: Community Council of New York.

Levinson, Sanford. 1988. *Constitutional Faith*. Princeton, N.J.: Princeton University Press.

Levitt, Peggy. 1996. "The Transnationalization of Civil and Political Change: The Effect of Migration on Institutional Ties between the U.S. and the Dominican Republic." Ph.D. diss., Massachusetts Institute of Technology.

Lewis, Edward. 1928. *America: Nation or Confusion? A Study of Our Immigration Problems*. New York: Harper and Brothers.

Liebow, Elliot. 1967. *Tally's Corner: A Study of Negro Streetcorner Men*. Boston: Little Brown.

Lien, Pei-te. 1995. "Contextual Change, Ethnic Identity, and Political Participation: The Case of Asian Americans in Southern California." Paper presented at the American Political Science Association meeting, Chicago, August 31–September 3.

———. 1994. "From Immigrants to Citizens and Beyond? The Political Participation of Asian Americans in Southern California." Paper presented at the American Political Science Association meeting, New York, September 1–4.

Lineberry, Robert. 1971. "Approaches to the Study of Community." In *Community Politics: A Behavioral Approach*, ed. Charles Boujean, Terry Clark, and Robert Lineberry, pp. 16–25. New York: Free Press.

Lippmann, Walter. 1965. *Public Opinion*. New York: Free Press.

Lipset, Seymour. 1960. *Political Man*. New York: Doubleday.

Lipsky, Michael. 1968. "Protest as a Political Resource." *American Political Science Review* 62 (December):1144–58.

Logan, John, and Gordana Rabrenovic. 1990. "Neighborhood Associations: Their Issues, Their Allies, and Their Opponents." *Urban Affairs Quarterly* 26(1):68–94.

Long, James. 1980. "The Effect of Americanization on Earnings: Some Evidence for Women." *Journal of Political Economy* 88 (June):620–29.

Longoria, Thomas, Robert D. Wrinkle, and J. L. Polinard. 1990. "Mexican American Voter Registration and Turnout: Another Look." *Social Science Quarterly* 71(2):356–61.

Lowndes, Vivien. 1995. "Urban Politics and Its Citizens." In *Theories of Urban Politics*, ed. David Judge, Gerry Stokes, and Harold Wolman, pp. 160–80. London: Sage.

Lutton, Wayne, and John Tanton. 1994. *The Immigration Invasion*. Petoskey, Mich.: Social Contract Press.

Lyon, Larry. 1987. *The Community in Urban Society*. Philadelphia: Temple University Press.

McAdam, Doug. 1989. "The Biographical Consequences of Activism." *American Sociological Review* 54 (October):744–60.

Macchiarola, Frank J., and Joseph G. Diaz. 1993. "Minority Empowerment in New York City: Beyond the Voting Rights Act." *Political Science Quarterly* 108(1):37–57.

McKay, James. 1982. "An Exploratory Synthesis of Primordial and Mobilizationist Approaches to Ethnic Phenomena." *Ethnic and Racial Studies* 5(4):395–420.

McKenzie, Roderick D. [1925] 1967. "The Ecological Approach to the Study of the Human Community." In *The City*, ed. Robert E. Park, Ernest Burgess, and Roderick McKenzie, pp. 63–79. Chicago: University of Chicago Press.

McNickle, Chris. 1993. *To Be Mayor of New York: Ethnic Politics in the City*. New York: Columbia University Press.

MacPherson, David, and James Stewart. 1989. "The Labor Force Participation and Earnings Profiles of Married Female Immigrants." *Quarterly Review of Economics and Business* 29(3):57–72.

Magnusson, Warren. 1990. "The Reification of Political Community." In *Contending Sovereignties: Redefining Political Community*, ed. L. B. J. Walker and Saul Mendlovitz, pp. 45–60. Boulder, Colo.: Lynne Riener.

Mahler, Sarah. 1995. *American Dreaming: Immigrant Life on the Margins*. Princeton, N.J.: Princeton University Press.

Mann, Evelyn, and Joseph Salvo. 1984. "Characteristics of New Hispanic Immigrants to New York City: A Comparison of Puerto Rican and Non–Puerto Rican Hispanics." Paper presented at the meeting of the Population Association of America, Minneapolis, Minnesota, May 3.

Marín, Gerardo, and Barbara VanOss Marín. 1991. *Research With Hispanic Populations*. Newbury Park, Calif.: Sage.

Marshall, Adriana. 1987. "New Immigrants in New York's Economy." In *New Immigrants in New York*, ed. Nancy Foner, pp. 79–102. New York: Columbia University Press.

Marshall, T. H. 1950. *Citizenship and Social Class and Other Essays*. Cambridge: Cambridge University Press.

Marx Ferree, Myra. 1979. "Employment without Liberation: Cuban Women in the United States." *Social Science Quarterly* 60(1):35–50.

Massey, Douglas. 1987. "The Ethnosurvey in Theory and Practice." *International Migration Review* 21(4):1498–1522.

———. 1986. "The Social Organization of Mexican Migration to the United States." *Annals of the American Academy of Political and Social Science* 487 (September):102–13.

———. 1981. "Dimensions of the New Immigration to the U.S. and the Prospects for Assimilation." *Annual Review of Sociology* 7:57–85.

Massey, Douglas, and Nancy A. Denton. 1993. *American Apartheid: Segregation and the Making of the Underclass*. Cambridge: Harvard University Press.

Massey, Douglas, and Jorge Durand. 1992. "Continuities in Transnational Migration: An Analysis of Thirteen National Communities." Paper presented at a conference on "New Perspectives on Mexico-U.S. Immigration," Mexican Studies Program, University of Chicago, October 23–24.

Massey, Douglas, and Kathleen Schnabel. 1983. "Recent Trends in Hispanic Immigration to the U.S." *International Migration Review* 17(2):212–44.

Mayo-Smith, Richmond. 1898. *Emigration and Immigration: A Study in Social Science*. New York: Scribner's.

Melucci, Alberto. 1989. *Nomads of the Present: Social Movements and Individual Needs in Contemporary Society*. London: Hutchinson Radius.

Mena, Camilio. 1986. "Legislación Electoral Ecuatoriana." In *Sistemas Electorales y Representación Política en Latinoamerica*, ed. Fundación Friedrich Ebert, pp. 75–117. Madrid, España: Graficos Geranios S.A.

Merton, Robert K. 1957. *Social Theory and Social Structure*. Rev. ed. Glencoe, Ill.: Free Press.

Milbraith, Lester, and Madan L. Goel. 1977. *Political Participation: How and Why Do People Get Involved in Politics?* 2d ed. Washington, D.C.: University Press of America.

Mill, John Stuart. 1873. *Considerations on Representative Government.* New York: Holt.

Miller, Mark J. 1989. "The Political Participation and Representation of Noncitizens." In *Immigration and the Politics of Citizenship in Europe and North America*, ed. William Rogers Brubaker, pp. 129–44. Lanham, Md: University Press of America.

———. 1981. *Foreign Workers in Western Europe: An Emerging Political Force.* New York: Praeger.

Miller, Steven, and David Sears. 1986. "Stability and Change in Social Tolerance: A Test of the Persistence Hypothesis." *American Journal of Political Science* 30(1): 214–36.

Mollenkopf, John Hull. 1995. "New York: The Great Anomaly." Paper presented at the meeting of the American Political Science Association, Chicago, August 31–September 3.

———. 1991. "Political Inequality." In *Dual City: Restructuring New York*, ed. John Hull Mollenkopf and Manuel Castells, pp. 333–58. New York: Russell Sage Foundation.

———. 1990. "New York: The Great Anomaly." In *Racial Politics in American Cities*, ed. Rufus Browning, Dale Rogers Marshall, and David H. Tabb, pp. 75–87. New York: Longman.

———. 1988a. "The Postindustrial Transformation of the Political Order in New York City." In *Power, Culture, and Place: Essays on New York City*, ed. John Hull Mollenkopf, pp. 223–58. New York: Russell Sage Foundation.

———. 1988b. "The Place of Politics and the Politics of Place." In *Power, Culture, and Place: Essays on New York City*, ed. John Hull Mollenkopf, pp. 273–83. New York: Russell Sage Foundation.

———. 1987. "The Decay of Reform: One Party Politics, New York Style." *Dissent* 34 (Fall): 492–95.

Montes Mozo, Segundo, and Juan Jose Garcia Vasquez. 1988. *Salvadoran Migration to the United States: An Explanatory Study*. Washington, D.C.: Hemispheric Migration Project, Center for Immigration Policy and Refugee Adaptation, Georgetown University.

Moore, David. 1993. "Americans Feel Threatened by New Immigrants." *Gallup Poll Monthly* 334 (July): 2–16.

Moore, Joan. 1984. "Effects of the Social Environment on Citizenship: A Comparison of Persons of Mexican Origin in San Antonio and Los Angeles." In *First National Congress on Citizenship and the Hispanic Community*, ed. Harry Pachón, pp. 24–41. Washington, D.C.: NALEO.

Morgen, Sandra, and Ann Bookman. 1988. "Rethinking Women and Politics: An Introductory Essay." In *Women and the Politics of Enlightenment*, ed. Ann Bookman and Sandra Morgen, pp. 3–32. Philadelphia: Temple University Press.

Muller, Thomas, and Thomas J. Espenshade. 1985. *The Fourth Wave: California's Newest Immigrants*. Washington, D.C.: Urban Institute Press.

Nagel, Joane. 1986. "The Political Construction of Ethnicity." In *Competitive Ethnic Relations*, ed. Susan Olzack and Joane Nagel, pp. 93–112. Orlando, Fla.: Academic Press.

———. 1982. "The Political Mobilization of Native Americans." *Social Science Journal* 19(3):37–45.

Nagel, Joane, and Susan Olzak. 1982. "Ethnic Mobilization in New and Old States: An Extension of the Competition Model." *Social Problems* 30(2): 127–43.

NALEO (National Association of Latino Elected and Appointed Officials). 1989. *The National Latino Immigrant Survey*. Washington, D.C.: NALEO Education Fund.

———. 1984. *Proceedings of the First National Conference on Citizenship and the Hispanic Community*. Washington, D.C.: NALEO Education Fund.

Naples, Nancy. 1991. "'Just What Needed To Be Done': The Political Practice of Women Community Workers in Low-income Neighborhoods." *Gender and Society* 5(4):478–94.

Nelson, Brent A. 1994. *America Balkanized: Immigration's Challenge to Government?* Monterey, Va.: American Immigration Control Foundation.

Newfield, Jack, and Wayne Barrett. 1988. *City for Sale: Ed Koch and the Betrayal of New York*. New York: Harper and Row.

Nie, Norman, G. Bingham Powell, and Kenneth Prewitt. 1969. "Social Structure and Political Participation: Developmental Relationships, Parts I and II." *American Political Science Review* 63(2):361–78 and 63(3):808–32.

North, David. 1987. "The Long Grey Welcome: A Study of the American Naturalization Program." *International Migration Review* 21(2):311–26.

Norton, Anne. 1988. *Reflections on Political Identity*. Baltimore: Johns Hopkins University Press.

Novack, Michael. [1971] 1973. *The Rise of the Unmeltable Ethnics*. New York: Macmillan.

Oboler, Suzanne. 1995. *Ethnic Labels, Latino Lives: Identity and the Politics of Re-Presentation in the United States*. Minneapolis: University of Minnesota Press.

———. 1992. "The Politics of Labeling: Latino/a Cultural Identities of Self and Other." *Latin American Perspectives* 19(4):18–36.

Oddone, J. M. 1986. "Regionalismo y nacionalismo." In *America Latina en sus ideas*, ed. Leopoldo Zea, pp. 201–38. Mexico, D.F.: Siglo Veintiuno Editores/ UNESCO.

Offe, Claus. 1985. "New Social Movements: Challenging the Boundaries of Institutional Politics." *Social Research* 52(4):818–68.

Okamura, Jonathan. 1981. "Situational Ethnicity." *Ethnic and Racial Studies* 4(4): 452–65.

Olsen, Marvin E. 1973. "A Model of Political Participation Stratification." *Journal of Political and Military Sociology* 1(2):183–200.

Olzak, Susan. 1983. "Contemporary Ethnic Mobilization." *Annual Review of Sociology* 9:355–74.

Ortiz, Vilma. 1991. "Latinos and Industrial Change in New York and Los Angeles." In *Hispanics in the Labor Force*, ed. Edwin Melendez, Clara Rodriguez, and Janis Barry Figueroa, pp. 119–32. New York: Plenum.

Pachón, Harry. 1991. "U.S. Citizenship and Latino Participation in California Politics." In *Racial and Ethnic Politics in California*, ed. Bryan O. Jackson and Michael B. Preston, pp. 71–88. Berkeley, Calif.: Institute of Governmental Studies.

———. 1989. *The National Latino Immigrant Survey*. Washington, D.C.: NALEO Educational Fund.

———. 1987. "Naturalization: Its Determinants and Process in the Hispanic Community: An Overview of Citizenship in the Hispanic Community." *International Migration Review* 21(2):299–310.

Pachón, Harry, and Louis DeSipio. 1994. *New Americans by Choice: Political Perspectives of Latino Immigrants*. Boulder, Colo.: Westview.

Padilla, Felix. 1990. "Latin America: The Historical Basis of Latino Unity." *Latino Studies Journal* 1(1):7–27.

———. 1985. *Latino Ethnic Consciousness: The Case of Mexican Americans and Puerto Ricans in Chicago*. Notre Dame, Ind.: University of Notre Dame Press.

———. 1984. "On the Nature of Latino Ethnicity." *Social Science Quarterly* 65(2): 651–64.

Papademetrious, Demetrios. 1983. "New Immigrants to Brooklyn and Queens: Policy Implications, Especially with Regard to Housing." Center for Migration Studies of New York for the Community Development Agency of the Human Resources Administration and Catholic Charities, Diocese of Brooklyn.

Pardo, Mary. 1990. "Mexican American Women Grassroots Community Activists: 'Mothers of East Los Angeles.'" *Frontiers* 11(1):1–7.

Park, Robert. 1925. "The City: Suggestions for the Investigation of Human Behavior in the Urban Environment." In *The City*, ed. Robert E. Park, Ernest Burgess, and Roderick McKenzie, pp. 1–46. Chicago: University of Chicago Press.

Park, Robert, and Herbert Miller. [1921] 1969. *Old World Traits Transplanted*. New York: Arno Press.

Pateman, Carole. [1980] 1989. "The Civic Culture: A Philosophic Critique." In *The Civic Culture Revisited*, ed. Gabriel Almond and Sidney Verba, pp. 57–102. Newbury Park, Calif.: Sage.

———. 1970. *Participation and Democratic Theory*. London: Cambridge University Press.

Patterson, Orlando. 1975. "Context and Choice in Ethnic Allegiance: A Theoretical Framework and Caribbean Case Study." In *Ethnicity: Theory and Practice*, ed. Nathan Glazer and Daniel P. Moynihan, pp. 305–49. Cambridge: Harvard University Press.

Pecorella, Robert F. 1994. *Community Power in a Postreform City: Politics in New York City*. Armonk, N.Y.: M. E. Sharpe.

Pedraza, Silvia. 1991. "Women and Migration: The Social Consequences of Gender." *Annual Review of Sociology* 17:303–25.
Peel, Roy V. 1935. *Political Clubs of New York City.* New York: Putnam.
Percheron, Annick. 1981. "Are American Studies on the Phenomena of Political Socialization at an Impasse? Chronicle of a Field of Research." *Année Sociologique* 31:69–96.
Perez, Lisandro. 1992. "Cuban Miami." In *Miami Now: Immigration, Ethnicity, and Social Change,* ed. Guillermo Grenier and Alex Stepick, pp. 83–108. Gainesville, Fla.: University Press of Florida.
Pesquera, Beatriz. 1993. "In the Beginning He Wouldn't Lift Even a Spoon: The Division of Household Labor." In *Building with Our Hands: New Directions in Chicana Studies,* ed. Adela de la Torre and Beatriz M. Pesquera, pp. 181–95. Berkeley: University of California Press.
Pessar, Patricia. 1987. "The Dominicans: Women in the Household and the Garment Industry." In *New Immigrants in New York,* ed. Nancy Foner, pp. 103–29. New York: Columbia University Press.
———. 1986. "The Role of Gender in the Dominican Settlement in the United States." In *Women and Change in Latin America,* ed. June Nash and Helen Safa, pp. 273–94. South Hadley, Mass.: Bergin and Garvey.
Peterson, Paul. 1981. *City Limits.* Chicago: University of Chicago Press.
Piore, Michael. 1979. *Birds of Passage.* New York: Cambridge University Press.
Portes, Alejandro, and Robert Bach. 1985. *Latin Journey: Cuban and Mexican Immigrants to the U.S.* Berkeley: University of California Press.
Portes, Alejandro, and József Böröcz. 1989. "Contemporary Immigration: Theoretical Perspectives on Its Determinants and Modes of Incorporation." *International Migration Review* 23(3):606–30.
Portes, Alejandro, and John Curtis. 1987. "Changing Flags: Naturalization and Its Determinants among Mexican Immigrants." *International Migration Review* 21(2):352–71.
Portes, Alejandro, and Ramón Grosfoguel. 1994. "Caribbean Diasporas: Migration and Ethnic Communities." *Annals of the American Academy of Political and Social Science* 536(May):48–69.
Portes, Alejandro, and Luis E. Guarnizo. 1991. "Tropical Capitalists: U.S.-bound Immigration and Small Enterprise Development in the Dominican Republic." Commission for the Study of International Migration and Cooperative Economic Development, Washington, D.C.
Portes, Alejandro, and Rafael Mozo. 1988. "The Political Adaptation Process of Cubans and Other Ethnic Minorities in the United States: A Preliminary Analysis." In *Latinos and the Political System,* ed. F. Chris Garcia, pp. 152–70. Notre Dame, Ind.: University of Notre Dame Press.
Portes, Alejandro, and Ruben Rumbaut. 1990. *Immigrant America: A Portrait.* Berkeley: University of California Press.
Portes, Alejandro, and Richard Schauffler. 1994. "Language and the Second Generation: Bilingualism Yesterday and Today." *International Migration Review* 28(4):640–61.

Portes, Alejandro, and Kenneth L. Wilson. 1980. "Immigrant Enclaves: An Analysis of the Labor Market Experiences of Cubans in Miami." *American Journal of Sociology* 86(2):295–319.

Portes, Alejandro, and Min Zhou. 1992. "Gaining the Upper Hand: Economic Mobility among Immigrant and Domestic Minorities." *Ethnic and Racial Studies* 15(4):491–522.

Power, Jonathan. 1979. *Migrant Workers in Western Europe and the United States*. New York: Pergamon.

Powers, Mary G., and John J. Mascisco, Jr. 1980. "Perfíl socio-demografico de los colombianos en la ciudad de Nueva York: censo 1970." In *El Exodo de colombianos: un estudio de la corriente migratoria a los Estados Unidos y un intento para proporcionar el retorno*, ed. Ramiro Cardona Gutierrez and Sara Rubiano de Velasquez, pp. 237–63. Bogotá, Colombia: Ediciones Tercer Mundo.

Ramirez, D. M. 1979. "Legal Residents and Naturalization: A Pilot Study." Mexican American Legal Defense Fund, San Francisco.

Raskin, Jamin B. 1993. "Legal Aliens, Local Citizens: The Historical, Constitutional and Theoretical Meanings of Alien Suffrage." *University of Pennsylvania Law Review* 141(4):1391–1470.

Rath, Jan. 1990. "Voting Rights." In *The Political Rights of Migrant Workers in Western Europe*, ed. Zig Layton-Henry, pp. 127–57. London: Sage Publications.

Reimers, David. 1992. *Still the Golden Door: The Third World Comes to America*. New York: Columbia University Press.

Reischauer, R. 1989. "Immigration and the Underclass." *Annals of the American Academy of Political and Social Science* 501(January):120–31.

Rich, Wilbur C. 1982. *The Politics of Urban Personnel Policy: Reformers, Politicians, and Bureaucrats*. Port Washington, N.Y.: Kennikat Press.

Richmond, Anthony. 1981. "Immigrant Adaptation in a Post-industrial Society." In *Global Trends in Migration: Theory and Research in International Population Movements*, ed. Mary Kritz, Charles B. Keely, and Silvano Tomasi, pp. 298–319. New York: Center for Migration Studies.

Rieder, Jonathan. 1985. *Canarsie: The Jews and Italians of Brooklyn against Liberalism*. Cambridge: Harvard University Press.

Riesman, David, and Nathan Glazer. 1950. "Criteria for Political Apathy." In *Studies in Leadership*, ed. Alvin Ward Gouldner, pp. 505–59. New York: Harper.

Rist, Ray C. 1978. *Guestworkers in Germany*. New York: Praeger.

Rodgers, Daniel T. 1987. *Contested Truths: Keywords in American Politics since Independence*. New York: Basic Books.

Rodriguez, Clara. 1994. "Challenging Racial Hegemony: Puerto Ricans in the United States." In *Race*, ed. Steven Gregory and Roger Sanjek, pp. 131–45. New Brunswick, N.J.: Rutgers University Press.

———. 1989. *Puerto Ricans: Born in the U.S.A.* Boston: Unwin Hyman.

Rodriguez, Orlando, Rosemary Santana Cooney, Angelo Falcón, Greta Gilbertson, Christopher Hansen, Arun Peter Lobo, Joseph Salvo, Vicky Virgin, and Kenneth Walzer. 1995. *Nuestra America en Nueva York: The New Immigrant His-*

panic Population in New York City, 1980–1990. New York: Hispanic Research Center.

Rogers, Rosemary. 1984. "Return Migration in Comparative Perspective." In *The Politics of Return: International Return Migration in Europe,* ed. Daniel Kubat, pp. 277–99. New York: Center for Migration Studies.

Rosberg, Gerald M. 1977. "Aliens and Equal Protection: Why Not the Right to Vote?" *Michigan Law Review* 75(April–May):1092–1136.

Rosenau, James N. 1974. *Citizenship between Elections: An Enquiry into the Mobilizable American.* New York: Free Press.

Rosenberg, Shawn. 1985. "Sociology, Psychology, and the Study of Political Behavior: The Case of the Research on Political Socialization." *Journal of Politics* 47(2):715–31.

Rosenbloom, Robert. 1981. "The Neighborhood Movement: Where Has It Come From? Where Is It Going?" *Journal of Voluntary Action Research* 10(2):4–26.

Rosenstone, Steven, and John Mark Hansen. 1993. *Mobilization, Participation, and Democracy in America.* New York: Macmillan.

Rouse, Roger. 1995. "Thinking through Transnationalism: Notes on the Cultural Politics of Class Relations in the Contemporary United States." *Public Culture* 7(2):353–402.

———. 1992. "Making Sense of Settlement: Class Transformation, Cultural Struggle, and Transnationalism among Mexican Migrants in the United States." In *Towards a Transnational Perspective on Migration,* ed. Nina Glick Schiller, Linda Basch, and Cristina Blanc-Szanton, pp. 25–52. New York: New York Academy of Sciences.

———. 1991. "Mexican Migration and the Social Space of Postmodernism." *Diaspora* 1(1):8–23.

Sahlins, Peter. 1989. *Boundaries: The Making of France and Spain in the Pyrenees.* Berkeley: University of California Press.

Sainz, Rudy Anthony. 1990. "Dominican Ethnic Associations: Classification and Service Delivery Roles in Washington Heights." Ph.D. diss., Columbia University.

Salvo, Joseph, and Ronald Ortiz. 1992. *The Newest New Yorkers: An Analysis of Immigration into New York City during the 1980s.* New York: Department of City Planning.

Sánchez, Luis Rafael. 1987. "The Flying Bus." In *Images and Identities: The Puerto Rican in Two World Contexts,* ed. Asela Rodriguez de Laguna, pp. 17–25. New Brunswick, N.J.: Transaction Books.

Sanders, Jimmy, and Victor Nee. 1987. "Limits of Ethnic Solidarity in the Enclave Economy." *American Sociological Review* 52:745–73.

Sanjek, Roger. 1988. "The People of Queens from Now to Then." Paper presented at a conference on "350 Years of Life in Queens," Queens College, Flushing, New York, April 16.

Sassen, Saskia. 1990. "Economic Restructuring and the American City." *Annual Review of Sociology* 16:465–90.

Sassen-Koob, Saskia. 1989. "New York City's Informal Economy." In *Informal*

Economy: Studies in Advanced and Less Developed Countries, ed. Alejandro Portes, Manuel Castells, and Lauren Benton, pp. 60–77. Baltimore: Johns Hopkins University Press.

———. 1985. "Changing Composition and Labor Market Location of Hispanic Immigrants in New York City, 1960–1980." In *Hispanics in the U.S. Economy*, ed. George Borjas and Marta Tienda, pp. 299–322. Orlando, Fla.: Academic Press.

———. 1979. "Formal and Informal Associations: Dominicans and Colombians in New York." *International Migration Review* 13(2):314–32.

Schlesinger, Arthur M. 1992. *The Disuniting of America: Reflections on a Multicultural Society*. New York: W. W. Norton.

Schmidt, Ronald J. 1992. "The Political Incorporation of Immigrants in California: An Institutional Assessment." Paper presented at the American Political Science Association meeting, Chicago, September 3–6.

———. 1989. "The Political Incorporation of Recent Immigrants: A Framework for Research and Analysis." Paper presented at the American Political Science Association meeting, Atlanta, September 3.

Schuck, Peter. 1989. "Membership in the Liberal Polity: The Devaluation of American Citizenship." In *Immigration and the Politics of Citizenship in Europe and North America*, ed. William Rogers Brubaker, pp. 51–66. New York: German Marshall Fund.

Schuck, Peter, and Rogers Smith. 1985. *Citizenship without Consent: Illegal Aliens in the American Polity*. New Haven, Ct.: Yale University Press.

Schumpeter, Joseph. [1942] 1975. *Capitalism, Socialism, and Democracy*. New York: Harper and Row.

Searing, Donald, Gerald Wright, and George Rabinowitz. 1976. "The Primacy Principle: Attitude Change and Political Socialization." *British Journal of Political Science* 6(1):83–114.

Sennett, Richard. [1974] 1992. *The Fall of Public Man*. New York: W. W. Norton.

Serra Santana, Emma. 1984. "Return of Portuguese: Goal or Retention of One's Identity." In *The Politics of Return: International Migration in Europe*, ed. Daniel Kubat, pp. 55–57. New York: Center for Migration Studies.

Shapiro, Michael, and Deanne Neaubauer. 1990. "Spatiality and Policy Discourse: Reading the Global City." In *Contending Sovereignties: Redefining Political Community*, ed. L. B. J. Walker and Saul Mendlovitz, pp. 97–124. Boulder, Colo.: Lynne Riener.

Shefter, Martin. 1988. "Political Incorporation and Containment: Regime Transformation in New York City." In *Power, Culture and Place: Essays on New York City*, ed. John Hull Mollenkopf, pp. 135–58. New York: Russell Sage Foundation.

Shils, Edward. 1957. "Primordial, Personal, Sacred, and Civil Ties." *British Journal of Sociology* 8(2):130–45.

Shorris, Earl. 1992. "Latinos: The Complexity of Identity." *NACLA: Report on the Americas* 26(2):19–27.

Shumsky, Neil Larry. 1992. "'Let No Man Stop to Plunder!' American Hostility to Return Migration 1890–1924." *Journal of American Ethnic History* 11(2):56–75.

Sibley, David. 1995. *Geographies of Exclusion: Society and Difference in the West.* London: Routledge.

Simon, Julian L. 1989. *The Economic Consequences of Immigration.* London: Basil Blackwell.

Simon, Rita James, and Susan Alexander. 1993. *The Ambivalent Welcome: Print Media, Public Opinion and Immigration.* Westport, Ct.: Praeger.

Skerry, Peter. 1993. *Mexican Americans: The Ambivalent Minority.* New York: Free Press.

Smith, Christopher. 1995. "Asian New York: The Geography and Politics of Diversity." *International Migration Review* 29(1):59–84.

Smith, Michael Peter. 1992. "Post-modernism, Urban Ethnography, and the New Social Space of Ethnic Identity." *Theory and Society* 21(4):493–531.

Smith, Robert. 1993a. "'Los Ausentes Siempre Presentes': The Imagining, Making, and Politics of a Transnational Community between New York City and Ticuani, Puebla." Ph.D. diss., Columbia University.

———. 1993b. "De-territorialized Nation-building: Transnational Migrants and the Re-Imagination of Political Community by Sending States." Paper presented at the American Political Science Association meeting, Washington, D.C., September 2–5.

Soja, Edward W. 1991. "Poles Apart: Urban Restructuring in New York and Los Angeles." In *Dual City: Restructuring New York,* ed. John Hull Mollenkopf and Manuel Castells, pp. 361–75. New York: Russell Sage Foundation.

Sonenshein, Raphael. 1993. *Politics in Black and White: Race and Power in Los Angeles.* Princeton, N.J.: Princeton University Press.

Soysal, Yasemin Nohoglu. 1994. *Limits of Citizenship: Migrants and Postnational Membership in Europe.* Chicago: University of Chicago Press.

Stacy, G. Palmer, and Lutton, Wayne P. 1986. *The Immigration Time Bomb.* Monterey, Va.: American Immigration Control Foundation.

Sullivan, Teresa. 1984. "The Occupational Prestige of Women Immigrants: A Comparison of Cubans and Mexicans." *International Migration Review* 18(4): 1045–62.

Susser, Ida. 1982. *Norman Street: Poverty and Politics in an Urban Neighborhood.* New York: Oxford University Press.

Suttles, Gerald D. 1972. *The Social Construction of Communities.* Chicago: University of Chicago Press.

———. 1968. *The Social Order of the Slum: Ethnicity and Territory in the Inner City.* Chicago: University of Chicago Press.

Sutton, Constance. 1992. "Transnational Identities and Cultures: Caribbean Immigrants in the United States." In *Immigration and Ethnicity: American Society—"Melting Pot" or "Salad Bowl"?,* ed. Michael D'Innocenzo and Josef Sirefman, pp. 231–41. Westport, Ct.: Greenwood Press.

———. 1987. "The Caribbeanization of New York and the Emergence of a Transnational Sociocultural System." In *Caribbean Life in New York City: Sociocultural Dimensions,* ed. Constance R. Sutton and Elsa Chaney, pp. 15–30. New York: Center for Migration Studies.

Tiao, Paul. 1993. "Non-citizen Suffrage: An Argument Based on the Voting Rights Act and Related Law." *Columbia Human Rights Review* 25(1):171–218.

Tilly, Charles. 1985. "Models and Realities of Popular Collective Action." *Social Research* 52(4):717–47.

———. 1979. "Repertoires of Contention in America and Britain, 1775–1830." In *The Dynamics of Social Movements: Resource Mobilization, Social Control, and Tactics*, ed. Mayer Zald and John D. McCarthy, pp. 126–55. Cambridge, Mass.: Winthrop.

———. 1978. *From Mobilization to Revolution*. New York: Random House.

———. 1973. "Do Communities Act?" *Social Inquiry* 43 (December):209–40.

Tocqueville, Alexis de. [1835] 1946. *Democracy in America*. Oxford: Oxford University Press.

Torres, Andrés. 1995. *Between the Melting Pot and Mosaic: African Americans and Puerto Ricans in the New York Political Economy*. Philadelphia: Temple University Press.

Treviño, Fernando M. 1987. "Standardized Terminology for Hispanic Populations." *American Journal of Public Health* 77(1):69–72.

Turner, Bryan. 1986. *Citizenship and Capitalism: The Debate Over Reformism*. Boston: Allen and Unwin.

Turner, Ralph. 1981. "Collective Behavior and Resource Mobilization as Approaches to Social Movements: Issues and Continuities." *Research in Social Movements, Conflicts and Change*, v. 4 (Greenwich, Ct.: JAI Press), pp. 1–24.

Turner, Victor. [1969] 1991. *The Ritual Process: Structure and Anti-structure*. Ithaca, N.Y.: Cornell University Press.

———. 1974. *Dramas, Fields, and Metaphors: Symbolic Action in Human Society*. Ithaca, N.Y.: Cornell University Press.

Ugalde, Antonio, Frank Bean, and Gilberto Cardenas. 1979. "International Migration from the Dominican Republic: Findings from a National Survey." *International Migration Review* 13(2):235–54.

Uhlaner, Carole, Bruce Cain, and D. Roderick Kiewiet. 1989. "Political Participation of Ethnic Minorities in the 1980s." *Political Behavior* 11(3):195–231.

Ui, Shiori. 1991. "Unlikely Heroes: The Evolution of Female Ethnic Leadership in a Cambodian Ethnic Enclave." In *Ethnography Unbound: Power and Resistance in the Modern Metropolis*, ed. Michael Buraway, pp. 161–78. Berkeley: University of California Press.

United Nations Population Fund. 1993. *The Individual and the World: Population, Migration, and Development in the 1990s*. New York: United Nations Population Fund.

United States Bureau of the Census. 1994. "We Asked—You Told Us: Place of Birth, Citizenship, and Year of Entry." Washington, D.C.: U.S. Department of Commerce.

———. 1993a. *Census of Populations: Persons of Hispanic Origin in the United States*. Washington, D.C.: U.S. Department of Commerce.

———. 1993b. *Census of Population Housing, Public Use Microdata Samples: Technical Documentation*. Washington, D.C.: U.S. Department of Commerce.

———. 1979. "Consistency of Reporting of Ethnic Origin in the Current Population Survey," technical paper no. 31. Washington D.C.: U.S. Government Printing Office.

United States Department of Labor. 1996. *Characteristics and Labor Market Behavior of the Legalized Population Five Years Following Legalization*. Washington, D.C.: U.S. Department of Labor.

United States Government. 1907. *Statutes at Large of the United States of America, 59th Congress, Vol. 37*. Washington, D.C.: U.S. Government Printing Office.

Urrea Giraldo, Fernando. 1982. "Life Strategies and the Labor Market: Colombians in New York City in the 1970s." Center for Latin American and Caribbean Studies, New York University, occasional paper no. 36. June.

Verba, Sidney, Kay Lehman Schlozman, and Henry Brady. 1995. *Voice and Equality: Civic Voluntarism in American Politics*. Cambridge: Harvard University Press.

Verba, Sidney, Kay Lehman Schlozman, Henry Brady, and Norman H. Nie. 1993. "Citizen Activity: Who Participates? What Do They Say?" *American Political Science Review* 87(2):303–18.

Verba, Sidney, and Norman H. Nie. 1972. *Participation in America: Political Democracy and Social Equality*. New York: Harper and Row.

Verba, Sidney, Norman Nie, and Jae-on Kim. 1978. *Participation and Political Equality: A Seven Nation Comparison*. New York: Cambridge University Press.

———. 1971. *Modes of Democratic Participation: A Cross-national Comparison*. Beverly Hills, Calif.: Sage.

Vietanen, Keijo. 1984. "Return Migration of the Finns from Overseas Countries." In *The Politics of Return: International Return Migration in Europe*, ed. Daniel Kubat, pp. 221–29. New York: Center for Migration Studies.

Vincent, Joan. 1974. "Brief Communications: The Structuring of Ethnicity." *Human Organization* 33(4):375–79.

Walaszek, Adam. 1984. "Return Migration from the USA to Poland." In *The Politics of Return: International Return Migration in Europe*, ed. Daniel Kubat, pp. 213–20. New York: Center for Migration Studies.

Waldinger, Roger. 1989. "Immigration and Urban Change." *Annual Review of Sociology* 15:211–32.

———. 1986–1987. "Changing Ladders and Musical Chairs: Ethnicity and Opportunity in Post-industrial New York." *Politics and Society* 15(4):369–402.

Waldinger, Roger, and Thomas Bailey. 1992. "Re-slicing the Big Apple: New Immigrants and African-Americans in the New York City Economy." *Policy Studies Review* 11(2):87–96.

Walker, R. B. J. 1990. "Sovereignty, Identity, Community: Reflections on the Horizons of Contemporary Political Practice." In *Contending Sovereignties: Redefining Political Community*, ed. R. B. J. Walker and Saul Mendlovitz, pp. 159–85. Boulder, Colo.: Lynne Riener.

Walzer, Michael. 1992. "The New Tribalism: Notes on a Difficult Problem." *Dissent* 39 (Spring):164–71.

———. 1990. "What Does It Mean to Be an 'American'?" *Social Research* 57(3): 491–514.

———. 1983. *Spheres of Justice: A Defense of Pluralism and Equality*. New York: Basic Books.

Ware, Alan. 1985. *The Breakdown of Democratic Party Organization, 1940–1980*. New York: Oxford University Press.

Welch, Susan, John Comer, and Michael Steinman. 1975. "Ethnic Differences in Social and Political Participation: A Comparison of Some Anglo and Mexican-Americans." *Pacific Sociological Review* 18(3):361–82.

———. 1973. "Political Participation among Mexican Americans: An Exploratory Analysis." *Social Science Quarterly* 53(4):799–813.

Wellman, Barry, and Barry Leighton. 1979. "Networks, Neighborhoods, and Communities: Approaches to the Study of the Community Question." *Urban Affairs Quarterly* 14(3):363–90.

Wells, Miriam. 1986. "Power Brokers and Ethnicity: The Rise of a Chicano Movement." *Aztlán* 17(1):47–77.

Whyte, William Foote. [1943] 1981. *Street Corner Society: The Social Structure of an Italian Slum*. Chicago: University of Chicago Press.

Wiarda, Howard. 1985. "The Dominican Republic: The Politics of a Frustrated Revolution." In *Latin American Politics and Development*, ed. Howard J. Wiarda and Harvey Kline, pp. 581–98. Boulder, Colo.: Westview.

Wilson, Hugh. 1993. "Black Politics: Towards a New Paradigm." Paper presented at the meeting of the New York State Political Science Association, Washington, D.C., April 23–24.

Wilson, James Q. 1962. "Politics and Reform in American Cities." *American Government Manual* 1962–1963, pp. 37–52.

———. 1961. "The Economy of Political Patronage." *Journal of Political Economy* 69(4):369–80.

Winnick, Louis. 1990. *New People in Old Neighborhoods: The Role of New Immigrants in Rejuvenating New York's Communities*. New York: Russell Sage Foundation.

Wirth, Louis. 1925. *The Ghetto*. Chicago: University of Chicago Press.

Wittke, Carl. 1952. *Refugees of the Revolution: The German Forty-eighters in America*. Philadelphia: University of Pennsylvania Press.

Wolfinger, Raymond. 1972a. *Politics of Progress*. Englewood Cliffs, N.J.: Prentice-Hall.

———. 1972b. "Why Political Machines Have Not Withered Away and Other Revisionist Thoughts." *Journal of Politics* 34(2):365–98.

———. 1965. "The Development and Persistence of Ethnic Voting." *American Political Science Review* 59(4):896–908.

———. 1963. "The Influence of Precinct Work on Voting Behavior." *Public Opinion Quarterly* 27(3):387–98.

Wolfinger, Raymond, and Steven J. Rosenstone. 1980. *Who Votes?* New Haven, Ct.: Yale University Press.

Wolpert, Czarina. 1984. "Returning and Remaining: Return among Turkish Immigrants in Germany." In *The Politics of Return: International Return Migration in Europe*, ed. Daniel Kubat, pp. 101–12. New York: Center for Migration Studies.

Wong, Morrison. 1986. "Post-1965 Asian Immigrants: Where Do They Come from, Where Are They Now, and Where Are They Going?" *Annals of the American Academy of Social and Political Science* 487 (September): 150–69.

Wrinkle, Robert D., and Lawrence Miller. 1984. "A Note on Mexican-American Voter Registration and Turnout." *Social Science Quarterly* 65(2): 308–14.

Yancey, William, Eugene Eriksen, and Richard Juliani. 1976. "Emergent Ethnicity: A Review and Reformulation." *American Sociological Review* 41(3): 391–403.

Yang, Philip. 1994. "Explaining Immigrant Naturalization." *International Migration Review* 28(3): 449–77.

Young, Crawford. 1976. *The Politics of Ethnic Pluralism*. Madison: University of Wisconsin Press.

Young, Iris Marion. 1990. "A Critique of the Ideal of Universal Citizenship." In *Throwing Like a Girl and Other Essays in Feminist and Social Theory*, pp. 114–40. Bloomington: Indiana University Press.

Yuan, Xiaoxia. 1986. "A Profile of Businesses in Elmhurst and Corona, Queens." M.A. thesis, Department of Sociology, Queens College, City University of New York.

Zhou, Min, and John R. Logan. 1989. "Returns on Human Capital in Ethnic Enclaves: New York City's Chinatown." *American Sociological Review* 54(5): 809–20.

Zorbaugh, Harvey Warren. 1929. *The Gold Coast and the Slum: A Sociological Study of Chicago's North Side*. Chicago: University of Chicago Press.

Index